Criminal Justice
Recent Scholarship

Edited by
Marilyn McShane and Frank P. Williams III

A Series from LFB Scholarly

Young Driver Accidents and Delinquency
Modeling and General Theories of Crime

Steven J. Ellwanger

LFB Scholarly Publishing LLC
New York 2006

*70114573

Library of Congress Cataloging-in-Publication Data

Ellwanger, Steven J., 1971-
  Young driver accidents and delinquency : modeling and general
theories of crime / Steven J. Ellwanger.
        p. cm. -- (Criminal justice recent scholarship)
  Includes bibliographical references and index.
  ISBN 1-59332-194-5 (alk. paper)
  1. Teenage automobile drivers--United States--Psychology. 2. Traffic
accidents--United States--Psychological aspects. 3. Traffic accidents--
Social aspects--United States. 4. Juvenile delinquency--United States.
I. Title.
  HE5620.J8E44 2006
  363.12'5108350973--dc22

                                                              2006019392

ISBN 1-59332-194-5

Printed on acid-free 250-year-life paper.

Manufactured in the United States of America.

For my wife Susan and son Ethan

TABLE OF CONTENTS

LIST OF TABLES

LIST OF FIGURES

Acknowledgements

I would like to thank Nicholas Lovrich, David Brody, Craig Parks, and the Division of Governmental Studies and Services of Washington State University for their inspirational, financial, and technical support. Without their support this work would not have been possible.

Preface

Modern industrial societies have become dependent on the automobile for both personal and commercial transportation. This dependence can in part be traced to social and economic forces that demanded more complex forms of social organization. This widespread dependence has not come without substantial social and economic costs, however, as measured in lives lost and property damaged. Of particular relevance is the disproportionate impact of the automobile on young drivers (16 to 24 years of age).

In response, state governments have adopted traffic safety education programs which aim to instill in novice drivers the knowledge, skill, and level of sensed personal responsibility found in older and more experienced drivers. This program theory, therefore, identifies the source of the problem as flowing from a personal deficit to be remedied through uniform pedagogy and curriculum. This program theory has come into question in recent years as a result of numerous evaluations which have failed to provide evidence in its support. To enhance our understanding, General Strain Theory and Self-Control Theory were tested for their explanatory power of this phenomenon. Consultation of these two theories was sought not only because each contends to be a superior "general" theory of crime/delinquency, but also because application of these theories to this phenomenon has largely been ignored in favor of more conventional definitions of crime and delinquency.

The results of the Simultaneous Regression Modeling techniques employed here reveal that both theories can claim intellectual province to this phenomenon. Counter to widespread belief, however, these general theories are not competitors, but instead distant cousins that when considered simultaneously enhance our understanding not only of young driver accidents and driving delinquency, but also of conventional crimes/delinquency. The results also provide support for the efficacy of traffic safety education after considering these individual level characteristics which spell numerous implications for the programming and delivery of effective traffic safety education.

CHAPTER 1

Institutions and Young Driver Accidents and Driving Delinquency

INTRODUCTION

This manuscript explores the efficacy of our society's concerted efforts to deal with a serious, unwelcome problem associated with our widespread societal dependence upon the automobile for our personal and commercial transportation. In the process of assessing the efficacy of "driver safety education" as a public policy countermeasure for addressing the problem of death and serious injury in the operation of motor vehicles by novice drivers, it will be seen that the systematic testing of two theories derived from the contemporary Criminal Justice literature will both enhance our societal understanding of this particular problem and deepen our disciplinary knowledge of the potential limitations of these important theories. This chapter lays out the historical context of the social problem under study here, and identifies the logic of a major public policy countermeasure developed to address that troublesome problem. Subsequent chapters will lay out the Criminal Justice theories in question, and develop the systematic tests of hypotheses derived from those theories with empirical data relating to driver safety education. The major benefit of this work is the development of novice driver psychological diagnostic instruments which could lead to the much more effective implementation of driver safety education programs in the United States and elsewhere in the world where traffic safety education problems are in evidence.

The modern automobile, with its high degree of reliable operation and instant mobility, has become an indispensable feature of the

American way of life. Heavy reliance upon the automobile in American society can be traced in part to social and economic forces that led to the development of increasingly complex forms of social organization. Indeed, as the American economy shifted from a rural agrarian base to a predominantly urban industrial foundation at the end of the 19th century, waves of foreign immigrants and migrants from rural communities flocked to the emerging metropolitan centers in pursuit of the fruits of the industrial revolution. The fundamental changes in the economy wrought by the industrial revolution would, in due time, require a fundamental change in social organization in American society.

Prior to the coming of the industrial revolution, agricultural societies were characterized by less complex forms of social organization that can best be described as "mechanical" in nature. These mechanical societies were relatively isolated from other social groups and tended to be rather self-sufficient with respect to most commerce in goods and services. As a result, there was relatively little division of labor and in most communities only a few persons carried out highly specialized functions. The capitalistic economy that fueled the industrial revolution, however, reflected the fact that the effective division of labor is the *sine qua non* of attending to the needs of large urbanized masses of people. The "scientific" division of labor permits a social organization to overcome limits on human cognition, improve the standard of living of organization members, and increase the leisure time available to those taking part in the collective enterprise in question (Gulick, 1937; Hummel, 1994; Taylor, 1912; Weber, 1968). Bureaucracy, as a form of social organization reflecting a scientific division of labor, thus emerged as the dominant form of social organization in modern industrial societies.

As bureaucracy has replaced less complex forms of social organization in American society, numerous segments of society have become increasingly dependent on each other in a highly organized division of labor. Thus, modern industrial societies are a product of economic and social conditions that have fundamentally altered the routine activities of its members to produce what scholars have termed "organic" societies where individuals have become highly dependent on others to provide for their own basic needs (L. E. Cohen & Felson, 1979; Durkheim, 1986). In contemporary American society the automobile is essential to the effective coordination of the division of labor between these segments by connecting raw materials with production processes and by transporting human capital (physical and intellectual) to the point of production and/or delivery.

In addition to the central role that the automobile plays in the American economy, changing social conditions have contributed further to its importance. The appearance of the nuclear family structure that accompanied the urban migration serves to bring together citizens in residential concentrations who once lived in extended families, but now have easy access to reliable and affordable transportation to pursue many forms of recreation and other leisure pursuits. In this socio-economic context the automobile has become a central and indispensable feature of modern industrialized societies—both in America and in most other industrialized societies. The widespread use of the automobile has not come without social and economic costs, however. Of particular relevance is the disproportionate impact of the automobile on young drivers who persistently contribute to and over represent the social and economic costs associated with its widespread use.

Problem Scope

The automobile has become the primary means of transportation in the United States for persons of all ages. In 2004, there were 198.9 million licensed drivers and 237.9 million registered vehicles whose owners logged nearly 3 trillion vehicle miles (National highway Traffic Safety Administration, 2004). Statistics compiled since the 1920s reveal that the prevalence of—and reliance on—the motor vehicle as the primary mode of transportation has come at substantial social and financial costs. As the recognition of this problem grew through the collection and compilation of traffic safety statistics, both the private and public sectors have intervened with attempts aimed at cost reduction. The result has been an ebb and flow of financial costs and social consequences of widespread dependence on the automobile in American society, starting in the 1920s. Despite various technological (e.g., improved braking systems), governmental (e.g., traffic laws), and social interventions (e.g., driver safety education programs), the

automobile continues to exact heavy economic and social costs—
especially among the nation's novice drivers.

Widespread recognition of the financial and social costs associated
with the automobile began to develop as early as the late 1920s. In
response to mounting fatalities and injuries associated with use of the
automobile, motor vehicle manufactures sought safety remedies on
technological and mechanical fronts. Indeed, the steady decline of
highway fatalities per vehicle mile traveled discernable in the period
1920-1950 was primarily the result of private initiatives that state
governments later codified. Despite the general belief among
manufactures that style—not safety—was what sold cars, they steadily
improved the safety of their vehicles by developing and installing
headlights, windshield wipers, rearview mirrors, and enhanced braking
systems. These technological and structural interventions were later
codified in both state and federal regulations (Porter, 1999: 99).

Social and technological forces continued to shape the accident
and fatality landscape beginning in the 1960s, at which point the
regulatory oversight of government came to the fore of safety
intervention efforts. Increased wealth, the appearance of multi-lane
interstate highways, further advances in automobile technology, and the
coming to driving age of a large wave of "baby boomers" would result
in increased automobile ownership, swelling levels of highway
congestion, and rising costs in terms of property damage, traffic
fatalities, and traffic injuries as motor vehicles became more affordable,
more powerful, and increasingly central to the economy and social
structure of American society. In response, Congress passed the
National Traffic and Motor Safety and Highway Safety Act(s) in 1966.
The Act(s) charged the National Highway Traffic Safety
Administration (NHTSA) with promulgating rules which would require
manufacturers to build safer vehicles. As a result, between 1966 and
1974 dozens of new, exacting standards were set for automobiles to
make them less prone to crash and to better protect passengers when
crashes occurred. Almost each year since 1969 has witnessed a decline
in highway death rates, an outcome at least in part attributable to these
safety regulations. In fact, traffic related fatalities have steadily
declined from 25.9 per 100,000 population in 1966 to 14.52 per
100,000 in 2004 (National highway Traffic Safety Administration,
2004).

Despite these positive trends, motor vehicle crashes continue to exact a heavy toll in deaths, injuries, and economic losses on American society. In fact, deaths and injuries resulting from motor vehicle crashes are the leading cause of death for persons of every age from 6 to 33 years old, while traffic fatalities account for more than 90 percent of all transportation-related deaths in the nation (National highway Traffic Safety Administration, 2004). In 2004 alone, 42,636 people lost their lives in an estimated 6,181,000 police-reported motor vehicle crashes. That figure represents 117 persons per day, or one person dying in a traffic accident every 12 minutes in the United States. Fatality and injury rates per 100 million vehicle miles traveled in 2004 were 1.46 and 100, respectively, and the economic cost associated with traffic crashes in 2000 was estimated to be in excess of $230 billion (National highway Traffic Safety Administration, 2004).

Young Drivers

The social cost of accidents borne by young drivers is one of the greatest health threats facing this segment of American society. In fact, according to the National Center for Health Statistics, motor vehicle crashes are the leading cause of death for 15 to 20 year-olds (based on 2002 figures, which represent the latest available data) (National Highway Traffic Safety Administration, 2005). Moreover, young drivers 16 to 24 years of age continue to disproportionately represent the social and economic costs associated with the use of the automobile. In fact, 15 to 24 year olds constituted 14.2 percent of the U.S. population in 2004, but represented 25 percent of all drivers involved in fatal crashes (National highway Traffic Safety Administration, 2004).

In contrast to other age groups, fatality rates per 100,000 licensed drivers for 15- to 20-year-olds were 63.8, compared to 46.3 (21- to 24-year-olds), 31.4 (25- to 34-year-olds), 27.0 (35- to 44-year-olds), 23.6 (45- to 54-year-olds), 20.7 (55- to 64-year-olds), 18.2 (65- to 69-year-olds), and 24.4 (70+ year-olds) (National highway Traffic Safety Administration, 2004). Economically, it is estimated that drivers 15 to 20 years of age were responsible for $40.8 billion of all police-reported accidents in 2002 (National Highway Traffic Safety Administration, 2002). More difficult to estimate—but every bit as important—are the costs associated with the loss of individual and generational years of life that extend beyond these immediate and more readily quantifiable costs.

Despite concerted governmental and industry attempts to reduce highway fatalities and injury accidents, recent estimates suggest that the contribution of young drivers to the annual number of traffic fatalities continues to grow nearly in step with their representation in the population. In fact, of the 196.2 million licensed drivers in the United States in 2003 (2004 data not available), 6.3 percent (11.6 million) were between 15 and 20 years of age, a 7.2 percent increase from 11.6 million young drivers in 1993 (National highway Traffic Safety Administration, 2004). In 2004, 7,898 15- to 20-year-old drivers were involved in fatal crashes—a 5 percent increase from 1994 (National highway Traffic Safety Administration, 2004).

Washington State Problem Scope

Similar to national trends, traffic fatalities in the State of Washington steadily decreased from 931 in 1968 to 761 in 1975. From 1975 to 1979, however, the state experienced sharp increases in the number of traffic fatalities to culminate in a state high of 1,034. Since that time, Washington has experienced steady declines to reach a record low of 563 traffic fatalities in 2004 (National highway Traffic Safety Administration, 2004).

The fatality rate per 100,000 licensed drivers in the state of Washington in 2001 was 9.08 as compared to a national average of 14.52. Similar to national trends, drivers 16 to 20 years of age accounted for 17.4 percent of all traffic fatalities in the state of Washington in 2004, while drivers 21 to 24 years of age accounted for 14.0 percent. Combined, these age groups accounted for 177 of the 563 traffic fatalities occurring in 2004—or 31.4 percent of all traffic fatalities (National highway Traffic Safety Administration, 2004), which is greater than twice their representation as a proportion of all licensed drivers in the state of Washington (14.1%) (Doane, 2004).

Contributing Factors of Young Driver Accidents

The disproportionate presence of young drivers—16 to 24 years of age—among the fatal and injury crash statistics has been a troublesome and perennial social problem, both at the national level and at the Washington state level as evidenced by annual traffic accident statistics. It is clear that both social and governmental forces are at play in the flow and ebb of collision and fatality rates among this group of novice drivers. In this regard, three factors have been identified by traffic safety researchers as potential contributors: human, environmental, and vehicular.

Type and Condition of Vehicle

When assessing the impact of different variables on the incidence of collision and fatality rates among young drivers, one must consider factors related to the vehicle. In fact, the International Automotive Engineering Congress estimated the relative role of the vehicle— including vehicle type, condition, and availability and use of safety restraints—to account for 6 percent of all accidents (International Automotive Engineering Congress, 1973). Of particular relevance is the tendency for younger novice drivers to prefer and operate motor vehicles that provide less protection and experience higher defect rates. In fact, for the state of Washington the Washington State Patrol found that the number of vehicle defects for drivers was greatest for those 15 to 20 years of age, and that the most common defect of 115,068 accidents reviewed was worn brakes and tires (Washington State Patrol, 1971).

In addition to the tendency for young drivers to own and operate vehicles with defective equipment is a marked preference for and ownership of motor vehicles which increase their exposure to risk. In fact, Trüstedt (1972) was the first researcher to note that young novice drivers tended to disproportionately own two-wheeled vehicles (mopeds and motorcycles) compared to those 24 years of age and over. The impact of this marked preference for two-wheeled vehicles on traffic fatalities was examined by Voas (1975) who found that drivers 24 years of age or younger accounted for 71 percent of all motorcycle accidents recorded in 1971. Findings such as these have led most observers familiar with traffic safety issues to conclude that this preference for two-wheeled vehicles results in an increased risk mainly for the young driver (Munsch, 1966).

In addition to young drivers tending to prefer and operate vehicles which increase their risk and frequency of collisions and fatalities, the tendency exists to own older vehicles which lack safety devices commonly associated with newer vehicles. The tendency also exists among this group of not using safety devices when they are available (e.g., seatbelts). Prior to the safety regulation of vehicles which began in 1966 with the passage of the National Traffic and Motor Vehicle Safety Act (NHTSA), manufacturers were not required by the federal government to install seatbelt assemblies in automobiles. With the passage of NHTSA, lap belts ("two point") and later shoulder ("three point") seatbelts were required by manufacturers beginning in 1967 (Porter, 1999).

The effectiveness of lap and shoulder belts in preventing fatal injury in severe motor vehicle crashes has been proven quite convincingly. In fact, these restraints which mitigate the impact of the "second collision"—the collision when drivers and passengers are being thrown around the auto interior or out of the vehicle—have been estimated to produce a life-saving rate of 45 percent. Many people would not buy seatbelts if they were optional, however, and do not wear them when they are available. In fact, in 1983, when seatbelt usage was voluntary everywhere in the United States, observational studies indicate that only 14 percent of drivers and front seat passengers used them (Porter, 1999: 110).

Safety restraint usage in Washington State from 1993 to 1998 supports earlier findings indicating a general reluctance among vehicle occupants to wear available safety restraints, especially young drivers. In fact, data from 1993 to 1998 indicate that safety restraint usage among passenger vehicle occupants was relatively low (only 48.9 percent). The differential rate of use of seatbelts among young and older drivers can be seen in the following statistics. While 54.6 percent of passenger vehicle occupants ages 15 to 20 injured or killed in 1998 were not using safety restraints, only 46 percent of crash victims 21 years of age or older were not using a safety restraint during that same period (Washington Traffic Safety Commission, 2001).

Attempts to increase safety restraint usage have occurred at both the behavioral and technological levels. Many observers of traffic safety phenomena believe that those who do not use safety restraints are acting irrationally and, therefore, must be protected from their lack of good judgment. Furthermore, the recognition of externalities flowing from the grief felt by family, friends, relatives, and strangers who experience or witness a premature death, along with the social and financial costs of dying on the highway—which the dead do not pay—has led to social and technological interventions designed to protect those who are unwilling or reluctant to protect themselves. By the end of 1986 all but one American state had adopted safety restraint laws, and increasing numbers of automobiles now come equipped with air bags which activate upon collision. However, because young drivers tend to own and prefer older, less well-equipped, and/or two-wheeled vehicles, the benefits of these technological advents are enjoyed disproportionately by older and wealthier drivers (Porter, 1999).

Alcohol and Drugs

Driving an automobile is a highly complex, psychomotor and perceptual task which is subject to impairment by any factor which significantly alters the physiological or psychological state of the organism operating it. Impairment of an organism's psychological and physiological driving abilities by drugs and/or alcohol is a function of the amount of change produced by the agents and the extent to which an individual is able to compensate for that effect. Our understanding of the degree of successful compensation achieved among young drivers is still in the developmental stage; however, our knowledge is fairly well developed on the condition and circumstances under which most young adults use alcohol and drugs, and these factors further distinguish young, novice drivers from older drivers. Drug and alcohol use among young drivers differs from that of older drivers in significant ways that increase the likelihood for collisions and fatalities to occur among this portion of the population.

In fact, the unfortunate confluence of low drug and alcohol tolerance, adverse environmental factors, lack of maturity in judgment, and a paucity of learned "behavior compensation" combines to increase the probability of collisions and fatalities among young drivers who use drugs and/or alcohol while operating motor vehicles dramatically. The Bureau of the Census (1995) and Wagenaar (1983) report empirical findings which support the idea that regular users of alcohol and drugs require higher doses to achieve any given "kick" than those who are infrequent users. As a result, intoxicant use has a greater impact among younger drivers whose tolerance levels are underdeveloped when compared to older and/or more frequent users. Evidence of this fact is borne out by statistics indicating that half of those arrested for "driving under the influence" are 25 to 39 years of age, but alcohol-related fatal highway crashes are more likely to be caused by those 16 to 24 years of age (Bureau of the Census, 1995; Wagenaar, 1983).

In addition to low tolerance levels, the confluence of environmental factors, maturity levels, and the absence of learned "behavioral compensation" combine to increase the frequency at which young drivers are involved in traffic collisions and fatalities. In fact, the National Commission on Marijuana and Drug Abuse (1973) found that the late teenage and early adult period—which encompasses the first eight or nine years of driving experience for most Americans—is a period when the use of drugs for all types has been rapidly increasing for some years. As a result, this is a period not only when many Americans are learning how to operate a motor vehicle, but also a period when individuals are "learning" to use drugs and/or alcohol through a variety of "behavior compensation" measures. It is clear that young drivers are ill-equipped to cope with traffic safety emergencies which often result from drug and/or alcohol use while driving (Voas, 1975: 65).

In addition to the correspondence of "learning" to use drugs and/or alcohol with learning to drive, environmental factors and low maturity levels increase the probability that young drivers will be involved in a higher proportion of traffic accidents and fatalities than other segments of the population. In fact, some have posited that young drivers— whose personalities and ability to cope with stress are still maturing— experience considerable levels of anxiety and stress vis-à-vis high school graduation, college, dating and marriage, and location of a first job. This stress is purported to lead to an increased propensity to use drugs/alcohol and engage in aggressive driving for relief. Lastly, because most young people live either with their parents or in supervised educational facilities—where substantial drug/alcohol use is not permitted—the automobile becomes either a method of getting to, or a locus where, drug/alcohol consumption is possible or unobservable by legal guardians (Voas, 1975: 65-6).

Personality and Other Person-Centered Characteristics

Drivers ages 18 to 24 would seem to possess the mental, sensory and psychomotor abilities necessary for safe driving. In fact, Baerwald (1965) found that visual acuity and the "field of vision" of drivers is negatively correlated with age, while the ability to see under night-driving conditions is best between the ages of 20 to 30, with reaction time being shortest among those 15 to 19 years of age. Similarly, Cronbach (1990) has demonstrated through longitudinal analyses that intellectual abilities tend to continue to rise at least until the age of 50. To answer why young drivers are overrepresented in collisions and fatalities—despite their comparatively higher psychomotor and mental and sensory advantages—researchers working in the area of accident and injury prevention have pointed to both sociological and psychological factors as important elements at play.

Indeed, some researchers have posited that the attitudes and values of young drivers, as well as their amenability to peer socialization, are significantly correlated with a young driver's likelihood of engaging in road traffic delinquency. For example, Klein (1971) found that the pursuit of success in competition, demonstration of self-reliance, display of aggressiveness and achievement of social status among young persons often manifests itself in various forms of delinquency seen as legitimate means for the self-expression of these values in youth (i.e., "youthful indiscretions"). Such behaviors are seldom observed among more mature persons. Support for the "social compensation" hypothesis is offered by Schuman et al. (1967) who found that of 288 unmarried drivers 16 to 24 years of age, those with a low level of education and history of poor occupational achievement were more likely to seek out danger on the road through aggressive driving behavior than those not sharing these characteristics.

In addition to the tendency for young drivers to use motor vehicles as a means for social compensation, the research literature on traffic safety suggests that an individual's social background may be an important contributing factor in road traffic delinquency. To be sure,

Carlson and Klein (1970) found that the driving behavior of young drivers was not only linked to the act of driving, but also to a wide range of attitudes and responses which apply to a wide variety of life situations. These inclinations, attitudes, and habitual responses are a result of socialization by the family and school which leads to the adoption of a "life style" that features negative attitudes towards authority, a heightened degree of conformity to peer norms, heightened level of aggressiveness, limited self-knowledge through critical introspection, and a confrontation relationship with the broader socio-political environment.

It is noteworthy that certain characteristics which are specific to young people having high accident rates correspond to those found in the general field of juvenile delinquency studied closely by scholars in Sociology and Criminal Justice. Road traffic delinquency is, therefore, only one particular form of the manifestation of the absence of successful socialization expressed by means of an instrument which in turn may considerably increase the consequences of the delinquent act itself (Gottfredson & Hirschi, 1990; Messrs, Tallqvist, Mäki, & Prigogine, 1975).

In addition to inadequate socialization (from the perspective of conformity with laws and social customs), other personality and person-centered characteristics also play into the overrepresentation of young drivers in the annual number of collisions and fatalities reported across the country. In fact, intelligence—at the extremes—and anxiety both receive theoretical and empirical support in this regard. These person-centered characteristics may be deleterious to the extent that they exert such a powerful and overriding effect on an individual's accident potential by rendering someone with all the necessary attributes, psychomotor skill, and physical fitness a bad risk. Indeed, Parry (1968) found that high anxiety is nearly as strong an influence on accident proneness as aggression. Parry also found that both aggression and anxiety levels vary across genders and age groups, and produce varying effects over time which makes different groups at different times in their lifecycles more or less prone to traffic accidents.

Aggression and anxiety scores are very high for males 17 to 24 years of age, not much lower for those 24 to 34 years of age, but steadily declined thereafter. In contrast, female aggression and anxiety scores do not covary in this way; in fact, aggression scores for females are generally much lower than those for males—more closely resembling the scores of males in the 44-54 year old age group. Anxiety scores among males and females, however, evince very different levels and trends over time. Anxiety scores for females are generally much higher than those of males throughout the life-span, and they fluctuate considerably over time. In fact, anxiety scores among males steadily decline during their driving years, while female anxiety scores steadily increase from 17 to 44 years of age, decline to their nadir at 44 to 54 years of age, then increase precipitously at 54 years of age and beyond (L. Shaw & Sichel, 1971).

Although intelligence is not sufficient to ensure safe driving, as personality defects can provide much of the impetus for irrational driving behavior, some degree of intellectual capacity is nevertheless necessary for the safe operation of a motor vehicle. Perhaps most importantly, intelligence at the extremes—extremely low or high— receives tangential empirical and theoretical support in the literature. In fact, Shaw and Sichel (1971: 388) conjecture that other personality defects such as selfishness, exhibitionism, or irritability can be accentuated by lower than average intelligence, while superior intelligence may become a liability as a result of low levels of stimulation associated with extended periods of driving—a stimulation needed to avoid frustration and/or inattention.

Exposure and Experience

When comparing accident rates of young and older drivers, two important factors to consider are those of *exposure* and *experience*. In fact, when two groups such as young and old drivers differ in accident rates, the differences may be attributed to differences in their exposure and/or experience rather than some person-centered or personality characteristic. Therefore, when making comparisons across driver age groups, attempts should be made to assess the impact of these two factors. In doing so, one finds a strong negative linear relationship between experience and collisions, while exposure between young and old drivers reveals conditions comparably favorable to younger versus older drivers.

Exposure refers to the extent to which a driver is exposed to the risk of accident involvement and is often measured in terms of *amount* and *type* of exposure to traffic events which create a risk of accident (Carroll, Carlson, McDole, & W., 1971: 18). Direct measures of exposure often include vehicle miles traveled, driving time, and traffic volume, while gasoline sales, car insurance premiums, miles of roadway, population, vehicle registration, and odometer readings are often used as indirect measures (Mills, 1975: 23). Studies have consistently shown that exposure measured in vehicle miles traveled per year is lower among young versus older drivers. In fact, Burg (1967) found that annual vehicle miles traveled increase until age 55 for males and 75 for females, while Pelz and Schuman (1971) found that average annual mileage increases only up to age 20, after which it remains more or less stable (Mills, 1975: 24-5). Despite their low exposure—at least in terms of distance traveled—younger drivers continue to experience higher accident and fatality rates than older drivers (Ibid., p. 25).

The exposure-based model predicting traffic collisions, fatalities and injuries exhibits explanatory power as evidenced by Jacqueline Bergdahl and Michael Norris (2002) who attempted to explain the convergence of fatality rates among males and females witnessed in the period 1982-1991. Their analysis suggests that the diminishing differences in fatality rates between males and females is not a result of convergence in risk-taking behavior, but rather that females have increased their exposure as measured in their proportion of licensed drivers and miles driven per year to more closely approximate male drivers. These more recent results suggest the importance of considering exposure during model specification, despite the counter-intuitive results provided in Mills' analysis (1975).

The type of exposure has also been shown to be important in explaining young driver accidents. Perhaps most importantly is the increased exposure of young drivers to night-time driving conditions and the increased number of vehicle occupants. This increased exposure to night-time driving conditions is implicated in fatal crash and accident rates in that it is the time of day usually associated with increased rates of alcohol and drug use, and is also a period of diminished visibility (Preusser, Williams, Zador, & Blomberg, 1984). Young drivers are also more likely to be transporting teenage passengers, a condition which serves quite often to distract driver attention. As these factors have empirically demonstrated increased risk for young drivers, a number of states have implemented graduated licensing programs which seek to mitigate their effects by delaying the age of full licensure while allowing new drivers to gain experience in relatively low-risk situations, i.e., driving during the day and with no teenage passengers (McCartt, Shabanova, & Leaf, 2003). Driving experience is typically defined as the time in years or months which have elapsed since a driver obtained a full driver's license. When adjusting for vehicle miles traveled, Harrington (1971) found that accident rates tend to decrease with increasing driving experience. With respect to young drivers, a self-report survey conducted every six months of students (N = 911) moving from their freshman to senior high school years indicated that the risk of a first accident is greatest during their first month of licensure—nearly twice that for the average of the remaining eleven months (McCartt et al., 2003). Mayhew and Simpson have demonstrated, however, that what may be more important—but is inextricably linked to experience—are individual levels of maturity. In fact, although experience and maturity may be related, maturity may be a person-centered characteristic that exerts an independent and significant influence on accident rates. After accounting for experience, Mayhew and Simpson (1991) found maturity to be relatively more influential in determining accident rates than experience because young novice drivers tend to have a higher propensity to engage in risk-taking behaviors and to make immature judgments.

Driver Training

Of all of the potential contributors to young driver accidents and fatalities, driver training appears to be the factor most amenable to government intervention. In fact, of those factors implicated in the overrepresentation of young drivers in the annual number of auto collisions and fatalities—type and condition of vehicle, alcohol and drugs, personality and other person-centered characteristics, and exposure and experience—driver training is the primary factor seen as amenable to the efforts of social intervention. It should, therefore, come as no surprise that both national and state governments have devoted considerable resources to educational programs in this field since the late 1920s. In fact, the driver education effort was so strong that within 18 years of its introduction, 90 percent of all high schools within the United States had adopted driver education courses which provided materials and methods consisting of classroom training and practice behind-the-wheel (Schlesinger, 1972, pp. 258-9). Despite its widespread adoption across the country, however, the immediate and long term effectiveness of these programs remains in question.

"Driver training" often refers to in-car practical instruction in driving a vehicle, while "driver education" is often taken to mean classroom instruction related to traffic safety. These two dimensions cover the process of bringing learner drivers from *ab initio* to a level of skill and knowledge sufficient to pass state driving tests (Quenault & Sten, 1975). While the effects of driving education probably tend to decline as experience contributes more to overall driving performance, the immediate and long-term effectiveness of driver education in reducing the rates of collisions and fatalities among young drivers is of considerable controversy. Indeed, studies of the impact of driver education and training on young driver accidents conducted by Harrington (1971) provide mixed results. To be sure, Harrington found that behind-the-wheel driver training among female novice drivers tended to reduce fatal and injury accidents per 1,000 drivers in the first year, but evidence with respect to effects on male novice drivers was less convincing. In fact, adjusted means for driving records between those participating in driver training were not significantly different than those who did not. Similarly, analysis of classroom instruction in traffic safety revealed that such instruction appeared to reduce fatal and injury accident rates among female novice drivers, while producing little or no effect among male novice drivers (Harrington, 1971).

A study conducted by McGuire (1969) of driving records of senior students attending two high schools in Orange County, California revealed similar results. Indeed, the comparison of population means for frequency of accidents, number of students involved in accidents, number of personal injuries, and estimated damage to a subject's car showed the differences in mean outcomes to be statistically nonsignificant. Most importantly, the two curricula and the attitudes among staff and students appeared to contribute little to these observed outcomes. These driver safety education inputs varied from extremely positive and comprehensive—consisting of 30 classroom hours, 3 hours behind-the-wheel, 12 to 14 hours in-car observation, and 12 to 14 hours of instruction on a driver simulator at School A—to extremely negative attitudes among students and staff and a comparably parsimonious curriculum—consisting of only 30 hours of classroom instruction being offered at School B.

Conversely, studies conducted by McFarland (1964), and by the Commission on Safety Education of the National Education Association suggest that driver training is highly effective. In a summary of various studies prepared by McFarland he concludes that the accident rate documented among trained drivers was only half as high as for those who were untrained through the first few years of driving (the time during which most people have most of their driving mishaps). Furthermore, these reports lead to the additional conclusions that trained drivers had fewer subsequent traffic violations and that classroom instruction supplemented by behind-the-wheel training was substantially more effective than classroom instruction alone (Schlesinger, 1972, p. 257). The Commission on Safety Education of the National Education Association (1961) provided additional support for driver training programs by concluding, based on the investigation of 26 evaluation studies, that drivers who were graduates of a high school course in driver education had fewer accidents and received fewer driving violations than drivers who were not graduates of a high school drivers safety education program.

To add further to the complex picture emerging of the effectiveness of driver safety education programs, a research review of nine high school driver education program evaluations on motor vehicle crashes, violations, and licensure rates suggests that high school driver education may actually exacerbate the problem of novice driver training. In fact, Vernick et al. (1999: 40-4; 40) concluded, through proportion relative risk assessment and ecological designs, that there is no convincing evidence that high school driver education reduces motor vehicle crash involvement rates for young drivers, either at the individual or community level. Perhaps more importantly, after accounting for licensure rates, the authors conclude that high school driver education may actually increase the crash involvement rates for young drivers (particularly males) by providing an opportunity for early licensure. A recent analysis of the impact of traffic safety education on a variety of outcomes—traffic stops, accidents, and risky driving attitudes/behaviors—on 1,209 novice drivers in Washington State revealed only modest and mixed results for the impact of traffic safety education. Lovrich, Stehr, Ellwanger, and Lin's (2003) analysis revealed that socio-demographic variables—gender, age, employment outside the home, miles traveled per week, high school population density, age upon receipt of license—and parental/peer environment had a greater influence over outcomes explaining ≈ 7.4% to 16.7% of the total variance, while traffic safety education variables—hours classroom instruction, hours behind-the-wheel, hours simulation, and graded or pass-fail courses—accounted for a modest amount of variance (≈ 2.3% to 5.6%). Moreover, the impact of traffic safety education on traffic stops, dangerous behaviors, and collisions was highly moderated by the type of practical instruction received—simulator or behind-the-wheel—and whether the course was graded or pass/fail.

Traffic Safety Education (A Program Theory) in Washington State

Government intervention aimed at solving the social problem of death and serious injury on the nation's roadways has come primarily through the adoption of a variety of automobile safety, transportation engineering, and traffic safety education programs. This diverse set of activities is due in part to the complexity or "wickedness" of the problem—that is, the problem includes many sources and spans several institutions (Guess & Farnham, 2000). Traffic safety education as a policy response was widely believed to be a factor in the equation of public safety that could be effectively manipulated by purposeful government action. As with so many other states, Washington adopted a traffic safety education program in 1963 which was initially voluntary, and later became mandated for those receiving a state-issued driver's license prior to 18 years of age.

The proponents of traffic safety education generally view the disproportionate representation of young drivers in the annual number of traffic fatalities and accidents as rooted in the absence of the knowledge, skills, and responsible behaviors and/or attitudes necessary for the safe operation of motor vehicles. The proper policy response, as viewed from this vantage point, is one which employs a uniform pedagogical approach consisting of a combination of classroom and applied field training aimed at instilling the necessary knowledge, skills, and responsible behaviors and/or attitudes within young novice drivers. To this end, the Revised Code of Washington (RCW) 28A.08 has granted authority to the *Office of the Superintendent of Public Instruction* (OSPI) for the formulation and implementation of a statewide public school traffic safety education program. The authorizing legislation—Revised Code of Washington 28A.220.010 (formerly known as 28A.08.005; 46.81.005)—requires that the OSPI formulate and implement a traffic safety education program that develops within the students of the state of Washington a knowledge of motor vehicle laws, promotes an acceptance of personal responsibility on public highways, develops an understanding of the causes and consequences of traffic accidents, and provides training in the skills necessary for the safe operation of motor vehicles. From this legislation, a program impact theory can be conceptualized (Ellwanger, 2004c) (see Figure 1.1). A traffic safety education program, as defined by the enabling legislation, is an "accredited course of instruction in traffic safety education consisting of two phases—classroom instruction and laboratory experience. The term "laboratory experience" in this instance consists of on-street, driving range, or simulator experience or some combination thereof ("Revised Code of Washington 28A.220", 1977).

Program Activities: Classroom Education and Laboratory Experience

To achieve the driver safety education program's conceptualization, pursuant the legislative authority granted it, the OSPI has established administrative authority through the Washington Administrative Code 392-153 ("Washington Administrative Code 392-153", 2001) (Ellwanger, 2004a) (see Figure 1.2). The administrative rule promulgates a thirty-hour *concurrent* classroom instruction requirement and a four-hour behind-the-wheel requirement. The classroom time element requires no less than thirty hours of contact time in a classroom setting with a certified teacher, and the laboratory experience requirement is to be met by providing not less than four hours of actual driving behind-the-wheel. Where simulation and/or off-street multiple car driving ranges are utilized, not less than three hours of actual driving behind-the-wheel per student shall occur; when simulation instruction is used, four hours of instruction equals one hour of actual driving. Lastly, when multiple car off-street driving ranges are used for instruction, two hours of instruction equals one hour of actual driving for the purposes of this administrative rule ("Washington Administrative Code 392-153", 2001, Section 032).

Traffic Safety Education Curriculum

Each school district, private school, and commercial driving school is authorized pursuant to WAC 392-153 to develop a locally-written curriculum including instruction in the following concepts: introduction to the highway transportation system; preparing and controlling the vehicle; maneuvering in limited space; signs, signals, and pavement markings; vehicle characteristics; human functions used in driving; roadway variations; intersections; management of time and space; lane changes; passing; nonmotorized traffic; internal factors affecting driving performance; physical factors affecting driving performance; alcohol and drugs; vehicle maintenance; planning for travel; limited visibility; reduced traction; special driving conditions; vehicle malfunctioning; avoiding and minimizing impact; post-crash responsibilities; legal responsibilities; highway transportation system improvement; fuel conservation; and motorcycle awareness ("Washington Administrative Code 392-153", 2001, Section 032) (Ellwanger, 2004b) (see Figure 1.3).

Testing

Given the presence of satisfactory course content and presentation, it is still necessary to test prospective drivers in the knowledge, skills, behaviors, and attitudes covered in instruction that are considered necessary for the safe operation of motor vehicles. Currently, prospective drivers who are under the age of 18 years must successfully complete a traffic safety education course—with individual service delivery units establishing performance criteria—and pass a state examination proctored by the Department of Licensing (DOL) before license receipt (Ellwanger, 2004d) (see Figure 1.4).

This examination—which consists of a written and a driving component—attempts to measure an individual's knowledge of motor vehicle laws and assess their ability to operate a motor vehicle safely. The knowledge and ability was theoretically obtained through the intervention of traffic safety education. To assess an individual's knowledge level, the Department of Licensing (DOL) administers a test of twenty randomly selected questions drawn from a computer test bank of five-hundred items. Assessments of the novice driver's ability to apply learning obtained in the classroom to real-world conditions then proceeds with a behind-the-wheel evaluation. Only after the prospective driver demonstrates proficiency in these two areas and passes a vision test is a state license issued.

Conclusion

Evolving social and economic conditions have made the automobile an indispensable feature of modern industrial societies. The increasing prevalence of and reliance upon the automobile to coordinate the basic activities of an "organic society" has not come without substantial social and economic costs, however. Traffic safety statistics compiled since the 1920s have led to an increased recognition of these costs, and public and private attempts have ensued in an attempt to alter them. Initially, structural engineering modifications and improved automobile technology served to reduce these costs, but in the latter part of the 20th century evolving social conditions—the emergence of multi-lane interstate highways, faster, more powerful and affordable automobiles—propelled the issue to the fore of government agendas as the widespread use of automobiles exacted record economic and social tolls in American society.

Contributing to the perceived need for purposeful government intervention was the increasing recognition of the disproportionate costs exacted by and distributed among young novice drivers. Attempts to identify and influence those factors most directly contributing to this overrepresentation have pointed to the role of knowledge, skill, ability, acceptance of personal responsibility, and an understanding of the causes and consequences of accidents as a primary factor that resides within the reach of governmental intervention. As a result, state governments have formulated and implemented traffic safety education programs as the most rational response to this social problem. These programs attempt to instill in novice drivers the necessary skills and attitudes for the safe operation of motor vehicles.

A careful examination of the potential factors contributing to this social problem reveals that the problem stems from many sources, and effective countermeasures likely span several social institutions. Of particular relevance is the role of person-centered and other personality traits that may exert such a powerful influence so as to render the intervention efforts ineffective. That is, a novice driver may receive the government intervention and demonstrate the necessary knowledge, skills, and ability to receive a state driver's license, but the effects of that treatment may be largely nullified by the presence of a person-centered characteristic or personality trait. These individual level variables may help explain the mixed, conflicting, and null results witnessed in traffic safety program evaluations conducted since the 1960s.

Road traffic delinquency can be considered one form of delinquency that is part of a broader, more general field of delinquency. Thus, we may look to theories of crime and delinquency that may be of utility in explaining driving delinquent behaviors that influence the formal outcomes—accidents and citations—typically used to evaluate the effectiveness of traffic safety education programs. Two theories offer particular promise in informing scientific inquiry in this area: Self-Control Theory and General Strain Theory. These two theories have demonstrated explanatory power for a wide range of criminal and delinquent behavior, but have not been used to explore various forms of driving delinquency despite their position as general theories. Not only do they purport to explain these behaviors, but they may be implicated in the discrepant findings of program evaluations as their omission would result in model misspecification. According to the logic of model specification and the core tenets of these theories, once we account for these individual level variables our empirical estimations of the effectiveness of traffic safety education should become more accurate and stable. Moreover, if one or both of these theories receives support in this area of behavior, then it would be possible to use this insight to further inform driver safety education program activities to increase their effectiveness.

Figure 1.1 — Traffic Safety Education Program Impact Theory

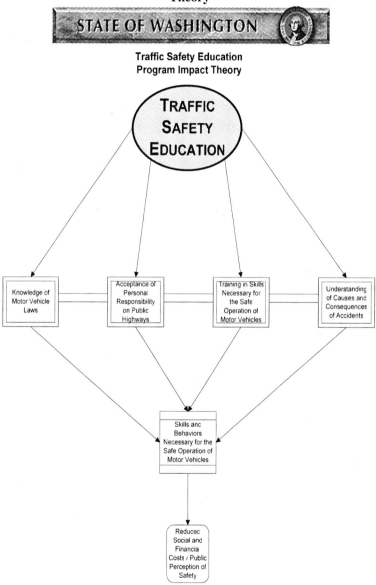

Figure 1.2—Traffic Safety Education Legislative and Administrative Authority

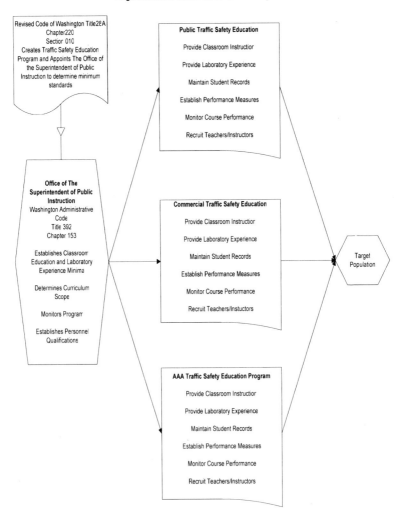

STATE OF WASHINGTON

Traffic Safety Education
Legislative and Administrative Authority

Revised Code of Washington Title28A
Chapter220
Section 010
Creates Traffic Safety Education
Program and Appoints The Office of
the Superintendent of Public
Instruction to determine minimum
standards

Office of The
Superintendent of Public
Instruction
Washington Administrative
Code
Title 392
Chapter 153

Establishes Classroom
Education and Laboratory
Experience Minima

Determines Curriculum
Scope

Monitors Program

Establishes Personnel
Qualifications

Public Traffic Safety Education

Provide Classroom Instruction

Provide Laboratory Experience

Maintain Student Records

Establish Performance Measures

Monitor Course Performance

Recruit Teachers/Instructors

Commercial Traffic Safety Education

Provide Classroom Instruction

Provide Laboratory Experience

Maintain Student Records

Establish Performance Measures

Monitor Course Performance

Recruit Teachers/Instuctors

AAA Traffic Safety Education Program

Provide Classroom Instruction

Provide Laboratory Experience

Maintain Student Records

Establish Performance Measures

Monitor Course Performance

Recruit Teachers/Instructors

Target
Population

Figure 1.3—Traffic Safety Education Logic Model

Traffic Safety Education
Logic Model

Inputs	Activities	Outputs	Outcomes		
			Initial	Intermediate	Long Term
Traffic Safety Education Program Provides Instructor Training Material Classroom Instruction and Laboratory Training with Vehicles Simulators and/or Driving Range	Provide Instruction or Highway Transportation and System Preparing and Controlling Vehicles Maneuvering in Limited Space Signs Signals and Pavement Markings Vehicle Characteristics Human Functions used in Driving Roadway Variations Intersections Management of Time and Space Lane Changes Passing Nonmotorized Traffic Internal Factors Affecting Driving Performance Physical Factors Affecting Driving Performance Alcohol and Drugs Vehicle Maintenance Planning for Travel Limited Visibility Reduced Traction Special Driving Conditions Vehicle Malfunctioning Avoiding and Minimizing Impact Post-Crash Responsibilities Legal Responsibilities Highway Transportation System Improvement Fuel Conservation and Motorcycle Awareness in 30 hours of classroom contact and 4 hours of behind the wheel instruction	Those Wanting a Washington State Driver's License prior to 18th birthday attend program	Knowledge of Motor Vehicle Laws Acceptance of Personal Responsibility on Public Highways Understanding of Causes and Consequences of Accidents Skills Necessary for the Safe Operation of Motor Vehicles	Decreased Collisions and Fatalities caused by 16-18 year Olds and within 16-25 year old age group	Reduced Social and Financial Costs Public Perception of Safety
Students Enroll in Public Commercial or AAA Traffic Safety Education Program			Modified Behavior and Knowledge	Safe and Responsible Driving	

Figure 1.4—Traffic Safety Education Service Utilization

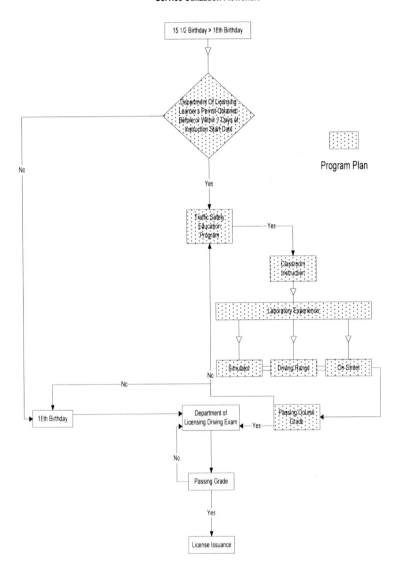

CHAPTER 2

Self-Control and Young Driver Accidents and Driving Delinquency

INTRODUCTION

The programmatic activities of contemporary traffic safety education programs reflect a policy framework that is a rational response to theories embraced by the national and state government(s) during the 1960s to address the disproportionate representation of young drivers in fatal and non-fatal automobile collisions. The regnant theory informing program structures and instructional activities at the state level is the belief that this overrepresentation can be explained in part by a lack of knowledge, skills, acceptance of personal responsibility, and failure to gain an understanding of the causes and consequences of auto accidents among young drivers ("Revised Code of Washington 28A.220", 1977). Such a program impact theory leads to the view that the social problem in question may be properly addressed through the implementation of uniform instructional pedagogy and curriculum aimed at instilling in young drivers the necessary knowledge, skills, attitudes, and sense of responsibility which approximate those of older, more experienced drivers.

Such an *indeterministic* view of young drivers—one that sees the future behaviors and outcomes of young drivers as malleable by the anvils and hammers of uniform governmental institutions and process—possibly overlooks individual level characteristics which may thwart or facilitate program outcomes as a consequence of deeply-seated individual differences across people who are the targets of the uniform programs and instructional activities. The emergence of nascent criminological theories recognizing variations in individual propensities to "deviate" from social and political norms may, as a consequence, be somewhat useful in explaining the often contradictory and/or null results witnessed in the extant evaluation studies of traffic safety education programs in the United States and elsewhere (Harrington, 1971; Lovrich et al., 2003; McGuire, 1969; Schlesinger, 1972).

Beyond these theoretical justifications for the inclusion of individual level characteristics in the study of traffic safety education program operations lie practical justifications in the field of intermediate sanctions pointing to the need to tailor program activities to client needs and/or characteristics to produce desired social outcomes (Annis, 1998; Bonta, 1996; Gendreau, Cullen, & Bonta, 1994; Harland, 1996). Empirical findings in a number of studies concerning various areas of deviance from social norms and legal restrictions on behavior indicate that program activities are often significantly moderated by important individual level characteristics that, once properly accounted for, have significant implications for the interpretation of program evaluations and subsequent programming.

Classical Criminology and Crime Control Policy

The role of science and rationality in informing criminal justice policy can be traced to the period of the Enlightenment. It was during the 18th Century that the seeds of classical criminology were sewn; crime control policy was reoriented in a fundamental way away from that of **retribution** toward that of **deterrence**. The impetus for this fundamental reorientation can be traced to emerging theories on the "causes" of crime and the concept of utilitarianism that was the regnant lexicon of Enlightenment reformers such as Cesare Beccaria (1738-1794) and Jeremy Bentham (1748-1832). To those two towering figures in the development of the modern-day discipline of Criminal Justice—and to other Enlightenment philosophers as well—crime control policies should be **rational** in the sense that they should be informed by appropriate theories on the causes of crime and should be crafted around the principle of **utility** which holds that the goal of public institutions should be bringing the greatest pleasure for the greatest number of citizens. Prior to the coming of the changes in intellectual thought occasioned by the European Enlightenment, the causes of crime were thought to derive from "spiritual explanations" and often ineffective and too frequently cruel criminal justice policies were developed to address the putative spiritual shortcomings of persons adjudged to be behaving outside the boundaries of social and or legal conventions. One of the most important sources for spiritual explanations of crime can be found in the theology of St. Thomas Aquinas (1225-1274), who argued that there was a God-given "natural law" that was revealed by observing people's natural tendency to do good rather than evil. Criminal justice policies that existed at this time reflected this "natural law" conception. According to this line of reasoning, individuals that commit crime (i.e., violate the criminal law) also commit sin (i.e., violate God's natural law).[1] This conceptualization of the basis of criminal law gave the state the moral authority to use many types of gruesome and horrible punishments; authorities (most often benevolent, but sometimes malevolent) could claim to be acting in the place of God during their infliction of pain and suffering on citizens under state control (Vold, Bernard, & Snipes, 2002: 14-5). The sanguine and seemingly cruel nature of these early punishments was also desirable, following this line of reasoning, for their apotropaic and/or symbolic qualities.

Drawing and quartering, mutilations, and breaking on the wheel, to name a few early punishments, were not usually employed with the intent of inflicting the most punishment possible on the condemned; instead, they were chosen for their ability to ward off the evil spirits (apotropaic) that would return for vengeance from the intentional killing of another, and for their symbolic qualities. For example, quartering the corpse after execution was believed to immobilize the spirit, while amputation of a hand for coining false money, arson, or murder was designed to make the culprit reflect on his or her misdeeds, in an attempt to literally or symbolically mete out *lex talionis* (the law of retaliation) in pursuit of retribution (Ellwanger, 2002; Newman, 1985).

In 1764, Cesare Bonesana, Marchese de Beccaria, would successfully reorient punishment from retribution to deterrence with his famous *Essay on Crimes and Punishment* (1819 [1764]) and become

---

[1] A brief review of Aquinas's ideas can be found in Vold, G. B., Bernard, T. J., & Snipes, J. B. (2002). *Theoretical Criminology* (5 ed.). New York: Oxford University Press, ch. 2.

known as the father of classical criminology (Allen & Simonsen, 1989). According to Beccaria, punishment was an evil act and should only be used to prevent some greater evil. This utilitarian perspective on the use of punishment would later combine with emerging theories on the causes of crime offered by Jeremy Bentham to provide the template from which *rationalistic* criminal justice policies would be cut.

Jeremy Bentham (1748-1832) began with Beccaria's premise that punishment was an evil that should be used only to prevent some greater evil, and he coupled to that idea with a new conception of the nature of crime. To him and other criminologists within the classical tradition, people are seen to possess *free will* and are thought to be *guided by reason and self-interest.* Thus, individuals were viewed largely as indeterministic and crime is seen to be in substantial part the result of ill-conceived (insufficiently rational) criminal justice policies. In fact, the "hedonistic calculus" offered by Bentham held that punishment should be moderated and made proportional, so as to negate whatever pleasure or gain was derived from the commission of a crime. The "hedonistic calculus" and the pleasure-pain principle upon which it rested would be the pole-star that guided the formulation of criminal justice policy until the late 19th Century. In due time significant challenges to this conception of crime and criminological thought emerged from the positivist tradition, challenges that were based on a much different conception of the causes of crime and deviance from social and legal norms.

Positivist Criminology and Crime Control Policy

The classical conception of human behavior—with its emphasis on choice in the service of self-interest—eventually gave way to a positivist conception of human behavior, or one that emphasized factors beyond the individual's immediate control. This view of social life suggests that humans are not self-determining agents free to do as they wish and as their intelligence directs. Instead, thinking and reasoning are actually processes of rationalization in which individuals often justify their predetermined courses of action rather than processes by which individuals freely and intelligently choose what they want to do (Gottfredson & Hirschi, 1990; Vold et al., 2002). Operating from this frame of reference, *positivistic* criminologists have attempted to identify the principal biological, psychological, and sociological determinants of crime.

The father of positivist criminology, Cesare Lombroso (1835-1909), was a physician who became a specialist in psychiatry and whose work was largely influenced by Charles Darwin's (1859) *The Origin of Species*. Writing in 1876, Lombroso proposed that criminals were biological throwbacks to an earlier evolutionary stage, or that criminals were *atavists* who were primitive and less highly evolved than their noncriminal counterparts. This particular theory of crime led Lombroso to search for those independent variables which increased the probability (not an absolute prediction) that individuals would violate the law—a politically defined dependent variable. Autopsies and personal observations led Lombroso to link head size and shape, asymmetry of the face, large jaws and cheekbones, unusually large or small ears that stand out from the head, fleshy lips, abnormal teeth, receding chin, abundant hair or wrinkles, long arms, extra fingers or toes, or an asymmetry of the brain to criminality (Ferro, 1972 [1911]).

Lombroso's approach, as do all other positivist approaches, led to endless classifications and clusters of independent variables as he encountered cases that did not fit his theory that physical anomalies with hereditary origins distinguish those with a propensity to commit crime from those without such a propensity. It was observed that offenders were not all alike, nor did they differ in the same ways from nonoffenders. Following the logic of biological and physiological determination, offenders had to be subdivided into different criminal populations with each being internally homogenous with respect to the causes of crime and different from other types on the same dimensions (Gottfredson & Hirschi, 1990: 47-50). This endless classification and clustering of independent variables with politically defined dependent variables (e.g., convictions for state defined crimes) has obfuscated rather than clarified the nature of crime and criminality as multiple-factor conclusions are advanced by students of various "disciplinary" orientations where all correlates and disciplines are *a priori* of equal significance. In the end, there is no method by which disciplinary disputes may be resolved following this particular path to understanding criminality in human societies.

Psychology, sociology, economics, and even classical approaches to the study of crime and criminality are implicated in this obfuscation. For the *classical and economic theorists*, the certainty, severity, and celerity of punishment are all correlates found to influence criminal propensities to varying degrees over a wide range of criminal offenses ranging from tax cheating, petty theft, drunk driving, and various forms of white-collar crime (Braithwaite, 2002; Grasmick & Bursik, 1990; Miller & Anderson, 1986; Paternoster & Simpson, 1996). For the sociologist working within the culture of the *deviance* tradition, it is the association with sub-cultures whose norms favor law violation (Becker, 1963; Sutherland, 1973) and teach methods of deviance and techniques of neutralization (Friedson, 1970; Sykes & Matza, 1957) which determine criminal propensities.

Sociologists working within the *strain* and *social disorganization traditions* point to other correlates and groupings, however. In fact, strain theorists point to the overriding emphasis on material wealth generated by the post-industrial cultural ethos without a commensurate emphasis on the means by which that wealth is achieved. Theorists working within this tradition note that structural strain—introduced by a capitalistic society that emphasizes goals over means and insufficient opportunities for legitimate economic achievement—increases criminal motivation as individuals pursue the goal of economic wealth through various modes of adaptation that lead to crime and other forms of delinquency (Farnworth & Leiber, 1989; Merton, 1938).[2] Institutional strain theorists have, however, implicated the institutional imbalance of power accorded the economy relative to the family and school. To these theorists, not only must there be *cultural regeneration* which reduces the pressures for materialistic success, but **institutional revitalization** of the family, school, and political system are necessary to increase their "drawing power" and ability to exercise informal social control (Messner & Rosenfeld, 2001).

Sociologists working within the *social disorganization* tradition draw from plant ecology to advance a "theory of human ecology" which views crime and criminality as being a function of the group to which the individual belongs, rather than the person themselves (Burgess, 1928; Park, 1936). Ecological criminology views the

---

[2] Robert K. Merton (1938) distinguished between "innovators" (criminals) or those who accepted the cultural goal of economic achievement but rejected the legitimate institutional means when experiencing structural strain, and "retreatists" (e.g., social outcasts and drug users) or those who rejected both the cultural goals and the legitimate institutional means.

physical structure of communities as shaping the "routine activities" (L. E. Cohen & Felson, 1979) of inhabitants in ways that affect the likelihood of crime and has been used to explain differences in crime rates within cities. Low economic status, ethnic heterogeneity, residential mobility, family disruption and urbanization have all been identified by theorists within this tradition as significant correlates of crime and criminality (Sampson & Groves, 1989; C. Shaw & McKay, 1942).

To this expanding list of social, economic, and biological correlates identified by competing disciplines, psychologists have added *personality traits*. Personality traits—unlike states of mind or conditions of being—are relatively stable behavioral predispositions and attitudes that persist over time and across situations (Nunnally & Bernstein, 1994). At first glance, the psychological approach appears to offer the promise of conceptual clarity by documenting the existence of latent traits and providing reliable measures that can be correlated with political definitions of crime to provide a measure of criminal propensity or "criminality" to specific persons. Thus, the psychological approach appears to offer a conceptual framework capable of producing the parsimony and leverage (King, Keohane, & Verba, 1994) in theory building which has heretofore evaded the sociological, economic, and classical approaches that have produced endless categories, typologies, and groupings of independent and dependent (politically defined) variables.

In this regard, *aggression* and *intelligence* are two personality traits that can be reliably measured and presumably correlated with cognate concepts to measure an individual's criminal propensity. A close inspection of the literature in this area, however, reveals that the psychological approach suffers pretty much the same centrifugal tendencies of endless sub-categorization and sub-groupings as the other positivist traditions have experienced. For example, the documentation of a rather significant inverse relationship between IQ and crime/delinquency has a long history with varied theoretical underpinnings.

Early theoretical explanations were largely influenced by the work of biological positivists who viewed criminals as evolutionary throwbacks. Thus, criminality was seen to be the result of feeblemindedness, or being "dull-witted" or "slow" (Goddard, 1972 [1914]). Although this theoretical explanation of low IQ leading to criminality has been largely dismissed among scholars, the empirical relationship between offending and low intelligence persists. Travis Hirschi and Michael Hindlelang (1977) reviewed a number of studies on the association between IQ and delinquency and concluded that it is at least as important as social class or race in predicting official delinquency, and more so in predicting self-reported delinquency. Later studies have found that more serious offenders have lower IQ scores than minor offenders (Blumstein, Farrington, & Moitra, 1985), and that low IQ scores among small children are associated with later offending when these children become adolescents and young adults (Lipsitt, Buka, & Lipsitt, 1990). At first glance, the promise of a unidimensional conceptual framework of criminality appears tenable regardless of the causal mechanism through which criminality leads to crime: low IQ → feeblemindedness → crime; or low IQ → adverse social conditions (e.g., social disorganization and strain) → crime.

Intelligence, much like aggression, fails to capture much of what we witness, and ultimately leads to endless sub-categorization and the identification of sub-groupings of independent and dependent variables. To be sure, measures of intelligence and aggression persistently correlate with politically specified measures of crime, yet both measures fail to account for some groupings of offenders. For aggression—which connotes activity, force, or violence—and for which significant positive correlations have been documented between measures of aggression and crime for adults (Huesmann, Rowell, Lefkowitz, & Walder, 1984), and for "characteristics of attacking behavior" such as disobedience, disorderliness, stubbornness, defiance, impudence, rudeness, quarrelsomeness, cruelty, bullying, and destruction of materials among juveniles (Gluek & Gluek, 1950), passive crimes employing fraud are neglected. Similarly, crimes by physicians, who possess presumably higher than average Intelligence Quotients, must be accounted for through various categorizations, *viz.,* white-collar criminals (Friedson, 1975; Jesilow, Pontell, & Geis, 1985).

Integrating Classical and Positivist Conceptions of Crime

The centrifugal forces produced by competing disciplines, along with the countless categorization and grouping of independent variables and politically defined dependent variables that has led to a deterministic portrait of the offender has produced competing conceptions of crime and divided disciplines. Each discipline has claimed intellectual ownership of particular criminological groupings; for example, sociologists within the social disorganization tradition are fond of correlating neighborhood crime rates with the physical structure of communities, while those sociologists within the structural strain tradition seek to explain the disproportionate crime rates witnessed among the lower class and between nations as flowing from an overemphasis on cultural goals vis-à-vis legitimate means.

According to Gottfredson and Hirsch (1989; , 1990), understanding the propensity to engage in crime, or "criminality," is the goal of each tradition and discipline. In pure classical theory, people commit criminal acts because of the universal tendency to enhance individual welfare. Thus, if criminals differed from noncriminals it was with respect to their location in or comprehension of relevant sanctioning systems. That is, those cut-off from the community will suffer less than those who are integrated, and/or those unaware of the natural and legal consequences of criminal behavior cannot be controlled to the degree that those aware are controlled (1990: 85). Positivist approaches also view criminality, or the propensity to engage in crime, as being external to the offender. Instead of an individual's location and/or comprehension of the relevant sanctioning system, however, criminality is **determined** by external biological, psychological, social, or economic correlates that increase individual propensities that reside beyond or outside the influence of the individual.

The theoretic simplicity and parsimony afforded the classical choice theory, along with the positivist's complexity (which recognizes relatively stable yet individual differences in propensity) were united by Gottfredson and Hirschi in *A General Theory of Crime* (1990) to provide conceptual clarity to the essence of crime and criminality which purports to account for individual differences in criminal and deviant behavior. According to them, the parsimonious classical theory, with its emphasis on social or external control, can and should be united with the positivists' collection of **tendencies** which recognize differences in individual propensities, but do so in a manner that recognizes that those influences are internal to the individual and subject to limited institutional influence.

A General Theory of Crime and Delinquency: Low Self-Control

Since its introduction in 1990, Gottfredson and Hirschi's *Self-Control Theory* has become one of the leading contemporary theories of criminal/deviant behavior (see Pratt & Cullen, 2000; Tittle, Ward, & Grasmick, 2003b; Unnever, Cullen, & Pratt, 2003; Vazsonyi, Pickering, Junger, & Hessing, 2001). The popularity of the theory was recently noted with a review of the **Social Science Citation Index** which revealed that since its introduction, a general theory of crime has received over 300 citations and is discussed in virtually every book on contemporary criminological theory (Pratt & Cullen, 2000). According to the theory's architects, the simplicity and clarity of the classical approach to the study of crime and delinquency offers promise as the foundation for informing scientific inquiry, but is anemic in that it overlooks the idea that people also differ in the extent to which they are vulnerable to the temptations of the moment (Gottfredson & Hirschi, 1990: 87). Accordingly, they advance a criminological theory which unites the classical and positivist traditions by recognizing that individual behavior is governed by both external influences—position in and understanding of relevant sanctioning systems—and internal individual differences which increase criminal propensities.

At the core of the theory lies the proposition that variation among individuals in their ability to exercise self-control in the face of temptation accounts for individual differences in criminal/deviant behavior. Self-control, a condition presumably affecting all humans, is purported to be the "master variable" which determines individual propensities to engage in crime/delinquency. Individuals low in self-control are theorized to succumb to the temptations of the moment, largely because they experience difficulty in anticipating the long range consequences of their behavior. In fact, because the pleasures to be obtained by a criminal and/or delinquent act are typically direct, obvious, and immediate, there should be little variability in individual ability to calculate the pleasures associated with crime. Conversely, the social, legal, and/or natural pains risked by it are not obvious, or direct, and are in any event greater removed from it. Thus, it follows that there should be considerable variability in individual ability to calculate potential pains associated with crime or delinquent acts. This is further complicated by the fact that pains, unlike pleasures, are not universal. That is, while everybody appreciates money; not everyone dreads parental anger or disappointment upon learning that some money was stolen (Gottfredson & Hirschi, 1990: 95). The architects of low Self-Control Theory argue that it is conceptually superior to traditional positivist approaches. In fact, Gottfredson and Hirschi (1990) argue that the positivistic approaches create unnecessarily complex explanations for why people are motivated to commit crime because they fail to acknowledge the **nature of crime and delinquency.** According to Gottfredson and Hirschi crime and "analogous" behaviors tend to entail simple choices and provide immediate pleasures. By recognizing the essence of most criminal actions, the theory provides a conceptual framework capable of predicting a wide range of behaviors across groups that is not constrained by context, i.e., political systems or sub-groupings of crimes and/or offenders.

Moreover, Gottfredson and Hirschi acknowledge that the presence of low-self control is indeterministic in the sense that it does not always produce crime, and that many other conditions may potentially affect whether crime does or doesn't occur. Nonetheless, they argue forcefully for the master status of self-control, contending that other conceptions popular among sociologists such as strain, peer influences, social bonds, or social disadvantages actually have little influence because self-control logically predates and supersedes these conditions. As a result, these variables are manifestations of low self-control considered to be social consequences that share a spurious rather than causal relationship with crime, e.g., low self-control → failure within the institutions of school, labor force, and/or marriage work → social disadvantages (see S. Baron, 2003; Gottfredson & Hirschi, 1990: 114, 232).

The Elements of Self-Control

According to Gottfredson and Hirschi (1990), a general theory of crime must rest upon a definition of crime that captures the essence of all sociopolitical definitions. To them, the study of crime and delinquency has become unnecessarily obfuscated by criminologists who approach their work by first acknowledging that not all crimes are alike. In fact, criminologists have approached the study of crime by employing classifications which distinguish between serious and trivial offenses (D. Elliot, Huizinga, & Ageton, 1985; Wilson & Herrnstein, 1985), between instrumental and expressive crimes (Chambliss, 1969), between victim and victimless crimes (Morris & Hawkins, 1970), between crimes **mala in se** and crimes **mala prohibita** (Samaha, 1990), and between person and property crimes (L. E. Cohen & Felson, 1979).

The consequence and implications of such an approach is to overlook the essence of crime while assuming that it is useful to study bank robbers differently from parking violators; that serious criminal acts somehow require causes of commensurate seriousness; and that offenders tend to be specialized (Gottfredson & Hirschi, 1990: 42-3). A more useful approach, according to the self-control paradigm, is to first recognize that all forms of crime and delinquency are acts of force and fraud undertaken in pursuit of self-interest. It is assumed within the self-control paradigm that **motivation** to commit crime is not variable; rather, all actors are rational and motivated to pursue their self-interest, including the commission of crime. What varies among individuals is their level of self-control, a trait which consists of several distinct elements subject to effective study.

First, Gottfredson and Hirschi (1990) state that criminal acts provide **immediate** gratification of desires. Thus, a major characteristic of people with low self-control is that they tend to respond to tangible stimuli in the immediate environment, and to have a concrete "here and now" orientation. In contrast to those with high self-control, those with low self-control tend to prefer the immediate and tangible stimuli afforded by criminal acts to more distal and uncertain stimuli provided through deferred gratification. Those high in self-control are more likely to consider and/or accurately calculate the costs and benefits associated with short-term misbehavior and/or defer gratification.

Second, criminal acts provide **easy or simple** gratification of desires. They "provide money without work, sex without courtship, revenge without court delays;" thus, individuals low in self-control tend to lack diligence, tenacity, or persistence in the course of action. Third, criminal acts tend to be **risky**, **exciting**, or **thrilling**, and involve stealth, danger, speed, agility, deception, or power. Thus, those low in self-control tend to be "adventuresome, active, and physical," while those high in self-control tend to be "cautious, cognitive and verbal." A fourth characteristic of crimes is that they require **little skill or planning and provide few or meager long-term benefits**. Thus, those low in self-control do not tend to possess or value cognitive or academic skills, while being unwilling and/or uninterested in preparing for long-term occupational pursuits. Fifth, crime often results in **pain or discomfort for the victim** as property is lost, bodies are injured, privacy is violated, and trust is broken. It follows that those low in self-control tend to be "self-centered, indifferent, or insensitive to the suffering and needs of others." Lastly, the major benefit of many crimes is not pleasure, but rather relief from momentary irritation. Those low in self-control, therefore, tend to "have minimal tolerance for frustration and little ability to respond to conflict through verbal rather than physical means" (Gottfredson & Hirschi, 1990: 89).

In sum, by recognizing the essence of crime—acts of force or fraud undertaken in pursuit of self-interest—and assuming that all individuals are rational and motivated to pursue their self-interest, including the commission of crimes (classical view of human nature), variation in crime and delinquency must be **a posteriori** an artifact of internal forces which capture the essence of criminal acts. Thus, individuals who lack self-control tend to be **impulsive (**here and now orientation), to prefer **simple tasks** (easy or simple gratification), to be **risk-seeking** (adventuresome as opposed to cautious), to enjoy **physical activity** (as opposed to cognitive or mental activity), to be **self-centered** (insensitive to the needs of others), and to possess a **temper** (little ability to respond to conflict through verbal rather than physical means) (Gottfredson & Hirschi, 1990: 90; Grasmick, Tittle, Bursik, & Arneklev, 1993: 8).

Sources of Self-Control

The sources of the immediate here and now self-centered orientation that characterizes those low in self-control are less well understood than the consequences of its presence. What the architects of Self-Control Theory do agree upon, however, is that it is not an artifact of training, tutelage, or socialization. In fact, the characteristics of low self-control tend to show themselves in the absence of nurturance, discipline, or training. That is, the causes of low self-control are negative rather than positive; self-control is unlikely in the absence of effort, intended or unintended, to create it (Gottfredson & Hirschi, 1990: 94-5). This indeterministic view of the sources of criminal propensities is at odds with positivist theories which view such sources as a result of learning, particular pressures, or specific defect. By acknowledging that children vary in their display of the manifestation of the characteristics of low self-control, and that their caretakers also vary in their ability and willingness to recognize the consequences of its presence and are able to correct it, child-rearing in the family is identified as the principal source of self-control.

The essence of human nature identified by those working within this tradition is one that views individuals as self-serving and opportunistic, or what some working within the arena of models of collective action have termed "dour" (Etzioni, 1996). Models of civil society—which have implications for the relationship between individuals and government—agree with self-control theorists that individuals are in fact born dour, but through molding efforts that begin at birth may be made "sanguine"—or to become *good* by nature. Civil society is thus centrally concerned with socializing children, through various institutions, to control individual self-serving impulses that might threaten the weal of the community and produce adverse long-term consequences for the individual.

Gottfredson and Hirschi (1990) point to the family as the primary institution of socialization into self-control, and child-rearing practices as the primary mechanism through which individuals are taught to consider the long-term consequences of their behavior and to think about how their behavior should be constrained by the rights and feelings of others. In short, effective child rearing practices include the assimilation of a community orientation, and the augmentation of the individual's time horizon when calculating consequences of behavior. The task of instilling self-control is borne by parents, and that task begins at birth.

For the effective instilling of self-control to occur, Gottfredson and Hirschi (1990) suggest that at a minimum parental management should include: (1) monitoring or tracking the child's behavior; (2) recognition of deviant behavior when it occurs; and, (3) consistent and proportionate punishment of the deviant behavior when it is recognized. These components of parental oversight allow parents (or guardians) to react appropriately to the behaviors of the child that are selfish, inconsiderate, immediately gratifying, and harmful to their future welfare. In doing so, they produce within the child a general orientation that increases the probability of a restrained or socially appropriate response throughout their life. The self-control orientation of the child is thought to be malleable during the first eight years of a child's life only; after that period of early childhood, Gottfredson and Hirschi argue that the degree of self-control exhibited in life becomes a relatively stable construct. They argue that children low in self-control relative to other children will grow up to be adults low in self-control relative to other adults, and that the level of self-control displayed in life choices is henceforth highly resistant to institutional interventions aimed at its modification.

Support for the mediation of child-rearing practices on crime and delinquency through self-control (child-rearing → self-control → crime and delinquency) has received some empirical support. The Gibbs et al. (1998) analysis of the retrospective accounts of parental management among 262 university students indicated a significant **indirect** relationship between their deviance index through a 40-item self-control scale and ineffective parental management, and a non-significant **direct** relationship between ineffective parental management once they controlled for self-control. This supports Gottfredson and Hirschi's contention that the effects of parental management on crime and delinquency are entirely mediated by self-control.

A recent path-analysis by Unnever et al. (2003) indicates that the mediating hypothesis may be inaccurate, while subsequent analyses on the administration of punishment by parents suggests limitations to the theory. In fact, subjecting responses from 2,472 middle school students to a path-analysis indicates there exists both an **indirect** and **direct** relationship between parenting practices and delinquency. This direct relationship between parenting practices and delinquency suggests that rival theories, **e.g.**, differential association and control theories, maintain their intellectual province in criminology by providing a theoretical framework to account for this relationship, **e.g.**, parents acting to determine the quality of their child's associations and/or limit the frequency of delinquent associations (Matsueda, 1982; Sutherland, 1973; Warr, 1993).

Similarly, Hay's (2001) analysis of parental monitoring and discipline on self-control and "projected delinquency" (or intentions to offend) among 197 urban high school students in a southwestern state, suggest that Gottfredson and Hirschi's (1990) narrow focus on the **extent** of punishment is a limitation of the theory. In fact, Hay's analysis suggests that the **context** and **manner** in which parents deliver punishment was significant in determining individual levels of self-control. Where punishment was perceived as fair and parents were not dependent of physical force during its administration, individuals were significantly more likely to report higher levels of self-control. Finally, a recent investigation of the structural sources of self-control conducted by Pratt et al. (2004), identified levels of community (dis)organization as a significant exogenous predictor of levels of parental supervision. Thus, parental supervision within the family is adversely affected by social disorganization.

Measuring Self-Control

Despite the outright rejection of positivistic approaches to the study of crime and delinquency by Gottfredson and Hirschi (1990) for reasons already noted, the first empirical test of the theory by Grasmick et al. (1993: 7) portrayed self-control as a *personality trait* predisposing individuals to criminal behavior, which is contrary to the self-control concept advanced by its architects (see commentary by Hirschi & Gottfredson, 1993). In fact, this psychological positivism rejects the logic of their theory of crime, which views self-control as the (general) cause of crime rather than a personality trait that leads to the commission of crime. Indeed, the theory of self-control views problematic traits of personality as only one of its possible by-products, just as other behavioral outcomes may be its by-product, e.g., school performance or drug use. These considerations of how a general orientation to self-interested behavior is translated into various traits and actions in Self-Control Theory have led to criticisms of tautology (Akers, 1991; Reed & Yeager, 1996). Gottfredson and Hirschi propose that these criticisms can be overcome by employing behavioral measures that are independent of crime; for example, they suggest whining, pushing, and shoving (as a child), and for adults smoking and drinking to excess, television watching in lieu of other activities, and experiencing difficulties in interpersonal relationships (Hirschi & Gottfredson, 1993).

Notwithstanding the positivistic tendencies experienced by theorists attempting to falsify the theory, and subsequent criticisms by its architects, the influence of low self-control on criminal and imprudent acts has largely been approached by employing the psychometric scale developed by Grasmick et al. (1993) (see Table

2.1). In fact, 11 of the 21 studies reviewed by Pratt and Cullen (2000) used this particular scale. The scale in question consists of the six components identified through the reading of Gottfredson and Hirschi's (1990) definition: **Impulsivity, simple tasks, risk-seeking, physical activities, self-centered,** and **temper.** Construct validation first proceeded by employing various combinations of items among college students purportedly tapping each component, with the goal of selecting 24 items—four for each of the six components.

The 24-item scale was then administered to a probability sample of adults in Oklahoma City. The survey instrument directed respondents to rate the level of agreement to each item using a four-point Likert-type scale. A subsequent exploratory principal components analysis of the 24 items which employed the **latent root criterion** and **scree discontinuity criterion** suggest the factor structure is best represented as a uni-dimensional trait consisting of the components identified by the architects of the theory of self-control. Measurement error was assessed using Cronbach's alpha (α); the researchers reported an internal consistency of .805 for the 24-item scale. Corrected-item total correlations suggest, however, that the reliability of the 24-item instrument can be increased by eliminating one item tapping the physical activities component, increasing the alpha coefficient to .812 upon this item deletion.

Subsequent exploratory and confirmatory analyses of the 24- and 23-item scale generally support the validity of the construct, yet there exists some disagreement regarding its dimensionality among scholars. Indeed, Nagin and Paternoster (1993), Piquero and Tibbetts (1996) and Arneklev et al. (1998), and Piquero et al. (2000) have all subjected the scale to subsequent exploratory factor analyses. Employing the **scree discontinuity criterion** (the criterion where if the largest drop in eigenvalues is between the first and second factor that evidence exists supporting the uni-dimensionality of the construct) or the **salient variable criterion** (which recognizes the practical significance of a variable's loading on a factor), these scholars find that the scale is indeed conformable to a single factor solution.

Confirmatory factor analyses of the scale have not been so amicable to the proposition that the trait is uni-dimensional as proffered by Gottfredson and Hirschi (1990), however. The implications of these findings are that the construct is best represented as a multi-

Table 2.1
Grasmick et al. Low Self-Control Scale Items

Item

Impulsivity
I often act on the spur of the moment without stopping to think.
I don't devote much thought and effort to preparing for the future.
I often do whatever brings me pleasure here and now, even at the cost of some distant goal.
I'm more concerned with what happens to me in the short run than in the long run.

Simple Tasks
I frequently try to avoid projects that I know will be difficult.
When things get complicated, I tend to quit or withdraw.
The things in life that are easiest to do bring me the most pleasure.
I dislike really hard tasks that stretch my abilities to the limit.

Risk Seeking
I like to test myself every now and then by doing something a little risky.
Sometimes I will take a risk just for the fun of it.
I sometimes find it exciting to do things for which I might get in trouble.
Excitement and adventure are more important to me than security.

Physical Activities
If I had a choice, I would almost always rather do something physical than something mental.
I almost always feel better when I am on the move than when I am sitting and thinking.
I like to get out and do things more than I like to read or contemplate ideas.
I seem to have more energy and a greater need for activity than most other people my age.

Self-Centered
I try to look out for myself first, even if it means making things difficult for other people.
I'm not very sympathetic to other people when they are having problems.
If things I do upset people, it's their problem not mine.
I will try to get the things I want even when I know it's causing problems for other people.

Temper
I lose my temper pretty easily.
Often, when I'm angry at people I feel more like hurting them than talking to them about why I am angry.
When I'm really angry, other people better stay away from me.
When I have a serious disagreement with someone, it's usually hard for me to talk calmly about it without getting upset.

dimensional trait, and that the scale should in fact be disaggregated into distinct sub-scales. Confirmatory factory analytic (CFA) techniques offer several advantages over exploratory approaches when testing the factorial validity of a measurement model. First, CFA's propose a measurement model to be tested and then assess the "fit" through various indices which either measure the amount of variation in the variance/covariance matrix accounted for by the model, or estimate the extent to which the model better represents the data in comparison to a null model where nothing is correlated. As such, this approach is more consistent with theory testing than exploratory techniques. Second, CFA's allow investigators to pinpoint areas of misspecification that may aid in improving future model fit. Lastly, CFA approaches estimate error terms for each of the several indicators of interest.

Subjecting the Grasmick et al. scale (1993) to both a single and six latent variable factor solution, Piquero et al. (2000) found that their conclusion regarding the uni-dimensionality of the self-control construct reached through EFA did not fit the data well, even though all loadings were statistically significant. A first- and second-order self-control six latent factor solution yielded statistically significant loadings for all indicators, as well as provided fit indices that suggest that modeling the construct as a first- or second-order multi-dimensional construct is most appropriate.

Additional support for the multi-dimensionality of the construct, as well as the factorial invariance of the scale across gender, five age groups, and across four nations, was documented among a sample of 8,417 participants from Hungry, the Netherlands, Switzerland, and the United States by Vazsonyi et al. (2001). A CFA analysis of the Grasmick et al. (1993) scale suggested a 22-item solution, but revealed unacceptable absolute and incremental fit indices. A first order six latent factor solution, however, revealed significant loadings for all 24 indicators, but modification indices suggested the deletion of two items due to correlated error terms. Results for the proposed and modified model reported acceptable absolute and incremental fit indices, suggesting the superiority of a multi-dimensional model while generally supporting the factorial invariance of the scale across sub-groups.

Behavioral versus Cognitive Self-Control Measures

Despite the popularity of the cognitive measure of self-control developed by Grasmick et al. (1993), and the relatively favorable psychometric properties reported by several independent investigators, Hirschi and Gottfredson (1993) contend that such measures severely restrict the range of independent and dependent variables. It is their contention that those who are particularly low in self-control are unwilling or unable to participate in surveys designed to validate the measures in question. The result, in their view, is seriously attenuated correlations occasioned by restricted ranges in test scores, ultimately producing findings which provide only modest support for their theory. The explanatory power of their theory, they argue, can be increased substantially by employing *behavioral* rather than *cognitive* measures—behavioral measures preferably based upon the direct observation of behavior rather than recall or archival records.

In this regard, sociologists Tittle, Ward, and Grasmick (2003b) examined the relative explanatory power of the popular 23-item cognitive scale developed by Grasmick et al. (1993) and a 10-item self-report behavioral measure of imprudent behaviors—marital arrangements, smoking, drinking, taking medicine with minor illness, overeating, using seat belts, etc.—which intentionally omitted criminal "acts of force or fraud for personal gratification" to avoid criticisms of tautology which would advantage the latter measure. The evidence obtained from 350 face-to-face interviews of randomly selected adults (18+) located in Oklahoma City contradict Gottfredson and Hirschi's claim that support for Self-Control Theory would be greater if researchers employed behavioral rather than cognitive measures. These investigators found that behavioral report data do not produce a significantly higher negative coefficient than do cognitive measures. Moreover, the low reliability ($\alpha = .62$) evidenced by the 10-item behavioral scale indicates that the contention that crime-analogous, imprudent behaviors are highly interrelated may be incorrect; thereby making it rather difficult to develop reliable behavioral measures.

The Empirical Status of Self-Control Theory

The intellectual province of Self-Control Theory in contemporary criminology remains vast as a result of the numerous empirical tests of the theory's reach since its introduction in 1990. Based upon this literature in Criminal Justice, it can fairly be said that a number of studies can be cited to generally support the hypothesized link between self-control and crime and delinquency. Despite variations in the form, method, and representation of the measurement model, and variations in the choice of outcome criteria (e.g., crimes of force, fraud, or juvenile delinquency), the influence of self-control as an underlying propensity on criminogenic and delinquent tendencies is well documented regardless of its source. Less well supported and understood is the claim that self-control is the "master variable" that often precedes a variety of life circumstances that give rise to crime and delinquency – e.g., self-control → failure in school and the labor force → economic deprivation (strain) → crime – and that once accounted for, self-control will cause previously significant correlations between crime and rival theories to disappear in accord with Gottfredson and Hirschi's "spuriousness" thesis.

Support exists for the inverse relationship between measures of self-control (V. S. Burton, Evans, Cullen, Olivares, & Dunaway, 1999; Cauffman, Steinberg, & Piquero, 2005; Grasmick et al., 1993; Keane, Maxim, & Teevan, 1993; Tittle & Botchkovar, 2005; Tittle et al., 2003b) and crimes of force and fraud (V. S. Burton et al., 1999; Grasmick & Bursik, 1990; Longshore & Turner, 1998), drunk driving (Keane et al., 1993), imprudent behaviors (V. S. Burton et al., 1999) and general deviance (Vazsonyi et al., 2001), automobile accidents (Junger & Tremblay, 1999), drug use (S. Baron, 2003), intentions to shoplift and drive drunk (Piquero & Tibbetts, 1996), and general law violations (Gibbs et al., 1998). Furthermore, a meta-analysis conducted by Travis C. Pratt and Francis T. Cullen (2000) suggests that the population effect size rho (ρ) for self-control and crime and delinquency/analogous behaviors is likely to be small to moderate (J. Cohen, 1988). In fact, the meta-analysis which included 126 effect size estimates derived from 21 studies—after detecting and correcting for serial correlation between statistically dependent estimates—revealed that self-control is an important predictor of crime and analogous behaviors, whether measured attitudinally or behaviorally with adjusted mean effect sizes of .262 and .278, respectively. Unequivocal empirical support for the "spuriousness" thesis is not forthcoming, however, while limited support exists for the proposition that low self control pre-dates and is related to a variety of social consequences. Stephen W. Baron's (2003) analysis of a sample of 400 Canadian homeless street youth in Vancouver, British Columbia reveals that various social consequences (unemployment, harmlessness, deviant peers, and deviant values) are related to self-control. Similarly, Evans et al. (1997), using survey responses from 555 adult residents in a Midwestern urban area, found that low self-control is related to diminished quality of interpersonal relationships with family and friends, reduced involvement in church, low levels of educational and occupational attainment, and possibly to unfulfilling marriages.

According to Gottfredson and Hirschi (1990), the relationship between social conditions and crime/delinquency (such as social disorganization, labeling, lack of economic opportunities, and social learning) documented by competing positivist theories is "spurious" because low self-control often predates these conditions, and once it is accounted for previously significant relationships between those traits or conditions and crime will disappear. Specifically, they argue that individuals with low self-control experience a range of negative social consequences because low self-control fosters failure in social institutions, activities, and personal relationships that require delayed gratification, planning, preferences for cognitive and verbal activities, and personal relationships that require delayed gratification, planning, preference for cognitive and verbal activities, and so on. Thus, individuals with low self-control have more difficulty making and keeping friends, are more likely to flock together with people who lack self-control and are thus similarly deviant (birds of the same feather flock together), are less able to suffer the demands of the school environment, experience more job instability and are less likely to ascend into white-collar occupations, tend to enter marriages destined to fail, and prefer to gravitate to the street.

The results of Evans' et al. (1997) and Baron's (2003) analyses provide limited support for Gottfredson and Hirschi's contention that low self-control is related to negative social consequences as each documents a substantive and statistically significant relationship. Because the data for each analysis are cross-sectional, however, causality cannot be inferred. It should be noted that the spuriousness thesis is consistently unsupported as evidenced by Pratt and Cullen (2000) whose meta-analysis revealed that social learning theory continued to explain a significant proportion of variation after controlling for self-control. Similarly, Baron's (2003) and Junger and Tremblay's (1999) analyses offered additional support for the role of social learning and classic strain in crime and drug use, and self-control theories in automobile accidents, respectively, in explaining a significant proportion of variation beyond self-control.

The spuriousness thesis has also been tested with competing rational choice and biological/neuropsychological paradigms. As with previous investigations of the spuriousness hypothesis, definitive evidence was not forthcoming. In fact, Cauffman et al. not only demonstrated that the effects of neuropsychological/biological factors were not mediated by self-control, but that the former perspective explained nearly twice the variance in offender status than did the former. In addition, these investigators demonstrated that our understanding of offender status can be enhanced when we consider both self-control and biological/neuropsychological perspectives simultaneously. Finally, Piquero and Tibbetts (1996) demonstrated that rational choice continued to predict intentions to drive drunk and shoplift after accounting for individual levels of self-control.

Conclusion

The dawn of the period of European Enlightenment brought with it an emphasis upon the incorporation of **rationality** in the design and implementation of social policy. Crime control and punishment philosophies that existed prior to that period emphasized the symbolic and apotropaic qualities of punishment for their retributive qualities. Criminal justice reformers during that period were successful in re-orienting criminal justice policy away from retribution and towards deterrence by emphasizing the utility of rational criminal justice policy. Central to their argument was that proportionality in punishment would lead to reductions in crime. That is, if the perceived costs of crime where greater than the perceived benefits ("Hedonistic Calculus"), then "rational" individuals would be deterred from committing crime.

The principle of deterrence, along with its concomitant indeterministic view of individuals, quickly fell from favor as the anticipated reductions in crime did not ensue as revealed by the enhanced reporting of early crime statistics. What later emerged was a deterministic view of individuals engendered by positivists—one that viewed individual futures as largely determined by environmental influences residing beyond the realm of "free will". Early efforts then focused on discerning biological and physiological characteristics that determined individual behavior beyond 'free will,' to mark the birth of positivist criminology. This positivist tradition quickly produced complex and sophisticated explanations of crime and delinquency sewn by competing traditions.

The implications of such complexity for informing social policy are numerous, and the suggested courses of action are often competing and/or contradictory. For example, *classic strain, social learning, labeling,* and *social disorganization* theories each prescribes various social policies for crime control and/or prevention, ranging from creating more legitimate job opportunities, recognizing and counteracting the values/neutralizing techniques of deviant sub-cultures, reducing the negative impact of formal criminal justice intervention, and stabilizing communities and/or deploying criminal justice resources. These examples are offered at the risk of over-simplification; many more "countermeasures" have been derived from these various theoretical foundations in criminology.

Self-Control Theory, which emerged in 1990, seeks to remedy the centrifugal tendencies of the positivistic tradition by recognizing the **nature of crime and delinquency.** Central to this approach has been the effort to unite the classical and positivist conceptions of crime and delinquency by recognizing that individuals are influenced by both internal and external variables, while abandoning sociopolitical definitions of crime. In doing so, Gottfredson and Hirschi argue that self-control as an underlying **predisposition** established early in life is the "master variable" that leads some to pursue easy and immediate pleasures through force or fraud; for them and their many followers in Criminal Justice and Criminology, that is the essence of all criminal and delinquent acts.

Despite contention of the theory's architects that that self-control is not a personality trait, early attempts to measure the propensity quickly followed a psychometric approach. The principal result of this work to measure the concept was a 24-item self-control scale developed by Grasmick et al. (1990) that has become the most widely used measure for testing the theory. Despite the panoply of methodological approaches adopted by researchers in this field, a substantial number of individual studies and meta-analytic analyses reveal significant and substantive support for the theory. Moreover, despite the contention by the theory's architects that behavioral measures are superior to cognitive ones, subsequent empirical analysis suggests that the predictive power of the theory cannot be significantly improved with such measures.

The promise of parsimony and conceptual clarity offered by the general theory of crime is an attractive lure that has gained a significant amount of attention and effort from many scholars. Parsimony as the standard by which scientific theory should be judged often comes at a cost to the complexity and richness that often characterizes social reality. More recent standards of scientific inquiry suggest that theories should be evaluated not so much for their parsimony, but for their **leverage**—or ability to explain as much as possible with as little as possible (King et al., 1994). Accordingly, this general theory of crime should be assessed for its superiority in relation to other competing theories. If the "spuriousness" thesis is supported, we can dismiss the competing theories and focus on the contexts and bounds of the general theory to determine its application and implications for social policy. Currently, the tenability of this promise appears to be beyond the reach of theory, however.

If we cannot readily dismiss competing theories in favor of Self-Control Theory, we must then assess the relative leverage—or explanatory power—of the theory in relation to its adversaries. In doing so, finite resources can be directed in a manner that produces the greatest net social benefit, in as much as many public policy problems we seek to understand such as crime are "wicked" or span several institutions and originate from diverse sources.

CHAPTER 3

Strain and Young Driver Accidents and Driving Delinquency

INTRODUCTION

Self-control theorists have documented the significant and relatively substantive relationship between low self-control and crime/delinquency, and "analogous behaviors." Through the lens of self-control theorists, individuals are seen to vary in their "propensity" to pursue immediate and simple gratification, a predisposition which is in part the residue of their short time horizon and absence of community orientation in rational decision-making. This pursuit of immediate and easy gratification is the essence of all politically defined criminal/delinquent and analogous acts which threaten the weal of the community and/or precipitate long term consequences for the individual. The promise of this general theory to scientific inquiry is vast—namely, a general theory which purports to explain a wide range of criminal and delinquent behaviors not bound by political context or conflicting narrow classifications.

A central tenet of the theory is that individuals are equally **motivated** to engage in crime and delinquent acts, as all persons are rational and motivated to pursue their self-interest. What differs across individuals, then, is their ability to exercise self-control in the face of temptation. Self-control as an individual propensity has been conceptualized by scholars as consisting of the core elements of **impulsivity**, a preference for **simple** and **physical tasks**, and a tendency to seek **risks**, be **self-centered** and possess a **temper**. It is argued that self-control pre-dates many of the social conditions which are the nexus of crime and delinquency within competing traditions. Low self-control moves persons with the propensity through the following path: low self-control→ various social consequences → adverse social conditions → crime and delinquency. The "spuriousness" thesis argues that after we account for individual levels of self-control, once statistically significant relationships revealed between various social conditions and crime and delinquency will likely disappear because self-control is the "master variable" at play in crime and delinquency.

In contrast to the self-control tradition, advocates of General Strain Theory argue that the "motivation" to engage in crime and delinquency is not equal and/or constant. Instead, various conditions have disparate impacts on individual levels of strain to provide motivation to engage in criminal or delinquent acts. The causal mechanism by which individual motivation is translated into criminal and delinquent acts is how an individual adapts to or copes with challenging stimuli: stimuli → strain → motivation → criminal or non-criminal adaptation/coping.

Classic Strain Theory: A Social Structural Theory

Writing in 1938, Robert K. Merton attempted to explain the great difference in crime rates witnessed in comparisons between America and Europe and across social classes within this country through a *social structural theory*. According to Merton, the culture of every society defines certain goals it deems "worth striving for" (Merton, 1968: 187). The dominant cultural goal of America is the accumulation of wealth, because wealth is equated with personal value and worth and is associated with a high degree of prestige and social status (Vold et al., 2002). The salience of this cultural goal is often captured in the American ethos with the dictum that society is egalitarian and that the "American dream" (Messner & Rosenfeld, 2001) is within the reach of those who are willing to work hard. Those who do not pursue this dominant cultural goal are typically degraded and characterized as either "lazy" or "lacking ambition."

Just as every culture defines certain goals that it deems worth striving for, so too do they prescribe the appropriate institutional means that individuals are to follow in pursuing these goals. Moreover, the most technically efficient methods of achieving the goal are generally ruled out. These means are based on the values of the culture, which in

American society can generally be defined as "middle-class values" or the "Protestant work ethic." The value set in question includes hard work, honesty, acquiring education, and the deferral of gratification; in addition, the most technically efficient means of acquiring some of these—force and fraud—are strictly prohibited (Merton, 1968: 187).

Because not all individuals can achieve the goals of the culture, sufficient emphasis must be placed on the institutional means. By emphasizing the socially acceptable institutional means, individuals receive an intrinsic satisfaction in the **pursuit** of the goal whether or not the goal is achieved; hence the power of the old bromide—"it's not whether you win or lose, it's how you play the game." American society, according to many social critics, emphasizes the goal of wealth without placing sufficient emphasis on the legitimate institutional means permitted, thereby placing the institutional means under considerable strain. To be sure, individuals who adhere to the legitimate institutional means—hard work, honesty, education, and deferred gratification—receive few social rewards unless some measure of wealth is ultimately achieved. Conversely, those who achieve wealth through the improper institutional means often receive the social rewards of prestige and social status, despite their wrongdoing. Awareness of this situation places those who are unable to achieve wealth through legitimate means under severe strain.

In addition to the social sources of individually experienced strain—a "cultural imbalance" emphasizing monetary success without a concomitant emphasis on the legitimate institutional means—Merton (1938) sought to explain the disproportionately high crime rates witnessed among the lower class by pointing to the distribution of opportunity within the social structure. According to Merton, opportunities for personal advancement within the social structure are concentrated in the higher classes, and they are relatively absent among the lower classes. Individuals within the lower class are likely to experience higher levels of strain than those in the upper class because only a small percentage of hard-working individuals within this class can ever expect to accumulate wealth through the use of established institutional means. Conversely, those within the upper class experience less strain as persons of modest talents can achieve a substantial degree of wealth with only moderate efforts (Vold et al., 2002).

When individual ambitions for wealth (or positively valued goals) are **frustrated** [sic.] (see V. S. Burton, Jr. & Cullen, 1992; Vold et al., 2002) individuals can respond through various modes of adaptation depending on their attitude toward the cultural goal and institutionalized means. When the strained individual continues to accept the cultural goal and the institutional means whether or not they succeed, the individual is termed a **conformist**. Most forms of crime occur, however, when an individual continues to accept the goal, but rejects the legitimate institutional means for a more technically efficient method, or through **innovation**. **Ritualism** as a mode of adaptation is typically found among the lower middle class who have rejected the cultural goal of wealth but continue to accept the institutional means for fear of losing the minimum level of success they have achieved. **Retreatism** occurs when individuals have rejected both goals and means and no longer pursue the dominant cultural goal of wealth nor act in accordance with institutionalized means. These individuals include "psychotics, autists, pariahs, outcasts, vagrants, vagabonds, tramps, chronic drunkards and drug addicts" (Merton, 1968: 207). **Rebellion** as a mode of adaptation occurs when the strained individual not only rejects the cultural goals and institutional means, but subsequently replaces those goals and means to live within an alternate culture, e.g., gangs and cults (Merton, 1938) (see Figure 3.1).

This social structural theory, while quite plausible, did not do well in accounting for non-utilitarian forms of crime witnessed among juvenile gang members, however. Responding to this noteworthy deficiency, subsequent strain theorists offered a potential explanation. To them, the non-utilitarian nature of most juvenile delinquency was represented an outright rejection and replacement of middle class values—ambition, responsibility, academic and athletic achievement, deferred gratification, etc.—by lower class youths frustrated in their attempts to achieve status among upper and middle class youths. This rejection and replacement of middle and upper class values with delinquent values serves as the vehicle by which the lower class youths could then achieve status among their peers and self worth (A. K. Cohen, 1955).

Merton's social structural theory of crime enjoyed considerable currency throughout the 1960s becoming the dominant criminological paradigm into the early 1970s (Cole, 1975). Considerable empirical support for the original conceptualization offered by Merton (1938),

Figure 3.1—Strain Modes of Adaptation

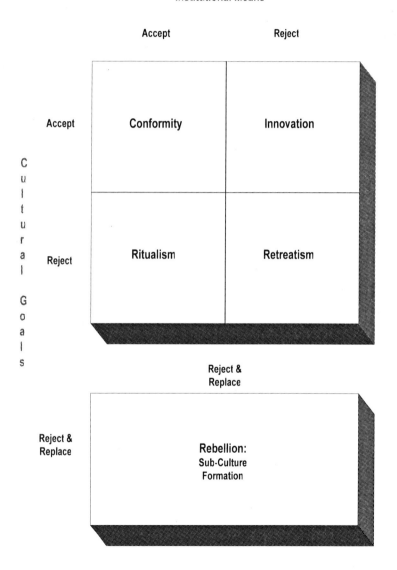

Institutional Means

Accept   Reject

	Accept	Reject
Accept	Conformity	Innovation
Reject	Ritualism	Retreatism

C u l t u r a l   G o a l s

Reject & Replace

Rebellion:
Sub-Culture
Formation

and for derivative theories offered by Cloward & Ohlin (1960) and Cohen (1955) (Hirschi, 1969; Kornhauser, 1978; Liska, 1971). In later years scholars cited "extra-empirical" forces as being responsible for catapulting the theory into preeminence despite sometimes conflicting empirical evidence calling the theory into question. In fact, this social structural theory offered professional rewards in the form of publishable "puzzles," while highlighting the cost of injustice—racism and poverty—during the liberal political climate of the 1960s (V. S. Burton, Jr. & Cullen, 1992: 2). Subsequently, the 1970s witnessed the advent of new theories of crime—principally labeling theory (Becker, 1963)—that would eventually relegate strain theory to the criminological dustbin until the paradigm underwent substantial revitalization in the 1990s.

General Strain Theory: A Reconstructed Social Psychological Theory

As new theories emerged and the Great Society Programs of the Johnson administration fell short of expectations, strain theories declined in popularity. This diminished popularity was not a result of empirical falsification, however. In fact, considerable empirical support existed for the theory (see D. S. Elliot, 1962; Fredricks & Molnar, 1969; Landis & Scarpitti, 1965; Palmore & Hammond, 1964; Rivera & Short, 1967; Short, Rivera, & Tennyson, 1965), especially where strain was measured as blocked opportunities rather than the disjunction between aspirations and expectations.

The moribund status of the major strain theories resulting from disagreement and difficulty associated with the conceptualization and measurement of the theory's central tenets led Francis T. Cullen (1983) to reinterpret Merton's original theory to advance an individual level social psychological derivative. According to Cullen, strain operates at both the aggregate level where the social structure fails to provide legitimate means to achieve cultural values (to explain rates and distribution of deviant behavior), and at the individual level where people in situations of social structural strain would feel frustrated, and those feelings would motivate them to act in deviant ways (Cullen, 1983: 36-7). Thus, at the individual level it is these feelings of frustration that are the actual cause of higher crimes rates—not the strain itself. The flow diagram would run as follows: strain →

frustration → negative affects (e.g., anger, depression, anxiety, disappointment, etc.) → crime and delinquency.

Identification of both a social and individual level of strain provided the grist that subsequent strain theorists would need to expand upon to offer a general theory of crime. At the individual level, Robert Agnew (1992) expanded the core tenets of the theory to identify additional sources of strain beyond the blockage of positively valued goals, while also focusing on the role of negative emotions experienced by the "strained" individual situated within negative relationships. According to Agnew, individuals experience strain when not treated the way they would like to be treated (1992: 50). Such relationships result in what is known as a "negative affect," most commonly characterized as anger or other unpleasant states which can lead to crime and delinquency (Agnew, 1992).

In addition to the **blockage** of some positively valued goal identified by classic strain theorists, such as monetary success or status, Agnew expands strain theory to identify two additional sources. The **removal** of some positively valued goal and/or the **presentation** of some "noxious" or negative stimuli are also identified as possible sources of negative affects. Crime and delinquency in the former are said to be the result of a coping response by the strained individual where he/she tries to prevent, recoup, substitute for, avenge, or manage the loss. Such an instance can be illustrated where an individual assaults the rival of their romantic partner's attention resulting from felt anger, or turns to drugs/alcohol to medicate their depression. In the latter, the strained individual seeks to escape, terminate, alleviate, or seek revenge against the source of the noxious or negative stimuli. The emotionally or physically abused adolescent who cannot legally leave the negative relationship provides an illustration, as they may manage their disappointment, depression, fear, and anger with delinquency and/or drugs.

Negative Affects and Coping

According to Agnew (1992: 59), each type of strain increases the likelihood that individuals will experience one or more of a range of negative emotions. These emotions include "disappointment, depression, and fear." Anger, however, is the most critical emotion identified by Agnew as it increases the individual's level of felt injury and gives rise to a desire for retaliation and revenge. Moreover, anger tends to lower inhibitions as strained individuals are inclined to believe that their aggression is justified (Agnew, 1992: 60). Agnew also acknowledges and moves beyond behavioral modes of adaptation, or coping strategies, to identify a variety of emotional and cognitive strategies ignored in previous tests of strain theory.

Behaviorally, Agnew (1992: 69) recognizes that innovation and rebellion are but two possible adaptations of individuals as they seek to achieve positively valued goals, protect or retrieve positively valued stimuli, or terminate or escape from negative stimuli. At the core of these non-vengeful behavior coping strategies lies "maximizing one's outcomes," "minimizing one's outputs," and "maximizing the other's inputs." When an individual blames their adversity on others, however, the tendency is to cope through vengeful behaviors which can be either delinquent (e.g., aggression) or non-delinquent. In the latter case, efforts can be aimed at minimizing the positive outcomes, increasing the negative outcomes, and/or increasing the inputs of others. **Cognitively**, individuals may reinterpret: adversity (deny the importance of a goal/value in an absolute sense), outcomes (deny existence of adversity by maximizing positive outcomes and/or minimizing negative outcomes by lowering standards or distorting estimates), and/or personal responsibility (convince themselves they deserve the adversity)(66-8). **Emotionally**, individuals may cope conventionally or delinquently by altering their state of consciousness to alleviate the strain (e.g., use of illegal drugs, indulgence in physical exercise, meditation, etc.)(69-70). The complexity of this coping typology suggests that many coping strategies exist, and that only some are delinquent.

Conditioning Factors of Strain on Delinquency

In addition to the various modes of adaptation that present serious measurement bulwarks for empirical tests of GST, conditioning factors that moderate strain and delinquent and conventional coping behaviors also exist. The conditioning factors arising from the impact of strain on delinquent and conventional coping strategies can be traced to internal and external factors that constrain individual adaptation strategies. Where initial goals, values, and the identities of the individual are comparatively favorable in both a relative and absolute sense, the individual will have more difficulty relegating the strain to an unimportant area of their lives.   Individual adaptations are also constrained by a wide range of traits that determine levels of sensitivity to objective strains and their ability to engage in cognitive, emotional, and behavioral coping.   Temperament, intelligence, creativity, problem-solving skills, interpersonal skills, self-efficacy, and self-esteem are just a few traits that are believed to influence an individual's strain threshold and affect the choice of either delinquent or non-delinquent coping strategies under stressful circumstances.

For example, studies reporting empirical findings for both youth and adult subjects indicate that individuals with high self-esteem are more resistant to stress (Averill, 1982; Compas, 1987; H. B. Kaplan, 1980; Rosenberg, 1990) and, therefore, less likely to respond to objective strain with delinquency or criminal activity (Agnew, 1992: 71).   Similarly, individuals high in self-efficacy are more likely to feel that their strain can be constructive behavioral coping strategies, and less likely to respond to strain with delinquency or criminal activity (Agnew, 1992: 71; Bandura, 1989).   Instrumental, informational, and emotional social support is also implicated in the choice of adaptations as it influences which strategy an individual is likely to adopt—behavioral, cognitive, and/or emotional.   Thus, individuals with high levels of conventional social support are more likely to cope in a non-delinquent or non-criminal manner.

Just as there are internal and external factors that constrain individual coping strategies making them either more or less likely to adopt delinquent or non-delinquent coping strategies in response to negative affects, so too do factors reside in the larger social environment with similar effects.   Individuals may be affected by the larger social environment according to the level of importance ascribed to a particular value/goal/identity and the relative insufficiency of opportunity to attain these values/goals/identities.   For example, the poor tend to overemphasize the importance of economic wealth and status, while experiencing few opportunities to achieve either.   The social environment may also limit an individual's ability to cope cognitively (non-delinquently) by means of information distortion and goal relegation by providing feedback regarding the true costs, benefits, and relative import of goals.   Poor parenting practices would be a common example (see: Agnew, 1992; Hay, 2001, , 2003) Lastly, an individual's social group may strongly influence their strain threshold (e.g., sub-culture of violence defining adverse environments to include "disrespect")(E. Anderson, 1999) and provide the techniques—social learning—for crime/delinquency, while the broader social environment may provide few opportunities to cope non-delinquently (e.g., children cannot legally leave the family to escape negative stimuli).

Issues in Testing General Strain Theory

As a general theory of crime, GST offers the promise of explaining a wide range of criminal and delinquent behaviors through a social psychological approach. In contrast to classic social structural strain theories, GST focuses on the psychological dimensions of the strained individual—negative affects—while expanding the sources of strain to include the removal or positively valued goals and the introduction of negative or noxious stimuli. The strained or stressed individual is believed to be **"motivated"** by his/her translation of frustrated ambitions into negative affects that precipitate adaptation through delinquent or non-delinquent coping strategies determined by internal/external constraints and the larger social environment. What GST promises in explanatory power for scientific inquiry, is, however, counterposed by conceptual and measurement bulwarks not commonly encountered by its rival paradigm (Tittle & Botchkovar, 2005; Wright, Caspi, Moffitt, & Paternoster, 2004)—Self-Control Theory (Gottfredson & Hirschi, 1990).

To be sure, in direct comparison to Self-Control Theory, GST suffers disproportionately the hazards of reification—whereby the central tenets of the theory are identified, conceptualized, and operationalized as stated or implied by the theory's architect(s)—by the scientific community whose interpretations often produce disparate findings. The source of these hazards is rooted in the complexity of the theory, well intentioned but misdirected interpretations where the architect is silent, and the situational orientation of the theory which greatly complicates measurement.

Conceptualization

Self-control has been conceptualized by its principal architects as a **"propensity"** to engage in acts of force or fraud flowing from an individual's inability or unwillingness to consider the distal and collective consequences of his/her actions. Self-control conceptualized as a propensity is considered to be a relatively stable construct consisting of: **impulsivity**, preference for **simple tasks** and **physical activity, risk-seeking, self-centeredness,** and **temper.** It is seen as a propensity which is established relatively early in life; most researchers believe this propensity is "fixed: by eight years of age. To the chagrin of its architects, measurement of self-control has been approached through psychological assessments conceptualizing self-control as a personality "**trait**" (Gottfredson & Hirschi, 1989) using the popular Grasmick et al. scale (1993). Despite the admonition of Gottfredson and Hirschi not to cast low self-control as a trait, the theory continues to enjoy considerable empirical support when self-control is measured with the Grasmick et al. scale. That measure continues to demonstrate predictive validity and factorial invariance across a wide range of subjects (see Chapter 2).

General strain theorists have conceived the construct strain as the "motivation" flowing from a wide-range of negative emotions experienced by the stressed or strained individual in response to the blockage of positively valued goals, the removal of positively valued stimuli, and/or the introduction of negative or noxious stimuli. The blockage of positively valued goals has traditionally been operationalized as the disjunction between aspirations and expectations, the disjunction between expectations and actual achievements, and the disjunction between fair outcomes and actual outcomes, as articulated by Agnew (1992). Numerous measures ranging from "noxious neighborhood conditions" (Mazerolle & Piquero, 1998) to "the loss of a relative" (Capowich, Mazerolle, & Piquero, 2001) and "the amount of physical and emotional abuse experienced by youth" in their households (Hay, 2001, , 2003; Leeper-Piquero & Sealock, 2000; Sigfusdottir, Farkas, & Silver, 2004) have been employed to represent negative stimuli and the removal of positively valued goals in tests of the theory.

<u>Measurement</u>

The specificity provided by Agnew (1992) in the operationalization of the blockage of positively valued goals has led theorists working within this tradition to focus on the *social circumstance* said to generate strain and delinquency—typically the disjunction between aspirations and opportunity—in their empirical tests of the theory (V. S. Burton, Jr. & Cullen, 1992). General Strain Theory also contains a psychological component which recognizes that "various social situations create a psychological state of "strain" (i.e., feelings of frustration, stress, or pressure) that lead to negative affects and motivation to engage in crime and delinquency across various domains of social life (work, leisure)(V. S. Burton, Jr. & Cullen, 1992: 8, 17).

Thus, testing "strain" from a psychological vantage first requires the documentation of innumerable social situations that are likely to evoke feelings of stress with significant variation among individuals, and the recognition that frustration or stress in one situation is not predictive of frustration or stress experienced in other situations or contexts (Agnew, 2001). That is, frustration or stress experienced by an individual is likely a function of the setting and coping resources available in that situation and social environment, and various situations provide different levels and types of coping resources (consider work and leisure) along with unique environmental demands.

As a result, a psychological approach to testing General Strain Theory requires context specific measures which allow individuals to assess the perceived level of adversity within the environment, while simultaneously considering the importance they attach to the value/goal and the coping resources available to overcome such adversity. To the extent that an individual values a particular goal/outcome, and an environmental condition exists which threatens that goal/outcome vis-à-vis insufficient coping resources, an individual is "strained," "stressed," or "frustrated." Thus, general measures used to test the limits of strain theory tend to inadvertently disadvantage the theory—a situation not experienced by Self-Control Theory.

"Dispositional" versus "Transitory" Negative Affects

According to Agnew (1992: 60), the mechanism by which strain is translated into crime and delinquency is through a wide range of negative affects. The negative affects identified by Agnew include the following experiential states: depression, disappointment, fear, and anger; the state of anger is considered the most critical emotion as it increases an individual's level of felt injury, and often creates a desire for retaliation and revenge. Subsequent tests by those working within the tradition have explored deeper dimensions of the theory to identify and operationalize a host of negative affects. In this regard it is noteworthy that recent efforts point to the value of casting strain as "**transitory**" rather than "**dispositional**" in theory testing. Agnew's (1992) relative silence regarding a "wide range" of negative affects, and identification of anger as the principal negative emotion which leads to aggression, have led theorists to focus on the role of anger, anxiety, and depression is tests of GST (Aseltine, Gore, & Gordon, 2000; Broidy, 2001; Capowich et al., 2001; Leeper-Piquero & Sealock, 2000; Mazerolle & Piquero, 1998; Sigfusdottir et al., 2004). Despite Agnew's (1992: 58-9) assertion that GST is more properly tested with "situational" measures—measures of negative affects emerging from particular incidents rather than dispositional measures— measures tapping enduring characteristics of an individual—many tests of the mediating role of anger and other negative affects have employed "dispositional" or general "trait" measures (Agnew, 2001; Mazerolle & Piquero, 1998). It is fair to say at this point in our progress toward understanding strain phenomenon that most empirical assessments have supported the role of anger in retaliatory aggression as a form of delinquent coping, while simultaneously highlighting the need to conceptually link negative affects with various forms of delinquent coping behaviors—a point on which GST is silent.

Empirical Status

Initial tests of GST focused on the direct relationship between strain and delinquency and drug use. Utilizing data from the first wave of the Rutgers Health and Human Development Project (HHDP), Agnew and White (1992) revealed that four measures of strain (negative life events; negative relations with adults; life hassles; parental fighting) were related to delinquency and drug use even after controlling for social control and differential association. Similarly, utilizing data from the first and second waves of the National Youth Survey (NYS), Paternoster and Mazerolle (1994) found that four (neighborhood problems; negative life events; negative relations with adults; and traditional strain) of five measures of strain shared a significant and positive relationship with delinquency even after controlling for social control and differential association.

More recent analyses have attempted to test the mediating role of various negative affects—especially anger—using general and situational measures, and other personality traits to highlight the need for context-specific measures and conceptual clarification of the theory. Mazerolle and Piquero (1997), using a composite measure, found that strain was related positively to anger and that anger increased the probability of intentions to engage in assault. Later, Mazerolle and Piquero (1998) examined the mediating effects of anger using the **temper** measure of Grasmick et al. scale (1993) on possible instrumental (shoplifting), escapist (drinking and driving), and violent (fighting) adaptations to strain. Using regression models, the authors found that not all types of strain (feelings of injustice, failure to achieve positively valued goals, and noxious stimuli) were significant predictors of anger. In fact, the only statistically and substantively significant predictor of anger was perceived equity on intentions to drive drunk and fight.

Attempting to assess the mediating impact of anger on intentions to drive drunk, shoplift, and fight revealed that anger only mediated strain with intentions to fight—not to drive drunk or shoplift—and that perceived equity remained a significant and relatively stronger predictor. According to Agnew (1992), the effects of strain on crime and delinquency are mediated by negative affects—especially anger. Thus, once significant and substantive relationships between measures of strain and crime/delinquency should either disappear or substantively decrease after accounting for the negative affect. Mazerolle and Piquero's (1998) analysis suggests that the mediating hypothesis stands in need of clarification and the impact of anger on crime and delinquency is dependent on the type of crime and delinquency. Mazerolle and Piquero (1998: 208) do note, however, that the mixed and limited support for the mediating impact of anger on intentions to shoplift and drive drunk could be related to the general trait anger measure they employed, which overlooks the more situational and dynamic nature of negative affects.

Despite the shortcomings of the dispositional anger measure employed by Mazerolle and Piquero (1998), subsequent analyses suggest that in fact the mediating hypothesis and the role of various negative affects in crime and delinquency requires careful revision. Using data from an "offending" population of juveniles in a residential drug-treatment program in a mid-Atlantic state (N = 150) revealed anger as a negative affect, which mediated the affects of strain on interpersonal aggression, but depression as a negative affect served no mediating role in predicting property offenses (Leeper-Piquero & Sealock, 2000).

Similarly, employing longitudinal data from 1988 (N = 1,208) to 1990 (N = 939) and variance/covariance structural modeling, Aseltine, Gore and Gordon (2000) investigate the role of anxiety and anger—using general trait measures—on three distinct types of delinquent behavior: aggression, non-aggressive delinquency, and marijuana use. This test of the "generality" of the theory in predicting crime and delinquency revealed that anxiety played no mediating role in the impact of family conflict, stressful life-events, and peer conflict on these three forms of delinquency. Perhaps more importantly, their results replicate previous findings regarding the role of anger: That anger as a negative affect is not related to non-aggressive forms of delinquency.

In an attempt to assess the impact of a "wide range" of negative affects on legitimate and illegitimate coping responses to strain and stress more accurately, Lisa Broidy (2001) subjugates thirty-two emotional responses to blocked goals and stressful events to a factor analysis. Employing the empirical **scree discontinuity test** (which identifies the greatest drop between eigenvalues as the appropriate solution), while considering the theoretical import of anger as the principal negative affect, the results of her analysis suggest that the "wide range" of emotions: feeling alone, anger, cheated, cranky, depressed, disappointed, frustrated, guilty, insecure, overwhelmed, resentful, scared, stressed, upset, worried, and worthless, coalesced into two factors (anger and other negative emotions), and that illegitimate coping (criminal/deviant) is more likely when the negative affect is anger. Conversely, non-angry responses to strain and stress were more likely to result in legitimate coping strategies.

Attempting to capture and assess the "situational," or state like nature of anger in response to strain, while estimating its influence on intentions to commit crime, Capowich, Mazerolle, and Piquero (2001) employ a situational measure of anger. The measure asked respondents to express what their level of anger would be if they were the character represented in scenarios covering intentions to shoplift, drive drunk, and fight. In addition to situational anger, the investigators included a negative emotions measure corresponding to being overwhelmed by life's demands. Consistent with GST predictions and prior tests, situational anger was a significant and positive predictor of intentions to fight (providing an adjusted R^2 of .267 in comparison to .009— where no measure of negative affects were included—to .019 for a model including only the negative emotions measure. The results highlight the need to consider the role of negative affects in aggressive forms of coping—especially situational anger.

General Strain, Other Personality Traits, and Trait-by-Situation Interactions

General Strain Theory recognizes that only some strained individuals turn to delinquent coping strategies, while others turn to conventional or non-delinquent coping strategies. Many factors are said to "condition" the response of the strained individual. Self-efficacy, self-esteem, problem-solving skills, and creativity are just a few factors purported to condition an individual's response to strain. Other factors potentially conditioning individual responses to strain are personality traits, as they may have a fundamental effect on the experience of and reaction to strain (Agnew, Brezina, Wright, & Cullen, 2002).

Psychologists have made considerable progress over the past twenty years in identifying the major personality traits that comprise the human personality. Some argue that these traits tend to cluster into several "master" or "supertraits," with some scholars arguing that personality can be described adequately in terms of five master traits ("the Big Five") while others have argued for three ("the big three"), with considerable overlap existing among several of the traits in question (see: Agnew et al., 2002; Block, 1995; Prior, 1992; Watson, Clark, & Harkness, 1994). Two of "the big three" personality traits which may theoretically condition the effects of strain on delinquency, while offering the promise of theoretical integration, is "constraint" and "negative emotionality" (Tellegen, 1985).

Constraint, as conceived by psychologists, is a personality trait which predisposes individuals to impulsivity, risk-seeking/sensation-seeking, rejection of conventional social norms, and egocentrism (Agnew et al., 2002; Tellegen, 1985). Negative emotionality, as conceived by psychologists, is a personality trait which predisposes individuals to view the actions of others as malicious and events as aversive. Individuals low in constraint and high in negative emotionality are thus more likely to experience the actions of others and their environments as malicious and aversive, respectively, and to be predisposed to act impulsively, egocentrically, and in a physical and delinquent manner. Moreover, these same individuals are more likely than others to select themselves into more "stressful" environments as these traits tend to illicit negative reactions by others, and transform their environments in ways that increase negative treatment by others (e.g., joining delinquent peer groups and being "tracked" into lower academic levels in school) (Agnew, 1992; Agnew & Brezina, 1997).

Using data from the second wave of the National Survey of Children (1981) (N = 1,031) featuring children 12 to 16 years of age, Agnew, Brezina, Wright, and Cullen (2002) investigate the relationship and conditioning role of constraint and negative emotionality on delinquency. Zero-order correlations revealed that six measures of strain (family strain; conflict with parents; parent's loss of control over feelings; school hatred; peer abuse; and neighborhood strain) were statistically and substantively correlated with the 11-item constraint/negative emotions scale—suggesting that these personality traits influence an individual's perception of/selection into uncommonly stressful conditions. The conditioning influence of constraint/negative emotions was investigated using Moderated Multiple Regression (MMR) to reveal that the impact of strain on delinquency is statistically moderated by these personality traits; although the statistical relationship documented is arguably substantively weak (β = .06) (J. Cohen, 1988). It is noteworthy that, the composite measure of strain remained the strongest predictor of delinquency, with the predictive strength being greater than twice that for the interaction or main constraint/negative emotions measure(s). The results of their findings led Agnew et al. (2002: 60) to conclude that linkages exist between strain and personality traits such as negative emotionality/low constraint that should be replicated and/or further investigated with more fully developed measures of constraint.

The linkage between constraint and negative emotionality, and the similarity of these two personality traits with the measure of low self-control developed by Grasmick et al. (1993), provide a promising area of study for increased understanding of this relationship and a potential avenue towards the theoretical integration of a an abundance of criminological theories that tend toward disciplinary fragmentation (Liska, Krohn, & Messner, 1989). To be sure, the Grasmick et al. scale is a 24-item multi-dimensional scale tapping items related to **impulsivity**, **egocentrism**, **risk-seeking**, and outwardly directed behavioral coping strategies that are aggressive in nature, captured in the sub-scales: **simple tasks**, **physical activity**, and **temper**.

Use of this scale also offers promise in assessing claims by GST's architects that the theory is more consistent with situational negative affect's measures—especially anger, and competing claims that trait measures share a relationship with state (trait-by-situation interaction) measures (Nunnally & Bernstein, 1994:   380).   For example, individuals presumably possess both trait anger and situational anger, and those high in trait anger may be more likely to be triggered by situational anger (Mazerolle & Piquero, 1998).   Thus, preliminary results suggested by Agnew et al. (2002) of the relationship between constraint/negative emotionality and strain and the low self-control scale developed by Grasmick et al. (1993) offer promise in more fully understanding   the   relationship   between   strain   and   these   two "supertraits" (theoretical integration) and/or comparative tests of the competing theories in explaining delinquent behaviors.

Automobile Accidents, Driving Delinquency, and General Strain

As a general theory of crime, GST offers promise in explaining a wide range of delinquent behaviors. Among these behaviors are delinquent coping actions and frames of mind adopted while operating a motor vehicle. Driving is one social situation whereby individuals experience a host of "frustrating" or "stressful" events in which automobile operators experience the blockage of positively valued goals, the removal of positively valued goals, and/or the introduction of negative or noxious stimuli to produce negative affects that lead to delinquent coping strategies for a variety of retaliatory, instrumental, or escapist reasons. Moreover, stressful or frustrating circumstances may disturb sufficiently cognitive processes to increase the probability of being involved in an accident.

In keeping with the situational orientation of the theory, a greater understanding of the sources and contexts likely to evoke negative emotions must be explored and documented in a manner which allows for a context-specific assessment based on individual interpretations of the importance they attached to a particular goal/value, their perceived amount and type of available coping resources, and the broader social environment within which they are immersed. Not only does this approach square with the situational orientation of the theory, but such exploration is necessary in the absence of previously developed measures which have tended to assess the role of traditional crime/delinquency—i.e., offenses against property and persons and vice and status—crimes and focus on the social dimension which entails the disjunction between aspirations and opportunity.

The universal status of this theory, a **general** theory of crime, means that it makes no distinction between its ability to predict various forms of crime/delinquency. A number of empirical analyses have demonstrated, however, significant limitations to the generality of this theory as it relates to non-aggressive forms of crime/delinquency. Delinquent coping behaviors adopted while operating a motor vehicle likely share an aggressive versus non-aggressive dimension that may be found to limit the generalizability when considering various forms of driving delinquency. Thus, an empirical test of GST in explaining driving delinquency must: 1) employ a novel context-specific measure; 2) investigate underlying dimensions of various driving behaviors; 3) and investigate the measure's relationship to negative affects experienced while operating a motor vehicle. Fortunately, the negative affects experienced while operating a motor vehicle are not likely to be as exhaustive as those experienced in other social situations (e.g., depression, and feeling alone and worthless).

Conclusion

General Strain Theory has experienced the ebb and flow of extra-empirical forces which have both contributed to and detracted from the theory's prominence and scientific exploration since the theory's early social structural conceptions. After a considerable period of scientific "inattention," strain theory experienced significant re-interpretation and re-conceptualization that extended the theory to include an individual social psychological dimension while augmenting the sources of strain to move beyond traditional social structural sources. This thoroughgoing re-interpretation and re-conceptualization revitalized scholarly interest to provide mixed empirical support for the theory. The mixed support registered to this point can be traced to the complexity of the theory, to well intentioned but misdirected efforts flowing from reification, and to issues in measurement which confound and disadvantage the theory.

Despite these substantial barriers to theory testing, GST continues to receive some forms of empirical support. Recent tests of the theory, however, point to the importance of casting social psychological strain as a context-situation bound response that is not predictive of stress or strain experienced across a broad range of social situations. Testing the theory, therefore, requires development and employment of measures that are context-specific if the theory is to be fairly tested. Recent tests of the theory also point to the relationship between strain and certain personality traits, and these connections offer promise of theoretical integration. Lastly, one important but relatively ignored form of delinquency—delinquency while operating a motor vehicle—has received little scholarly attention from the strain perspective (probably because of the absence of situational measures) despite its theoretical explanatory promise.

CHAPTER 4

Analytic Strategy

INTRODUCTION

Logical positivism is not the only form of social scientific inquiry aimed at creating empirically-based representations of social reality. Logical positivism can be distinguished from interpretive and critical social science by both its goals and methods (Neuman, 1997; Ragin, 1994). When describing the characteristics of positivistic social science it is often useful to compare it with these competing approaches, to appreciate nuanced differences in epistemology. In reality, none of these traditions exist in pure form, in practice because researchers often mix or employ multiple approaches to achieve triangulation on complex analytical problems (Almond, 1990; King et al., 1994; Neuman, 1997; Ragin, 1994).

Broadly speaking, logical positivism is the primary form of scientific inquiry often associated with the natural sciences. This tradition argues that there is an organized method for combining deductive logic with precise empirical observations of natural phenomena (including human behavior) in order to discover and confirm a set of probabilistic causal laws that can be used to predict general patterns of outcomes (Neuman, 1997: 63). Similar to how the approach is used in the natural sciences, logical positivism in social science relies on an established method—the scientific method (hypothesis testing, rules of evidence, and observational techniques adopted by the scientific community)—to formulate tentative representations of social reality subject to replication by other researchers. The purpose of research within this tradition is to discover natural laws in order to explain, control, and predict outcomes of interest. By comparison, the purpose of interpretive and critical social science is generally to understand more fully and describe in meaningful ways complex social action, or to expose and alter arguably unjust power imbalance, respectively. The advocates of interpretive social science tend to view the portrayal of social reality as inherently subjective and beyond objectification. Advocates of critical social science tend to view social reality as being constructed by powerful groups who employ science as the handmaiden facilitating the domination of marginalized groups that cannot command the resources to produce their own versions of scientific proof.

These varying goals and rival assumptions have significant implications for the design of social scientific inquiry. Interpretive and critical social science research—because they are interested in describing complex social phenomena or identifying and altering the imbalance of power (Almond, 1990; King et al., 1994; Neuman, 1997; Ragin, 1994; Rosenau, 1992)—is considerably less structured than logical positivism, and is rarely involved in theory testing (Ragin, 1994: 81-130). Designing scientific inquiry on the basis of these approaches thus requires focusing on a small number of cases usually selected for their anticipated similarity or differences. The purpose is to create a representation of reality that enhances understanding of certain aspects through non-random case selection and *qualitative techniques*. Principal investigative methodologies associated with these research efforts include participant observation, in-depth interviewing, fieldwork, and ethnographic study—all of which seem to immerse the investigator in the research setting to uncover the "deeper meaning" and contextual significance of social phenomena for individuals found within the social settings of interest.

In contrast to interpretive and critical social scientific research, designing scientific inquiry with an eye on discovering natural laws based on stable and pre-existing patterns of order for the purpose of explanation, prediction, and control requires a very different approach to evidence collection and assessment and to the selection of techniques of investigation. Despite the *prima facie* conceptual demarcation between logical positivism and the critical and interpretive approaches resulting from different goals, analytic techniques, and preferred types of evidence collected, considerable "interplay" exists between the approaches in the creation of social scientific knowledge. Indeed, the critical and interpretative approaches often advance theory by identifying commonalities (patterns of order) that exist across cases, while unanticipated diversity requires identification or construction of theoretical frameworks to account for such anomalous findings. It is the development and enhancement of theoretical frameworks that provide the principal grist to be milled by those working within the positivistic tradition.

Where critical and interpretative theorists are generally concerned with data enhancement, positivistic social scientists are most often concerned with condensing data by distilling peculiarities identified by critical and interpretive theorists. They typically pursue theory identification and the testing of specific hypotheses by focusing their investigation on a few attributes or features across many cases. Looking across many cases allows for the construction of social representations that are "purified" as the peculiarities of individual cases are averaged out in the aggregation process. What becomes clear in the process is a general pattern (Ragin, 1994: 131). Social scientists working within this tradition are primarily interested in identifying patterns that exist *between* attributes and features of the cases in question (variables). Identification of covariation between features and attributes allows the investigator to construct parsimonious representations (models) which specify significant relationships and allow for predictions based on the strength of the relationship obtaining between the attributes or features. Where covariation is non-extant, or where the observed relationship runs counter to the propositions of the theory being tested, qualitative techniques are often employed to refine or enhance social representations (hence another interplay between research traditions).

Explanation and prediction are the primary goals of logical positivism, and the replication (and refinement) of reported findings contributes to accuracy of social representations as independent and repeated tests of falsifiable propositions either support or refute their existence as natural laws. Previous studies attempting to identify those variables that contribute to the overrepresentation of young drivers in the annual number of auto-collisions and traffic fatalities witnessed in the United States have identified a host of plausible factors at play: experience, exposure (amount and type), gender, opportunity (e.g., Graduated Driver's Licensing Laws), type of vehicle, and vehicle ownership have all received attention in this regard. State and federal government intervention efforts have, however, emphasized the role of knowledge, skill, understanding of the causes of and consequences of automobile accidents, and the acceptance of personal responsibility among young drivers (see Chapter 1). The mixed, conflicting, null, and/or modest results witnessed in the evaluation of traffic safety education programs in reducing young driver accidents and fatality rates suggests that important variables may not be included in the theoretical frameworks henceforth developed, or that the proposed relationships do not exist in reality. Two sociological theories of crime and delinquency–Self-Control and General Strain Theory—offer promise in identifying those variables existing in nature that share a relationship with various forms of driving delinquency and young driver accidents (see Chapters 2 & 3). Not only do these competing theories offer promise in the identification of theoretically important variables for inclusion during model specification, but both theories offer promise for a more nuanced understanding of the role that traffic safety education might play in young driver accidents and driving delinquency. In fact, several testable propositions may be developed from the core tenets of these theories which will serve as the basis for the creation of new knowledge regarding the role that these previously identified variables share with young driver accidents and driving delinquency. If stable and pre-existing patterns in nature are to be elucidated that will allow for accurate predictions and future replications, however, several design principles consistent with the positivistic research tradition must first be observed.

Construct Measurement: Self-Control and Strain

Reliability

All basic sciences are concerned with establishing functional relationships among important variables. Before functional relationships can be established, however, the variables of interest must first be measured in valid and reliable ways. These variables can be distinguished by the extent to which they are concrete and observable, or latent and abstract. Where variables are concrete and observable, the scientist simply employs observation or other readily accepted methods to measure a variable of interest. With respect to the social sciences, gender is frequently included in models because of the social and physiological differences between males and females that likely share a direct or indirect relationship with the outcome of interest and the trait is readily observable and concrete. That is, the observer and research participant can measure the variable through ocular inspection and the trait in question is concrete, or unlikely to change over repeated measurements. Here the task of variable measurement is relatively straightforward and not likely—note, however, that measurement estimates remain a matter of estimated probability of accurate classification—to suffer measurement error.

Another observable and concrete variable associated with humans is height. In comparison to gender, the scientist typically employs a yardstick or measuring tape to discern an individual's height. This variable, although relatively concrete, is likely to change over time depending on the subject's age—increasing from adolescence to adulthood, and decreasing (slightly) as some skeletal support system cells and some organs experience atrophy near the end of the lifecycle. Measurement of this particular variable is relatively straightforward—using conventional instruments—but its estimation is more likely to suffer measurement error than is the specification of gender. That is, although the variable is readily observable (can be discerned with a conventional instrument), the measure can be confounded by the reading of the instrument (the angle at which the observer takes the reading), the application of the instrument (is it resting on the ground at the time of the reading), the composition of the instrument (expansion and contraction of wood and metal with changes in temperature), the time of the reading (individuals are slightly taller after long periods of sleep as tissue and joints re-hydrate), etc.

To the extent to which a variable is latent and abstract it is referred to as a "construct." A construct is something created by scientists (put together from their own imaginations) because it is not a readily observable phenomenon. A construct reflects a hypothesis (often incompletely informed) that a variety of behaviors will correlate with one another in studies of individual differences and/or will be similarly affected by experimental manipulations (Nunnally & Bernstein, 1994: 85). Juvenile delinquency is such a social construct, one which is commonly investigated by researchers interested in understanding adult criminality (Hirschi, 1969), criminal histories (Sampson & Laub, 1990), and "career criminality" (Wolfgang, Figlio, & Sellin, 1972). In contrast to gender and height, juvenile delinquency is not readily observable and concrete.

To measure juvenile delinquency, the investigator must propose a set of hypotheses regarding a variety of behaviors that would be theoretical manifestations of the trait. The extent to which individuals vary along this dimension, and the extent to which the hypothesized behaviors correlate, is the extent to which the investigator can marshal empirical evidence to document the existence of the social construct and develop a reliable measure. For example, theoretical manifestations of juvenile delinquency may include school truancy, frequent fighting, smoking, and drug and/or alcohol use. Adolescents are likely to vary considerably with respect to these behaviors, and the linear combination of these behaviors can be used to score an individual relative to others on the construct of "juvenile delinquency."

Latent and abstract variables such as this are more likely to suffer measurement error as individuals being observed frequently modify their behavior in response to process of observation, as instruments are often inappropriately applied (the limits of the instrument are not understood—e.g., applying a food thermometer to measure human temperature will lack the necessary range and precision), and specific individual and environmental conditions (distractions, noxious environments, physiological conditions, etc.) will influence perceptions and responses (For more on the sources of systematic and random measurement error see Nunnally & Bernstein, 1994). Because the goal of all the social sciences is to document patterned social phenomena and functional relationships, two basic concerns tend to pervade social science research: 1) developing useful and reliable measures of individual constructs; and, 2) finding functional relationships between and among measures of different traits and constructs (Nunnally & Bernstein, 1994).

The systematic measurement of the trait of self-control has proceeded by identifying the theoretical manifestations of the dimensions identified by Gottfredson and Hirschi (1990)—namely, impulsivity, preference for simple tasks and physical activities, risk-seeking, egocentrism, and possession of a volatile temper. The most widely adopted measure of self-control in the field of criminology was developed by Grasmick et al. (1993) (Pratt & Cullen, 2000). The Grasmick et al. instrument's factorial structure has been replicated over various groups and numerous settings (see Chapter 2). Self-Control Theory posits that individuals vary in their "propensity" to engage in crime and delinquency, and that self-control is trait-like in that it is a relatively stable characteristic which is resistant to change after the age of eight. In addition, this psychological propensity is not greatly influenced by either context or situation. Given this background, the scale developed by Grasmick et al. (1993) will be used in this analysis. General Strain Theory, in contrast, is more situation- and context-bound, a fact that complicates theory testing in that if the theory is to not be unduly disadvantaged, investigators must develop and employ measures that attempt to measure the social psychological response of individuals to context and situation-specific events and/or stimuli (see Chapter 3). Therefore, before a test of General Strain Theory can proceed with respect to young driver accidents and driving delinquency, a measurement instrument must be developed *de novo*. Because instrument development employing psychometric principles is guided by a host of highly structured methodological considerations, the subsequent chapter will outline the measure strategy employed and describe the empirical development of a potential measurement model (see Chapter 5).

Validity

Developing reliable measures of individual constructs is the first step leading toward the creation of scientific knowledge. The second step entails finding functional relationships between these variables. For example, it is of little utility to measure an individual's level of self-control or strain experienced while operating a motor vehicle if the ultimate goals of logical positivism cannot be achieved. That is, if we are going to explain, control, and predict behaviors/events then we must validate the trait measurement instrument with an outcome of interest (discover functional relationships). To use an example from the natural sciences, if we develop a measure of an individual's weight—a floor scale (this is only one method)—of what interest is this measure? The utility is that it likely predicts an individual's height, age, and health. That is, the measure correlates with other variables of interest in nature (functional relationship). The measurement of an individual's level of self-control and strain is of little utility if it cannot predict another outcome of interest. In this case, various forms of driving delinquent behaviors that potentially increase an individual's risk for accidents and citations are the outcomes of interest. If these functional relationships can be established, empirically, governmental interventions can be informed by these findings to *possibly* increase their effectiveness in reducing the injuries and loss of lives associated with the operation of automobiles (see Chapters 1, 2, and 3).

Case Selection

The goal of logical positivism is to discover and elucidate relationships that exist in nature for the purpose of explanation, control, and prediction. The most accurate representation of these relationships is achieved by measuring these variables among all cases within the population of interest. In the case of this study we would be interested in measuring self-control and context-specific strain experienced while operating a motor vehicle among *every* individual 16-24 years of age. Limits on time and financial resources necessarily prevent such a comprehensive investigation, of course. Fortunately, sampling theory prescribes well-researched and widely accepted principles that, if faithfully followed allows the investigator to draw conclusion regarding what is taking place in the population of interest.

According to sampling theory, dependable conclusions regarding the relationships existing among variables in the population can be derived from a sample—a subset of cases or elements selected from a population—if they are **representative**. A sample is said to be representative if the selection of cases for analysis possess characteristics that accurately reflect the composition of the larger population from which the sample was drawn. To increase the likelihood that a sample will be representative of the original population, case selection should employ **simple random sampling**. The simple random sampling procedure requires that all individuals included in the population of interest be identified (**sampling frame**) and that each individual within that population enjoy an equal chance for inclusion (For more on sampling theory, see Bohrnstedt & Knoke, 1994; Neuman, 1997) .

Finite limits on time and money necessarily require that artificial boundaries be drawn with respect to the sampling frame. The consequences for scientific inquiry and for the generalization of findings gleaned from the sample can be minimized, however, by drawing boundaries based on sound theory. For example, one could investigate the relationship between these variables among all individuals 16-24 years of age within the United States (since we are concerned with state and national government interventions), or we could limit our investigation to a particular region, state, or municipality. According to the proponents of Self-Control Theory and General Strain Theory, there is no theoretical reason that individuals 16-24 years of age in the state of Washington would differ significantly from individuals 16-24 years of age in other states. Thus, due to constraints on time and money, all drivers 16-24 years of age in Washington State were included in the sampling frame provided by the Washington State Department of Licensing, and simple random sampling techniques were employed to increase the likelihood of representativeness of the cases selected for the study.

Sample Size

A common misconception among the lay public is that the larger the sample size the more accurate the results of any study. Unnecessarily large samples unduly increase research costs, and a large sample that is not representative of the original population will not produce accurate results. Determining how large a sample should be can be addressed in two ways. One common method is reliance upon convention. Convention, or a commonly accepted amount, is not an arbitrary standard, but rather one based on sound past experience. Convention typically determines sample size where researchers for various reasons (e.g., convenience or lack of precise information) do not employ statistical calculations. In contrast, the second method for determining sample size employs specific statistical calculations based on working assumptions regarding the parameters of the population of interest and the demands of the statistical tests to be used in analyzing the results. For example, if theory-testing entails documentation of differences across ethnic groups (e.g., Latinos, blacks, Asians, and Native Americans) in a static population where few minorities are present it is necessary to see a far larger sample than would be the case if ethnic subgroup comparisons were not necessary.

A defining characteristic of logical positivism is *hypothesis testing*. Hypotheses are links in a theoretical causal chain that take the form of verbal statements regarding the relation of variables in nature that are informed by a theory. Through hypothesis testing, scientific knowledge is accumulated as theoretical postulates are advanced that test the core propositions of theories. With each test, empirical evidence is examined to determine the extent to which the purported relationship in nature is supported by empirical observation or refuted by lack of same. Where empirical evidence is found to support a theory, it remains in contention among other competing theories. If, however, the theory in question is continually refuted over time, it is gradually eliminated from consideration as a true representation of social phenomena. This process of *falsification* stems from Popperian logic (1962) which recognizes a fundamental asymmetry—namely, that a hypothesis can never be completely *proved*, only disproved. Disconfirming evidence shows that predictions are wrong, but positive or confirming evidence cannot summarily dismiss alternative hypotheses that may make the same prediction.

Following this logic, if a relationship among variables is purported to exist in nature, one must ensure that the selected sample is large enough to reveal it that relationship. The ability to detect meaningful relationships is referred to as statistical **power**. Because hypothesis testing includes the explicit, or implicit, testing of two proposition: One proposition hypothesizes the existence of no relationship between two variables—the null hypothesis (H_o)—and the other hypothesizes the existence of a relationship—the alternative hypothesis (H_1)—the researcher is concerned with two types of potential error. One type of error occurs when he/she mistakenly rejects the null (concludes that the relationship exists in nature when in fact is does not) which is a function of the *a priori* alpha level (α) [typically .05 in the social sciences] which is referred to as Type I error, and the other where he/she fails to reject the null (concludes that no relationship exists in nature when in fact it does) referred to as Type II error (β).

Because the investigator is concerned with creating an accurate representation of social reality, either type of error is undesirable. Researchers and consumers of research often emphasize Type I error without giving sufficient attention to Type II error in study design (Hunter & Schmidt, 1990). The relationships between the theoretical constructs advanced here have not been previously documented; consequently, convention provides no guidance in determining sample size. It is clear, however, that the commission of a Type II error could have detrimental consequences for the application of General Strain Theory in understanding those factors contributing to young driver accidents. As a result of this consideration, the second method (statistical calculation) is used to ensure sufficient statistical power in the sampling process employed for this study.

As will be discussed in considerable detail later, the primary statistical technique of investigation to be employed to test the relationships obtaining among the constructs and traits of interest is Structural Regression Modeling. Unfortunately, issues of statistical power in Structural Regression Modeling are not well understood and can vary considerably across the model (D. Kaplan, 1995). Structural Regression Modeling does, however, rely on the general linear model for estimation. As such, it is closely akin to Hierarchical Linear Regression (HLM). HLM is a variant of general linear modeling that assess the ability of each level of the model to account for a significant proportion of variation after partialling the influence of variables residing at lower levels. Cohen and Cohen (2003) have outlined procedures for determining sample size for HLM based on assumptions regarding the population effect size and the number of independent variables included in the model. Assuming a small population effect size (.10), while accounting for self-control and other important demographic and opportunity variables in model construction, indicates that a sample size of 228 will ensure sufficient power (see Table 4.1— Hierarchical Linear Regression Power Computation). Assuming a modest response rate (15%)—based on the length of the survey questionnaire and the nature (social-psychological) of the measurement models—in conjunction with the power estimation estimates, a sample of 2,000 drivers 16-24 years of age were randomly selected by the Washington State Department of Licensing for participation in the study reported here.

Data Collection

Surveys containing the Grasmick et al. (1993) self-control measurement model and the "Driving Frustration" General Strain Theory measurement model to be developed in Chapter 5 were mailed to all 2,000 subjects under the Institutional Review Board approval 8061 (see Appendices F and G) in two waves. In the first wave, an incentive to increase individual participation rates was offered by automatically entering those who completed and returned the survey by October 29, 2004, into a lottery where five individuals would be randomly selected to receive one of five $100.00 awards. This

Table 4.1
Hierarchical Linear Regression Power Computation

Model Level and Variables:	Computational Formula and Computation:
Model A: Gender Ethnicity: Caucasian (Yes/No) Total Model A = 2	To determine n* for an F test on ratio of variances of two predictors: sR2 = R2Y.AB - R2Y.A: 1. Set the significance criterion to be used, a. 2. Set desired power for the F test. 3. Identify the number of IVs to be included in Set A, in Set B. 4. Identify the alternate hypothetical ES in the population for which n* is to be determined μ (Estimation based on theory, intuition, or conventional values, e.g., small, medium, large effect sizes)
Model B: Own Vehicle GDL Urban Area Economy Car Experience Miles per Week Total Model B = 6	5. Identify anticipated error variance, that is, $(1 - R^2_{Y.ABC})$: $$f^2 = \frac{R^2_C = R^2_{Y.ABC} - R^2_{YA} - R^2_{YB}}{1 - R^2_{Y.ABC}}$$

Model C:
Self-Control:
  Impulsivity
  Simple Tasks
  Risk-Seeking
  Physical Activities
  Self-Centered
  Temper
 	
Total Model C = 6
	$$f^2 = \frac{.10}{1 - .20} = .125$$
	
	$$n^* = \frac{L}{f^2} + K_A + K_B + K_C + 1$$

Model D:
Driving Frustration:
  Progress Impeded
  Irregular Traffic Flow
  Law Enforcement Presence
  Road Construction
  Discourteous Driving Behavior
  Restricted Field of Vision
 	
Total Model D = 6
	Where:
	n* = necessary sample size
	L = desired power for the given K_c (number of variables in model C)
	and the desired power level $(1 - \beta)$
	
	$$n^* = \frac{25.86}{.125} + 2 + 6 + 6 + 6 + 1 = 228$$

incentive was offered due to the length (83 questions) and nature of the survey (social-psychological) that may discourage participation. Participants of the second wave mailing were not eligible for this participation incentive.

Included in the survey were important demographic variables shown in previous studies to be related to young driver accidents and citations: Amount and type of exposure, participation in a Graduated Licensing Program, gender, ethnicity, experience, vehicle type and ownership (see Chapter 1). Also included were 18 items (items 53-70) measuring individual driving behaviors that are theoretical consequences identified or deduced from Self-Control and/or General Strain Theory while operating a motor vehicle. The sources of these items include a risky driving scale developed by Kidd and Huddleston (1994) and other driving behaviors obtained in a personal interview (Joireman, 2004).

Structural Equation Modeling

Structural Equation Modeling (SEM) is a statistical technique that takes a confirmatory (i.e., hypothesis-testing) approach to testing for the presence of relationships among observed and latent variables. Compared to classical general linear modeling approaches—zero-order correlations, Analysis of Variance (ANOVA), Exploratory Factor Analysis (EFA), Multiple Regression, etc.—SEM attempts to represent a "causal" process that generates observations on multiple variables (Bentler, 1988) by explicitly stating and subsequently testing models. It is this explicit *a priori* model specification and subsequent testing, along with simultaneous estimation and goodness of fit assessments used to infer causality, that set SEM apart from classical linear models.

To be sure, classical linear models are essentially descriptive in nature (e.g., Exploratory Factor Analysis and Multiple Regression) in that the models are fit to raw data so that hypothesis testing is difficult if not impossible (Byrne, 2001; Raykov & Marcoulides, 2000). Conversely, SEM specifies a model—statements regarding the relationships among variables—and then assesses the plausibility of the specified relations established within the model against the observed data (variance/covariance matrix). It is this *a priori* model specification and subsequent assessment of *goodness of fit* between the hypothesized population level variance/covariance matrix (Σ) implied by the model and the observed sample variance/covariance matrix (S) that is most consistent with the goals of logical positivism and inferential statements regarding the relation of variables beyond the sample data.

Classical linear models are also not readily amenable to assessing the direct and indirect relationships obtaining among variables, except indirectly through multiple model specifications. It is this simultaneous estimation that allows the investigator to make nuanced "causal" statements guided by theory and logic with increased confidence— especially among higher-order moments—by isolating the putative cause from extraneous influences and measurement error that is not enjoyed with classical linear models (Hoyle, 1995). Lastly, SEM offers the advantage of increasing point estimate accuracy by estimating error in explanatory variables that is ignored with classical linear modeling techniques. The latent nature of the variables under investigation (i.e., self-control, strain while operating a motor vehicle, and driving delinquency) significantly increases the likelihood for measurement error and/or measurement model misspecification that may lead to serious inaccuracies where sizeable errors are present. Thus, SEM offers several advantages not enjoyed with classical linear models that appear to make it the most appropriate statistical technique for this investigation.

Central Theoretical Hypotheses

Control Variables

Hypothesis 1: The previously mentioned environmental, opportunity, and individual level variables identified in the research literature share a significant relationship with an individual's self-reported number of accidents and citations: amount of driving (miles per week); type of exposure (urban versus rural driving); participation in a Graduated Driver Licensing (GDL) program; type of vehicle (i.e., economy car), ownership of a vehicle, gender (male as reference group), ethnicity (Caucasian as the reference group), months driving experience in the following direction:

Miles per Week → Self-Report Accidents and Citations (+)
Urban Driving → Self-Report Accidents and Citations (+)
GDL → Self-Report Accidents and Citations (-)
Economy Car → Self-Report Accidents and Citations (-)
Vehicle Ownership → Self-Report Accidents and Citations (+)
Ethnicity → Self-Report Accidents and Citations (-)
Gender → Self-Report Accidents and Citations (+)
Driving Experience → Self-Report Accidents and Citations (+)

The number of self-reported accidents and citations received among young drivers has been shown to be a function of exposure (Bergdahl & Norris, 2002; Carroll et al., 1971). Exposure measured in the *amount* and *type* of driving conditions experienced by an individual, is said to increase an individual's risk of accidents while increasing opportunity for traffic delinquency, *ceteris paribus*, as those who drive more miles per week are more likely to experience an increased number of traffic events that create a risk for an accident. Similarly, those who drive in dense urban areas are not only theoretically more likely to experience traffic events that create a risk of accident, but they are also more likely to receive a formal traffic citation for traffic delinquency as policing and traffic law enforcement remains predominantly a local activity (Gaines & Kappeler, 2003).

Graduated Driver Licensing programs—which restrict driving behaviors for adolescent drivers under certain conditions and times— are informed by opportunity theory. According to the programmatic theory of GDL, young drivers are more likely to drive in nighttime conditions and with an increased number of vehicle occupants. Nighttime driving conditions increase the likelihood for accidents and citations as visibility is reduced and it is the time of day most often associated with the use of drugs and the consumption of alcohol (Preusser et al., 1984). Similarly, adolescent drivers are more likely to have teenage passengers with them than do adults, a factor that often distracts their attention away from safe vehicle operation (McCartt et al., 2003). GDL programs thus represent an attempt by the state authorities to reduce the opportunity for accidents and citations among young drivers by restricting behaviors to create low-risk driving environments where novice drivers can gain valuable experience under maximally safe conditions.

Vehicle ownership and type of vehicle are also theoretically related to an individual's number of accidents and citations received. Type of vehicle with respect to small, fuel-efficient economy cars likely share a relationship with an individual's number of accidents and citations as larger more powerful vehicles increase the opportunity to respond to traffic events in an instrumental manner (e.g., passing a slow moving vehicle on a mountain road), while reducing the perceived potential individual costs associated with retaliatory (tail-gating) driving behaviors. The latter logic is rooted in rational choice theory—which views individuals as utility maximizers—which would argue that ownership of larger, more powerful vehicles increases the likelihood that an individual will engage in retaliatory behaviors as the vehicle creates a greater sense of safety—should an accident occur—then is experienced by those driving smaller, fuel-efficient cars (Porter, 1999). Rational choice theory would also predict that those who own their own vehicle would theoretically be more likely to engage in traffic delinquency as the potential social costs stemming from an accident (guilt and embarrassment) are significantly less than for those drivers who rely on the goodness of others to provide an opportunity to drive (Grasmick & Bursik, 1990).

Gender and ethnicity are theoretically and empirically related to an individual's number of reported traffic accidents and citations received. Sociologists and anthropologists have documented the existence of distinct cultures (values, beliefs, and ideals) and sub-cultures among various ethnic groups that theoretically may influence individual driving behaviors to a substantial extent. For example, criminologists have pointed to the cultural values of collective weal emphasized by the Japanese culture as one factor contributing to the nation's comparatively low crime rates (Braithwaite, 1985). Similarly, sociologists have documented the existence of a sub-culture of violence among African Americans living in inner cities. According to this theory, behavior is governed by a code which emphasizes being treated with respect—being treated "right" or being granted one's "props" (proper due). When another individual "disses" (disrespects) another, it is considered an indication of an intention to attack; consequently, it is likely to call forth a preemptive first strike (E. Anderson, 1999).

Lastly, physiology and socialization likely influence driving behaviors among males and females for a number of reasons (see Chapter 1) (Gottfredson & Hirschi, 1990; Klein, 1971; Parry, 1968; L. Shaw & Sichel, 1971)

Hypothesis 2: The statistically and substantively significant variables identified with Hypothesis 1 are reduced to practical or statistical nonsignificance after including measures of individual self-control and context-specific strain experienced while operating a motor vehicle.

The previously identified individual, environmental, and opportunity variables highlighted in early investigations of young driver accidents (see Chapter 1) possibly overlook the role that individual level self-control and context-specific strain variables may play in accident and citation frequencies. Including measures of individual level self-control and strain experienced while operating a motor vehicle may reduce these important control variables to practical or statistical nonsignificance. Reductions in practical and statistical significance of these variables would provide evidence for the import of including individual level psychological predisposition measures during model specification when attempting to assess their influence.

Measurement Models

Hypothesis 3: Self-Control is best represented as a second-order factor consisting of six first-order factors: Impulsivity, preference for simple tasks, high risk-seeking, preference for physical activity, self-centered thinking, and arousal of temper.

Gottfredson and Hirschi (1990) have argued that self-control is a uni-dimensional "predisposition." Despite the admonition of the theory's architects to cast self-control as a personality trait, Grasmick et al. (1993) developed a 24-item psychometric scale tapping the six distinct dimensions identified by Gottfredson and Hirschi. Subsequent exploratory analyses of the scale have revealed that the scale is indeed conformable to a single factor solution—using the scree discontinuity criterion and/or the salient variable criterion (see Chapter 2) (Arneklev et al., 1998; Nagin & Paternoster, 1993; Piquero et al., 2000; Piquero & Tibbetts, 1996). Subsequent confirmatory factor analyses have suggested, however, that the factor structure is best represented as a second-order construct consisting of the six first-order constructs identified by Gottfredson and Hirschi (Piquero et al., 2000; Vazsonyi et al., 2001), and that this six-construct structure is invariant across several sub-groups.

Hypothesis 4: Strain experienced while operating a motor vehicle ('Driving Frustration') is best represented as a second-order construct consisting of the six first-order constructs identified in Chapter 5: Progress impeded, irregular traffic flow, law enforcement presence, road construction, discourteous driving behavior, and restricted field of vision.

General Strain Theory is a social psychological theory of adult crime and juvenile delinquency which recognizes that the psychological strain experienced by individuals resulting from the blockage/removal of positively valued goals and/or the introduction of negative stimuli creates "motivation" to engage in crime and delinquency. This theory stands in stark contrast to that offered by self-control theorists who argue that all individuals—because they are rational—are equally motivated to engage in crime and delinquency (what differs then is individual levels of restraint or self-control). What's more, General Strain Theory contains a social component in that stress or strain experienced in one environment is not predictive of stress or strain experienced in other situations and contexts. Accordingly, individual levels of strain experienced while operating a motor vehicle should vary according to specific driving situations and contexts. Specifically, the amount of stress or frustration experienced while operating a motor vehicle can best be represented as a second-order factor consisting of the six first-order factors identified in Chapter 5.

Full Structural Model

Hypothesis 5: Low self-control shares a significant and positive relationship with driving delinquency.

Gottfredson and Hirschi (1990: 49) have argued that automobile accidents (and presumably citations) are the residue of a host of driving behaviors: speeding, drinking, tail-gating, inattention, and reckless risk-taking. As a result, individuals low in self-control are significantly more likely to engage in driving delinquent behaviors, and it is these specific behaviors that are more predictive of accidents and citations than individual levels of self-control: low self-control → driving delinquency → accidents and citations (or that the influence of self-control on accidents and citations is mediated by driving delinquent behaviors). This proposition tests the generality of the theory in that Self-Control Theory has not previously been used to explain driving behaviors and formal driving outcomes.

Hypothesis 6: Individual levels of strain experienced while operating a motor vehicle share a significant and positive relationship with driving delinquency and automobile accidents and citations.

General Strain Theory predicts that individual motivation to engage in crime and delinquency varies significantly across contexts and situations in response to the removal or blockage and/or introduction of negative stimuli (Agnew, 1992). For some individuals, situations or contexts experienced while operating a motor vehicle may be more stressful than that experienced by others, and it is the experienced strain that, in conjunction with the social context in which it occurs, "motivates" individuals to engage in crime and delinquency. Thus, driving situations and contexts which remove or block positively valued goals and/or introduce negative stimuli should predict driving delinquent behaviors as individuals attempt to retrieve, prevent loss, or escape the blockage or removal of positively valued goals and/or the introduction of negative stimuli.

Hypothesis 7: General Strain Theory explains a significant amount of variation in driving delinquent behaviors after accounting for individual levels of self-control.

Disenchantment with classical criminology to produce anticipated reductions in crime and delinquency gave way to a deterministic view of the individual. In contrast to the classical conception, individuals do not possess "free will" that can be readily influenced by the manipulation of perceived costs and benefits of crime and delinquency. What has emerged is a deterministic view of the individual which suggests that behaviors are "determined" to a certain extent (a probability) by variables that if identified by those working within the positivist tradition can be manipulated to produce desired results. As positivists have raced to identify the correlates of crime/delinquency, centrifugal forces have fragmented the field of criminology as scholars have pointed to variables variously rooted in social ecology, biology, psychology, and economics. The complexity of the scholarship produced by researchers associated with the positivist tradition has often confounded legislators and agency-based policymakers seeking simple and uniform policies aimed at reducing crime/delinquency.

In *A General Theory of Crime*, Gottfredson and Hirschi (1990) unite the classical and positivistic traditions by arguing that all individuals are rational and equally motivated to commit crimes and/or engage in delinquency, but that what differs within an individual is their level of restraint (or self-control) exercised in the face of temptation. Furthermore, self-control is argued to be the "master variable" that precedes those identified by positivist criminologists: peer influences, social bonds, social disadvantages, and even strain. Specifically, the advocates of Self-Control Theory argue that individuals with low self-control experience a range of negative social consequences as they typically experience failure in prominent social institutions (i.e., work, school, and marriage), prefer activities that are physical and provide immediate gratification, and seek personal relationships with others who are similarly deviant "birds of the same feather flock together." Thus, social disadvantage (classical strain), delinquent associations (social learning), weak social bonds (control and life-course theory) are all pre-dated by individual levels of self-control. As a result, these relationships are actually "spurious" and should disappear after accounting for individual levels of self-control. This hypothesis tests the "spuriousness" thesis advanced by Gottfredson and Hirschi (1990) with respect to General Strain Theory in explaining driving delinquency and young driver accidents and citations.

Hypothesis 8: Low self-control is positively correlated with situational strain experienced while operating a motor vehicle.

Lamenting over the disciplinary fragmentation characterizing criminology since the emergence of the positivistic tradition, Liska, Krohn, and Messner (1989) have urged those working within the field to strive toward theoretical integration. To this end, they have outlined forms of reasoning and specific criteria for theory development and hypothesis testing that lead toward theoretical integration. With respect to Self-Control and General Strain Theory, early investigations by Agnew, Brezina, Wright, and Cullen (2002) on the role of two psychological "super traits" and situational strain suggest that *end-to-end* integration of Self-Control and General Strain Theory may be a tenable goal of theoretical integration.

Using secondary data analysis techniques with data taken from the National Survey of Children (1981) (N = 1,031) involving a sample of children 12 to 16 years of age, Agnew, Brezina, Wright and Cullen (2002) employed Moderated Multiple Regression (MMR) to investigate the potential moderating impacts of "constraint" and of "negative emotionality." Constraint, as conceived by psychologists, is a trait that predisposes individuals to impulsivity, risk-seeking/sensation-seeking, and rejection of conventional norms (Agnew et al., 2002; Tellegen, 1985). Negative emotionality, as conceived by psychologists, is a trait which predisposes individuals to view the actions of others as malicious, and to see life events as aversive. Consequently, individuals low in constraint and high in negative emotionality are more likely than others to experience the actions of other people and their immediate environments as malicious and aversive, respectively, and to be predisposed to act impulsively, egocentrically, and in a physical manner. Moreover, evidence suggests that individuals are more likely to select themselves into comparatively more "stressful" environments as these traits tend to illicit negative reactions by others, in turn transforming their environments in ways that actually increase negative treatment by others and thereby reinforcing predispositions toward misanthropic suppositions (Agnew, 1992; Agnew & Brezina, 1997).

The moderating impact of constraint/negative emotionality on strain and delinquency documented by Agnew, Brezina, Wright and

Cullen (2002) suggest that attempts at theoretical integration may bear precious theoretical fruit. Consistent with this logic is the potential interplay between trait (dispositional) and situational (transitory) personality traits. That is, General Strain Theory argues that context or situational strain creates a psychological sense of strain (that translates into some negative affect such as anger, depression, anxiety, etc.) that is moderated by the situation in which it occurs. Thus, it is highly situational and transitory. Self-Control theorists argue for the enduring predisposition to engage in crime and delinquency that is a result of impulsivity, egocentrism, a preference for simple and physical tasks, a volatile temper, and persistent pursuit of risk-seeking activities. This view recognizes the trait or dispositional state of an individual personality and also covers several of the dimensions of "constraint" and "negative emotionality" investigated by Agnew et al. (2002). Psychologists have recognized that there often exists an interplay between trait and state, or that these two factors in human behavior often share a relationship (Nunnally & Bernstein, 1994: 380). For example, individuals presumably possess both trait anger and situational anger and those high in trait anger may be more likely to be triggered by situational anger (Mazerolle & Piquero, 1998). This *logical coherence* between Self-Control and General Strain Theory provided by psychologists and criminologists, thus, satisfies the criterion for potential end-to-end theoretical integration of Self-Control and General Strain Theory—with respect to operating a motor vehicle—provided by Liska et al. (1989).

Hypothesis 9: The effect of Traffic Safety Education on young driver accidents and driving delinquency is moderated by situational strain experienced while operating a motor vehicle.

Traffic safety education programs adopted by state governments beginning in the 1960s—in an attempt to reduce the overrepresentation of young drivers in the annual number of traffic fatalities and collisions—have viewed this serious and ongoing social problem as one which is amenable to amelioration through the adoption of a uniform pedagogy and curriculum of study designed to address cognitive and experiential deficits. This approach is informed by a program theory which views the problem as one arising from the absence of sufficient skill, knowledge, personal responsibility, and an understanding of the causes and consequences of automobile accidents.

Thus, states have adopted traffic safety education programs that attempt to instill in young drivers the operational skills, the factual knowledge, and the sense of responsibility for safe vehicle operation that approximates that found in older drivers. To this end, adolescent drivers are required to complete in-class and laboratory training meant to provide the skill and knowledge sufficient to pass state driving tests (Quenault & Sten, 1975).

Subsequent analyses of traffic safety education programs in reducing accident and citation rates among young drivers have provided mixed, conflicting, and/or null results (Harrington, 1971; Lovrich et al., 2003; McGuire, 1969; Schlesinger, 1972). Some studies have even suggested that high school driver education may actually exacerbate the problem by providing an opportunity for early licensure (Vernick et al., 1999). General Strain Theory offers promise in increasing our understanding regarding the impact of traffic safety education outcomes. Specifically, the effects of traffic safety education may be either facilitated or thwarted (moderated) by individual levels of situational strain experienced while operating a motor vehicle. Confirming evidence supporting this hypothesis would have serious implications for traffic safety education program activities, perhaps including the adoption of activities aimed at more complete diagnosis of novice driver traits and the incorporation of individually tailored treatments in driver safety education programs.

CHAPTER 5

Development of a 'Driving Frustration' Scale

INTRODUCTION

Self-Control (Gottfredson & Hirschi, 1990) and General Strain Theory (Agnew, 1992) are two broad theories that purport to explain a wide range of criminal behaviors. In the former, crime is conceptualized as the result of the pursuit of immediate, certain, and easy benefits, while the latter views crime and delinquency as an individual response to the blockage/removal of positively valued goals, and/or the repeated presentation of negative stimuli. Driving infractions and automobile accidents—as viewed through the self-control lens—are one class of events that are analogous to crimes. In the case of at fault accidents, they tend to be correlated with speeding, drinking, tail-gating, inattention, and risk-taking. Under the self-control paradigm, at fault automobile accidents are likely the residue of a host of delinquent driving behaviors in pursuit of immediate and certain benefits (Gottfredson & Hirschi, 1990: 42). Conversely, General Strain Theory views automobile accidents as the result of negative emotions that lead to outwardly directed coping mechanisms aimed at preventing and/or retrieving loss, or escape, termination, alleviation, and/or seeking of revenge for the removal and/or presentation of positive and negative stimuli, respectively (Agnew, 1992).

Self-Control Theory has received considerable empirical support where measured with the 24-item scale developed by Grasmick et al. (1993), or variants of that scale attempting to measure the theory's core elements, in explaining a significant proportion of variation in a wide-range of criminal and delinquent behaviors, including drug use (S. Baron, 2003), drunk driving (Keane et al., 1993), and crimes of force and fraud (Longshore & Turner, 1998; Tittle et al., 2003b). Despite disagreement regarding the dimensionality of the construct and the superiority of cognitive versus behavioral measures (V. S. Burton et al., 1999; Delisi, Hochstetler, & Murphy, 2003; Grasmick et al., 1993; Piquero et al., 2000; Vazsonyi et al., 2001), the 24-item scale developed by Grasmick et al. (1993) remains the most widely used measure (Pratt & Cullen, 2000). Several exploratory and confirmatory factor analyses have been reported supporting the predicted factor solution to various degrees (Delisi et al., 2003; Piquero et al., 2000; Vazsonyi et al., 2001).

Strain theory, in contrast, has suffered from a relative lack of conceptual clarity (Agnew, 1992) and generality (Agnew, 1992, , 2001; Merton, 1938; Messner & Rosenfeld, 2001) associated with a universal measure, while various operationalizations of the theory have produced conflicting findings (Farnworth & Leiber, 1989). The first step in assessing the relative reach of these competing theories in explaining various forms of driving delinquency is to document and elucidate the factor structure of the proposed construct, or the contexts and correlates associated with individual levels of contextual driving strain.

'Driving Frustration'

Driving frustration can be conceived as a personality trait related to stress. Stress has been operationalized by Barrett and Campos (1991) as any organism-environment relationship where it is appreciated by the organism as having the potential for exceeding the organism's resources (Lazarus & Folkman, 1984), and that serves to disorganize the organism's behavior and/or thought processes. Thus, frustration is subsumed and subordinate to the general category stress which is contained within the family of emotions (Barrett & Campos, 1991). Frustration as a form of stress that serves to disorganize the organism's behavior and/or thought processes is then most appropriately housed within the general strain tradition of criminology.

General Strain Theory can be traced to Robert K. Merton (1938) who attempted to explicate the disproportionate rates of crime and delinquency within the United States and among the lower class from a **personal disorganization** perspective by arguing that crime is an individual response to the blockage of positively valued goals. Robert

Agnew (1992) moved beyond this structural interpretation—where crime and delinquency was viewed as a consequence of structural influences introduced by a capitalistic society that emphasized goals over means and insufficient opportunities for legitimate economic achievement—to advance a general theory of strain which operates at the individual level, while recognizing that the removal of positively valued goals and/or the introduction of negative stimuli may precipitate crime and/or delinquency.

According to the tenets of General Strain Theory, not only may an individual engage in crime and delinquency when positively valued goals are blocked as individuals adapt through various modes, but the removal of positively valued stimuli and/or the introduction of negative stimuli are also implicated in crime and delinquency as they too are possible sources of negative affects—or a wide range of negative emotions. The negative emotions of individuals experiencing the blockage or loss of positively valued goals, or the introduction of negative stimuli, are implicated in crime and delinquency as individuals try to prevent and/or retrieve losses, or escape, terminate, alleviate, and/or seek revenge for the removal and/or presentation of positive and negative stimuli, respectively. Drawing from General Strain Theory and psychological definitions of stress, the role frustration in driving delinquency can be operationalized as the removal or blockage of positively valued goals, and/or the presentation of negative stimuli that would likely disorganize the organism's behavior and/or thought processes.

Driving frustration is, however, a much narrower; more situation- or context-bound source of frustration than general strain and/or stress. While individuals may experience general frustration and/or stress, driving frustration can be defined as a more frequent and intense frustration experienced while operating a motor vehicle. By analogy to anxiety, there is a general condition or trait of anxiety, but there are also context-specific anxieties such as test-taking or speech-giving anxieties felt by some people but not others. While somewhat correlated with trait anxiety, these context-specific anxieties are much more predictive of emotional responses and behaviors within these specific contexts than measures of general anxiety (Deffenbacher, Oetting, & Lynch, 1994). Driving frustration is akin to the latter; it is the extent to which frustration is experienced in driving-related contexts. In an attempt to measure the potential dimensions which constitute contextual driving frustration, a pool of items was generated from a reading of the literature and discussions with driver safety education professionals covering a broad range of situations. Those high in driving frustration would be expected to become frustrated more frequently and experience higher levels of frustration.

The Role of Frustration in Accidents and Driving Delinquency

Driving frustration may adversely affect young drivers in two specific ways. First, young drivers who do experience driving frustration would theoretically be more likely to view specific adverse situations and/or particular environmental conditions as overwhelming or insurmountable; as a result, their thought processes are likely to become relatively disorganized. In this manner, driving frustration could potentially sufficiently disturb thought processes so as to interfere with attention, perception, information processing, and motor performance in ways that would increase the likelihood of violating a traffic law and/or causing an accident. Secondly, the blockage or removal of positively valued goals, or the introduction of negative stimuli, may result in the increased likelihood of violating a traffic law or causing an accident as young drivers may cope outwardly through aggressive or impulsive behaviors. Tailgating, engaging in risk-taking maneuvers, or aggressive verbal or physical behavior could all be done either for hostile or instrumental reasons arising from driving frustration.

In illustration of these psychological dynamics, researchers have pointed to the role of traffic congestion and dense traffic patterns in increasing the incidence of 'road rage' as drivers experience high levels of frustration while behind the wheel. Frustration resulting from dense traffic and road congestion acts to block the goal-directed behavior of the driver (Shiner, 1998). In response, some of the drivers may respond instrumentally and/or with emotional aggression. In the former, the driver responds in a manner to simply remove the obstacle from one's way, e.g., passing a slow moving vehicle on a blind curve, while in the latter, the driver becomes emotionally aggressive and expresses one's anger to the frustrator, e.g., tail-gating a slow driver. Aggression resulting from frustration in the case of instrumental aggression is not mediated by anger; instead, frustration leads to instrumental aggression (frustration → instrumental aggression), while emotional aggression is mediated by anger in response to a frustrating situation (frustration → anger → emotional aggression).

The impact of driving frustration on individuals and their driving behavior is also likely to be a function of driving experience and exposure as well as psychological predispositions. Driving experience and exposure likely share an inverse relationship with an individual's tolerance, or their 'frustration threshold' for annoying driving conditions. Drivers who are high in experience and prior exposure have probably experienced more frustrating situations with more frequency than have novice drivers. Increased experience with and frequency of exposure to frustrating driving contexts is likely to heighten an individual's threshold as repeated and frequent exposure reduces sensitivity to and modifies behavior in response to the adverse consequences (i.e., tickets, accidents, and expressed social disapproval) flowing from negative outward directed coping mechanisms such as reckless risk-taking, aggressive driving, and general violation of traffic laws (Lajunen & Parker, 2001).

An individual's frustration threshold may also influence driving behavior in a manner which reduces their likelihood of engaging in driving delinquency. Those experiencing high levels of frustration to contexts or conditions that are perceived to reside in the realm of nature or fate—as compared to contexts or conditions viewed as controllable or purposeful such as the behavior of other road users and choice of route—may reduce their driving delinquency frequency as compared to persons with higher thresholds (Agnew, 2001).

Item Generation

Potentially frustrating driving situations were generated from several sources. First, research has been performed in the areas of driver anger and aggressive driving. Perhaps most notably, Deffenbacher et al. (1994)—using a five-point scale in Likert format and TRYSYS key cluster analysis (Tryon & Bailey, 1966)—generated a 33-item driver anger scale ($\alpha = .90$) consisting of six sub-scales. The reliabilities for the sub-scales **discourtesy, illegal driving, hostile gestures, slow driving, traffic obstructions,** and **police presence range** from .78 to

.87. A confirmatory factor analysis conducted by Lajunen, Parker, & Stradling (1998) of Deffenbacher's driving anger scale administered among 270 British respondents produced a 21-item, three factor scale labeled the *United Kingdom Driver Anger Scale* consisting of **progress impeded**, **reckless driving**, and **direct hostility**. The impact of and responses to frustrating driving contexts may include or exclude anger as a mediating variable, and therefore can result in a host of delinquent driving behavior behaviors. Enhanced risk-taking and general law violation may occur as a form of instrumental aggression to overcome the blockage of goal directed behavior, or aggressive driving behavior borne of anger at others or unkind fate may take place (Stone, 2002). As a result, items from the Deffenbacher et al. Driving Anger Scale (1994) and the United Kingdom Driving Anger Scale (Lajunen et al., 1998) that included situations which either blocked or removed positively valued goals or introduced negative stimuli, were adopted and/or modified to tap driving frustration. In addition, potentially frustrating driving situations were generated from personal experience and interviews with traffic safety education professionals. The result was a 54-item instrument containing a wide range of potentially frustrating stimuli (see Appendix A).

Formal Likert Scaling Method

The subjects were 216 (96 males, 119 females) students enrolled in criminal justice/political science courses at Washington State University during the Spring 2004 semester. Courses surveyed during this phase included POL S 316 (American Public Policy) N = 35; POL S 101 section 1 (American National Government) N = 90; POL S 101 section 3 (American National Government) N = 29; and CRM J 403 (Violence Toward Women) N = 62. Participants ranged in age from 17 to 36 years with the mean, median, and mode ages = 21.21, 21, and 20 years, respectively. The study protocol was approved by the Washington State University Institutional Review Board (IRB No. 6013) (see Appendix E) and participation was voluntary. Administration of the survey occurred during regularly scheduled class time and participants were compensated on a per class bases through additional points—the amount determined by individual instructors/professors—being added to their cumulative course grade.

Participants were asked to indicate how characteristic each statement was of their response to the behavior of other drivers and to road conditions which they believed to be affecting them, using a Likert scale anchored along 7 points (1 = Extremely Uncharacteristic; 2 = Moderately Uncharacteristic; 3 = Slightly Uncharacteristic; 4 = Uncertain; 5 = Slightly Characteristic; 6 = Moderately Characteristic; 7 = Extremely Characteristic). Thus, strain and the negative affect (frustration) were combined into a single measure.

This is important because Agnew (1992) has distinguished between strain and negative affects. Unfortunately, this has led to the use of objective strain and general trait measures in most tests of the theory (Agnew, 2001; Capowich et al., 2001; Mazerolle, Piquero, & Capowich, 2003). These measures overlook the "situational" orientation of the theory, however. In fact, measures which simultaneously capture the subjective strain and affective response of an individual to a particular situation do a much better job predicting crime/delinquency, than do the former, as demonstrated by Capowich, Mazerolle, and Piquero (2001).

These investigators were able to document the relative superiority of a "situational anger" measure in predicting intentions to fight in comparison to both their objective strain and general anger measures, by asking individuals how angry they would be if they were the individual represented in a particular vignette. Similar to this approach, appropriate-aged subjects were asked to indicate how characteristic each statement was of them using a 7-point Likert scale, where each item attempted to tap the subjective "frustration" experienced by road users to specific driving situations. This is consistent with subsequent elaboration of theory which recognizes that *subjective* measures tend to be more appropriate because they attempt to measure how an individual actually feels (Agnew, 2001). Additionally, subjective and emotional responses are closely linked in that the individual subjectively perceives a strainful event, condition, or belief which is followed by affective response (Agnew, 2001: p. 322).

Finally, given the **absolute** nature of an individual's response to the stimuli, i.e., I get frustrated when…, and the absence of a frame-of-reference that accompanies absolute versus **comparative** responses, i.e., stimulus A is more frustrating than stimulus B, anchors were employed to specify the meaning of the response scale in an attempt to reduce unwanted error that may arise from differences in implicit bases of comparison (Nunnally & Bernstein, 1994: 51-2). Seven points were chosen to overcome "response compression" sometimes found to be present in 5-point scales, and to avoid overwhelming the respondents by making overly fine distinctions within the stimuli.

Subjects were informed prior to the administration of the instrument that the questionnaire was lengthy, with multiple items appearing to be similar. As a result, the administrator requested that only those students who felt they possessed the necessary endurance and willingness to read thoroughly and answer accurately each question participate in the study. Because of the long format and **prima facie** similarity of several stimuli, special attention was paid to allowing sufficient time (a minimum of 30 minutes) to allow all study participants to complete the questionnaire without a sense of "time pressure." All completed questionnaires collected contained a 100% response rate to all stimuli. Additional measures were introduced to reduce biases or distortions in the estimation of an individual's true score (score obtained under ideal testing conditions) potentially occurring through individual **response styles**.

Two threats to accurate assessment of context specific driving frustration occurring through individual response styles of particular relevance are those emanating from *social desirability* and *acquiescence bias*. Social desirability bias, which occurs when a subject attempts to respond in a socially desirable way, was addressed by ensuring anonymity by requiring participants to detach the 'informed consent form' containing personal information from the questionnaire upon completion. Social desirability bias may likely influence subject responses as participants imagine the researcher applying some social standard of acceptability.

Perhaps the more important threat to unbiased measurement is the threat posed by acquiescence bias, or the tendency to agree with a particular statement. Where items are keyed in the same direction, measurement of a trait—in this instance driving frustration—may become confounded with an individual's propensity to acquiesce with survey items. As a result, the form is in fact measuring two factors rather than just one—driving frustration <u>and</u> acquiescence. The consequence of yea- and nay-saying is to define the trait in narrow terms which in turn limits correlations with variables of interest to the general trait, while causing the trait to correlate with variables that are not of interest. Attempts to overcome threats posed by an individual's willingness to acquiesce were addressed by following the traditional point of view that the number of items keyed "yes" and "no" should be balanced (Nunnally & Bernstein, 1994: 314). To this end, a balanced number of "I do..." and "I don't..." stems were followed by the context-specific stimuli, despite the added difficulty in interpretation and analysis.

The **scaling model**—or internally consistent plan for developing and applying a new measure—adopted was provided by Rensis Likert (1993). Formal Likert scaling procedures impose an internally consistent logic for the construction of scales rooted in the domain-sampling model. The domain-sampling model considers any particular measure to be composed of responses from a random sample of items drawn from a hypothetical domain of items. From this theoretical vantage, if a form is measuring a particular concept or construct then the items used to measure the purported concept or construct should all be highly correlated (Cronbach, 1951; Nunnally & Bernstein, 1994).

The construction of scales employing formal Likert methods requires assembling a collection of homogenous items purporting to measure the construct of interest. Judges—N $\geq$ 100—then rate their agreement with each item. Corrected item-total correlations—where the influence of the item is partialed—for each item are then assessed according to their association with the total score. Following the logic of the domain-sampling model, items with negative or low corrected item-total correlations $\leq$ .30 are not part of the domain, and/or contain unacceptable levels of measurement error, and should be discarded (Nunnally & Bernstein, 1994: 301-04). Only after scales are assessed for their content homogeneity and measurement error should the scale be re-applied to a new population and subsequently factor analyzed to explore dimensionality within the item set.

Item Analysis

Following the scaling model proposed by Likert, all corrected item-total correlations were inspected. Corrected item-total correlations for all fifty-four items ranged from .05 to .48, while corrected item total-correlations for items 4, 8, 13, 15, 23, 30, 35, 47, and 52 ranged from .05 to .23. Following the logic of the Likert scaling model, these nine items were identified as residing outside the domain of interest, or containing unacceptable amounts of measurement error. Rather than discard the items, the investigator chose to include the items in the revised form to act as "distractors" in subsequent scaling data collection. Including distractors is one method used to prevent a response bias known as the "good subject effect" where the respondent tries to please the investigator by providing the responses they believe he/she would like. By including questions that appear to be unrelated, the respondent is less likely to be aware of the purpose of the study, thereby reducing the likelihood of creating a "demand characteristic." The result was the retention of forty-five items eligible for factor analysis, and nine items included to serve as distractors.

Factor Analysis

The revised form was then administered to an independent sample of students registered in criminal justice/political science courses in the Spring of 2004. The subjects were 237 (140 males, 97 females) ranging in age from 18 to 24 years, with the mean, median, and mode ages = 20.53, 20, and 19, respectively. Courses participating during this second phase of the instrument development included: CRM J 105 (Realizing Justice in a Multi-Cultural Society) N = 22; CRM J 420 (Law of Evidence and Criminal Procedure) N = 30; CRM J 150 (Organizational Environment of Criminal Justice) N = 51; POL S 305 (Gender and Politics) N = 20; CRM J 330 (Crime Control Policies) N = 61; CRM J 101 (Introduction to the Administration of Criminal Justice) N = 53. Sample size and its relation to the number of variables to be factor analyzed in this instance achieved the minimum five-to-one ratio recognized to sufficiently minimize the chance of "overfitting" the data, or deriving factors that are sample specific (Hair, Anderson, Tatham, & Black, 1995: 373-74). Additional precautions were taken to ensure independence of observations and prevent recall by asking subjects prior to administration if they had previously participated in the study at an earlier time in another course. Those indicating previous participation were granted the extra credit and excluded from participation.

Principal Axis (Common Factor) Extraction

Using SPSS 11.5.1, responses to the 45 items were subjected to a principal axis factor analysis. Principal axis extraction was selected to reduce the probability of capitalizing on errors in measurement typically enjoyed by the alternative method—principal components analysis. Indeed, principal axis analysis accounts for unique variance (u^2) by inserting values < 1 into the diagonal of the correlation matrix (**R**), thereby acting on the assumption that the constructs are broader than the measures being used to define them. This process is superior to that employed in principal components analysis which substitutes a value of 1 (unity diagonal) into (**R**) (Nunnally & Bernstein, 1994) which has the effect of biasing estimates upward. In fact, a common factor (principal axis) solution containing the same number of factors as compared to a component (principal components) solution will (1) estimate correlations better; (2) produce smaller residual correlations and, as a consequence, (3) produce a smaller root mean square error (RMS) (Snook & Gorsuch, 1989).

Using the default SPSS 11.5.1 communality (h^2) estimation procedures, estimations were substituted within the diagonal positions of (**R**) with values < 1. Although extraction through principal axis sometimes prevents convergence between the observed and estimated matrices due to the increased number of estimations associated with the additional parameters (Nunnally & Bernstein, 1994), extraction convergence was achieved after only fourteen iterations, or within the **a priori** limit of twenty-five. After fourteen iterations, twelve common factors with eigenvalues > 1 were revealed that cumulatively explained 59.57% of the variance prior to rotation (see Appendix B).

Rotation

After factor extraction, the solution may be made more interpretable by employing an orthogonal or oblique rotation. Although considerable controversy surrounds which approach is most appropriate in any given instance, orthogonal solutions are typically advocated for their relative simplicity in interpretation. While oblique rotations provide clearer factor solutions, those solutions come at some cost to interpretability (Nunnally & Bernstein, 1994). Orthogonal rotations maintain the 90° coordinate system used to derive the original structure loadings, and are lauded for allowing simple interpretation of the total variance explained through summation of the sums of squares factor loadings. This approach assumes, however, that the factors identified are themselves uncorrelated.

Conversely, oblique rotations begin with the 90° principal axes structures, but may provide a solution where the distance between the principal axes is less than 90° if some or all of the factors are correlated. This approach confounds interpretability of the total variance explained because of "overlap," but provides a clearer factor solution. Because the investigator is most interested in accurately representing the factor structure for the purpose of subjecting the measurement model to a confirmatory factor analysis using a probability sample, an oblique rotation was employed using Promax rotation with Kappa 4—or the power most commonly used (Loehlin, 1998; Nunnally & Bernstein, 1994)—to maximize the spread (variance) of pattern elements on the factors (Hendrickson & White, 1964) with convergence being achieved in 23 iterations.

Factor Selection

Multiple methods were employed to determine the number of factors to extract. According to the **latent root** criterion, only those factors with eigenvalues greater than one are considered significant (Guttman, 1954; Kaiser, 1970). According to this rationale, any individual factor should account for the variance of at least a single variable if it is to be retained for interpretation. Accordingly, twelve factors were eligible for extraction (see Appendix B). Because the Kaiser-Guttman rule has been shown to be biased upwards to account for less variance than purported (Cliff, 1988), the scree test and salient criteria (.30 minimum factor value) were also employed to determine the appropriate number of factors to extract.

The scree test is used to identify the optimum number of factors that can be extracted before the amount of unique variance—factors consist of common and unique variance—begins to dominate the common variance structure. This analysis is achieved by plotting the latent roots against the number of factors in their order of extraction. Factors are extracted in the order of their proportion of common variance accounted for—and identifying that point at which too large a proportion of unique variance would be included is the goal of the scree test. Despite the practical simplicity of this criterion, no definitive number of eligible factors could readily be discerned. As a result, the Kaiser-Guttman rule, and scree test and the salient variable[3] criterion were all used to determine the number of factors to be extracted. The salient variable rule recognizes the practical, rather than statistical, significance of a variable's relation to a factor.

Because the factor loading of a variable represents the correlation of a variable to the factor, the squared loading is the amount of the variable's total variance accounted for by the factor. Thus, a loading of .30 translates to approximately 10 percent explanation, or a standard of practical significance broadly recognized in the social sciences (J. Cohen et al., 2003). Applying all three criteria, six factors were extracted that explained 42.7% of the total variance in the un-rotated solution, after variables 42, 31, 46, and 50 were eliminated because they cross-loaded—or nearly shared practical significance with one or more factors. The principal axis oblique rotation factor solution is summarized in Table 5.1 with the structure (**S**) and pattern (**B**) elements.

Factor Correlation Matrix

The factor correlation matrix (**Φ**) reveals that factors 1 through 5 are all positively correlated, with magnitudes ranging from a low of .197 between factors 4 and 5 ($\cos\Phi = 78.6°$) to a high of .552 between factors 1 and 2 ($\cos\Phi = 56.5°$). The relationship between these factors and factor 6 is not as clear, however. Factor 6 is not substantively correlated with any other factor as evidenced with magnitudes ranging from .033 ($\cos\Phi = 88.1°$) between factors 4 and 6 and .213 ($\cos\Phi = 77.7°$) between factors 5 and 6, while being negatively correlated with factor 1 -.098 ($\cos\Phi = 95.6°$). Given that nine of the fifteen non-

---

[3] A salient is a variable having a value on a factor of at least .3 (Nunnally & Bernstein, 1994).

Table 5.1—'Driving Frustration' Scale Items

Item by Factor	Structure Element	Pattern Element
Factor 1: Progress Impeded		
Eigenvalue = 8.76		
5. I don't get frustrated when another driver will not heed my attempt to merge into traffic.	.524	.731
7. I don't get frustrated when a bicyclist is riding in the middle of the lane and slowing traffic down.	.589	.621
10. I don't get frustrated when a driver is holding up traffic by being slow to park.	.486	.509
11. I don't get frustrated when someone hastily pulls into oncoming traffic, causing the flow of traffic to unnecessarily slow.	.578	.471
16. I don't get frustrated when a slow vehicle on a winding road will not pull over to allow others to pass.	.462	.365
Factor 2: Irregular Traffic Flow		
Eigenvalue = 2.79		
39. I get frustrated when the driver in front of me makes a turn without signaling.	.552	.678
40. I get frustrated when someone runs a red light.	.472	.656
41. I get frustrated when the driver in front of me repeatedly drifts across the marked road lines.	.582	.578
29. I don't get frustrated when a portion of a vehicle which is pulled off to the side of the highway remains in my driving lane.	.532	.506
34. I get frustrated when the driver in front of me appears to be uncertain about his/her actions.	.585	.470
19. I don't get frustrated when I cannot pass another vehicle because a driver in the passing lane is driving too slowly.	.507	.300
Factor 3: Law Enforcement Presence		
Eigenvalue = 2.39		
51. I get frustrated when a law enforcement official pulls me over.	.721	.814
27. I get frustrated when I see a law enforcement official watching traffic from a hidden position.	.621	.663
28. I don't get frustrated when a law enforcement official appears to be following me.	.607	.628
Continued		

110

Table 5.1—'Driving Frustration' Scale Items Continued

Item by Factor	Structure Element	Pattern Element
Factor 4: Road Construction		
Eigenvalue = 1.87		
9. I get frustrated when I encounter road construction which halts my progress.	.764	.842
12. I don't get frustrated when I encounter road construction with detours.	.630	.667
Factor 5: Discourteous Driving Behavior		
Eigenvalue = 1.84		
36. I don't get frustrated when at night, the person immediately behind me is driving with their bright lights on.	.646	.727
25. I don't get frustrated when at night, a driver who is approaching does not dim their bright lights.	.637	.653
22. I get frustrated when someone backs out in front of me without looking.	.612	.582
Factor 6: Restricted Field of Vision		
Eigenvalue = 1.58		
17. I don't get frustrated when the condition of the roadway is so poor that it is difficult to see its markings.	.593	.538
18. I don't get frustrated when my defroster is unable to keep my windshield clear at all times.	.517	.516
54. I get frustrated when it is raining so heavily that it is difficult to see.	.590	.462
6. I don't get frustrated when a vehicle remains in my "blind spot" for an extended period.	.364	.454

redundant elements in the variance/covariance factor correlation matrix—excluding the communality estimates h^2—present magnitudes $\geq .30$, oblique rotation appears to be the most appropriate method of rotation despite the increased difficulties associated with interpretation.

Factor Scores

Although one could calculate and assign to individuals an **individual factor score**[4] on the latent variable using their observed variable scores, the investigator is more interested in calculating **composite factor scores** for the purpose of determining which types of contextual driving situations evoke the highest levels of frustration. Derivation of factor scores suffers, however, from **indeterminacy**. Factor indeterminacy means that an infinite set of factor scores can be calculated which are all consistent with the factors' loadings resulting from more unknowns than equations, e.g., $X + Y = 10$ has an infinite number of solutions. Consequently, investigators are requested to follow the conventions existing within their respective disciplines. To this end, sub-scale scores were calculated by computing the mean for each scale and these computations are summarized in Table 5.2.

In reviewing the factor scores provided in Table 5.2, the findings indicate that driving frustration is greatest in contexts where individuals perceive other road users to be engaging in discourteous driving behaviors. Stimulus 36 (frustration experienced when an individual is driving immediately behind another with their bright lights on) is the item that generates the highest average level of frustration. Irregular traffic flow and progress impeded were the sub-scales which recorded the second and third highest average contextual driving frustration scores.

Driving frustration in contexts where individuals believed that conditions and other road-users that adversely affected their driving could not be avoided or were socially permissible were comparatively lower than those perceived to be purposeful and/or avoidable. For example, the factor score for experienced levels of driving frustration to road construction was 4.29 as compared to 5.19 and 5.20 for progress impeded and irregular traffic flow, respectively. Road construction

---

[4] Individual Factor Scores conceptually represents the degree to which each individual scores high on a group of items that load high on a factor. Thus, an individual who scores high on several variables that have large loading for a factor will obtain a higher factor score for that factor showing that he/she possesses a particular characteristic represented by the factor to a higher degree than others. For more on calculating Individual and Composite Factor Scores, see: Nunnally & Bernstein (1994) and Loehlin (1998).

Table 5.2—'Driving Frustration' Factor Scores

Factor 1: Progress Impeded

5. I don't get frustrated when another driver will not heed my attempt to merge into traffic.	5.37
7. I don't get frustrated when a bicyclist is riding in the middle of the lane and slowing traffic down.	5.46
10. I don't get frustrated when a driver is holding up traffic by being slow to park.	4.45
11. I don't get frustrated when someone hastily pulls into oncoming traffic, causing the flow of traffic to unnecessarily slow.	5.33
16. I don't get frustrated when a slow vehicle on a winding road will not pull over to allow others to pass.	5.35
Mean	**5.19**

Factor 2: Irregular Traffic Flow

39. I get frustrated when the driver in front of me makes a turn without signaling.	5.11
40. I get frustrated when someone runs a red light.	5.43
41. I get frustrated when the driver in front of me repeatedly drifts across the marked road lines.	5.21
29. I don't get frustrated when a portion of a vehicle which is pulled off to the side of the highway remains in my driving lane.	4.71
34. I get frustrated when the driver in front of me appears to be uncertain about his/her actions.	5.21
19. I don't get frustrated when I cannot pass another vehicle because a driver in the passing lane is driving too slowly.	5.52
Mean	**5.20**

Factor 3: Law Enforcement Presence

51. I get frustrated when a law enforcement official pulls me over.	5.34
27. I get frustrated when I see a law enforcement official watching traffic from a hidden position.	4.38
28. I don't get frustrated when a law enforcement official appears to be following me.	4.91

Continued

113

Table 5.2—'Driving Frustration' Factor Scores Continued

Item by Factor	Frustration Mean
Mean	**4.88**
Factor 4: Road Construction	
9. I get frustrated when I encounter road construction which halts my progress.	4.38
12. I don't get frustrated when I encounter road construction with detours.	4.21
Mean	**4.29**
Factor 5: Discourteous Driving Behavior	
36. I don't get frustrated when at night, the person immediately behind me is driving with their bright lights on.	6.03
25. I don't get frustrated when at night, a driver who is approaching does not dim their bright lights.	5.53
22. I get frustrated when someone backs out in front of me without looking.	5.89
Mean	**5.82**
Factor 6: Restricted Field of Vision	
17. I don't get frustrated when the condition of the roadway is so poor that it is difficult to see its markings.	4.97
18. I don't get frustrated when my defroster is unable to keep my windshield clear at all times.	5.02
54. I get frustrated when it is raining so heavily that it is difficult to see.	4.71
6. I don't get frustrated when a vehicle remains in my "blind spot" for an extended period.	4.29
Mean	**4.75**

contains elements of both of these factors in that it often results in irregular traffic flow and almost always threatens the goal directed behavior of a driver by extending driving time and/or altering routes. Similarly, environmental and vehicular conditions which negatively affect a driver by reducing visibility were only slightly higher than those reported for frustration to road construction, but comparatively lower than discourteous driving behavior of others.

Variable Relationships

When interpreting factor solutions derived from oblique rotations, one must consider both the structure elements (**S**) and pattern elements (**B**). A factor structure consists of product-moment correlations between each of the **F** factors and **V** variables. When the factors are uncorrelated, or when an orthogonal rotation has been employed to elucidate the factor structure, the structure and pattern elements are identical: **S** = **B**. Oblique rotations, however, result in overlapping variance between the variables and the factors. As a result, the influence of other factors must be partialed before interpretations can be made between a factor and the variable(s) of interest. Pattern elements are the *higher* higher-order product-moment correlations that make these interpretations possible. As such, they represent a change in a variable per unit change in a factor, holding all other factors constant. Conversely, structure elements reflect the relation between a variable and a factor, ignoring other factors (Nunnally & Bernstein, 1994: 500-01). The structure and pattern elements are provided in Table 5.1.

In reviewing Table 5.1, the results suggest that stimulus 5 (becoming frustrated when another driver will not heed the respondent's attempt to merge) is the "effect" most strongly influenced by the latent construct **progress impeded** (with a pattern element of .731), while stimulus 16 is the effect least influenced by the progress impeded factor with a **B** = .365. The greatest effects flowing from frustration experienced to **irregular traffic flow** are stimuli 39 and 40, or frustration experienced by respondents when other drivers make a turn without signaling (39) and when another driver runs a red light (40) with **B** = 6.78 and 6.56, respectively.

The greatest manifestation of frustration flowing from the latent constructs **law enforcement presence** and **road construction** indicated by the instrument are stimuli 51 (becoming frustrated when pulled over by a law enforcement official) and 9 (becoming frustrated when encountering road construction which halts progress). The greatest effects and relationship to the latent constructs **discourteous driving behavior** and **restricted field of vision** are stimuli 36 (becoming frustrated when a person is driving immediately behind a respondent with their bright lights on) where **S** = .646 and **B** = .727, and 17 (becoming frustrated when the condition of the road is so poor that it is difficult to see its markings) where **S** = .593 and **B** = .538.

Reliability

An important criterion by which psychometric instruments are evaluated is that of their estimated degree of reliability. Attempts to estimate an individual's "true" score necessarily includes both systematic and random error. The impact of the former is of less concern to psychometricians than the latter because systematic sources of error affect all observations equally and therefore have no effect, by definition, unless the scale has a meaningful zero—since it affects only the location of the scale mean. Conversely, random error is extremely problematic in that it complicates the lawfulness in nature of relationships (Nunnally & Bernstein, 1994: 213). Furthermore, attempts may be made to limit sources of random error, while the sources of systematic error are often unidentifiable and/or difficult to correct. Psychometric scales are, therefore, evaluated by their degree of reliability, or the extent to which they are "free of random error."

Although several methods of reliability estimation exist, the type of data available here and the conditions under which the data were obtained ultimately guide the selection and use of a particular method. Given that the questionnaire item data are continuous, and that the observations were obtained without a sense of "time pressure," Cronbach's alpha (α) (1951)[5] is the most suitable method for assessing the "internal consistency" of the Driving Frustration Scale and each of its composite sub-scales.

The theoretical underpinnings of Cronbach's alpha are rooted in the domain-sampling model discussed above. Extrapolating from this model, Cronbach argued that if a form is measuring a particular concept or construct, then the items used to measure the purported

---

[5] Cronbach's alpha may be obtained through: $\left(\dfrac{k}{k-1}\right)\left(1 - \dfrac{Sy^2 - \sum\limits_{i}^{k} Si^2}{Sy^2}\right)$ where k = number of items on the form; Sy^2 = variance in test scores; Si^2 = individual item variances.

construct should all be highly correlated (Cronbach, 1951). From this vantage, Cronbach viewed each item on a form as a form itself sampled from the domain of all possible forms; thus, the 23-item driving frustration form, and its concomitant sub-scale items, are all miniature forms representing the construct "driving frustration." The scale, along with each of its six sub-scales, may all be evaluated by their degree of internal consistency—or estimates of reliability based on the average correlation among items within the test. Sub-scale and instrument coefficient α's are summarized in Table 5.3, along with corrected item-total correlations, or item-form correlations obtained after partialing the influence of each item.

Assessment of Reliability

In reviewing the driving frustration sub-scale and instrument reliability coefficients obtained through the Cronbach's α assessment of sub-scales and the overall scale, several observations are in order. First, the six sub-scales possess only modest reliability estimates, ranging from .61 to .71, while the scale reliability estimate of .81 is relatively high for the 23-item instrument and deemed to be at an acceptable level for basic research concerned with predictive or construct validation. In fact, Nunnally and Bernstein (1994) note that in the early stages of predictive or construct validation research, that considerable time and energy can be saved working with instruments that have only a modest reliability (e.g., .70.) by documenting the predictive validity of the scale before additional time and effort are directed at increasing reliability estimates. After the predictive validity of the instrument has been established, the investigator may calculate what the magnitude of the validity coefficient will be after corrections to attenuation have been made to reflect the desired reliability levels. Before the scale can be used to make decisions regarding individuals, however, reliability estimates for the instrument and its sub-scales would have to be raised to a minimum of .90, with .95 being more desirable (Nunnally & Bernstein, 1994: 264-65).

   Increasing reliability is best achieved through increasing test length, assuming that the average correlation among the new items is no less than the average correlation of the existing items. Using the

Table 5.3—'Driving Frustration' Sub-Scale and Instrument Reliability Estimates

Item by Factor	Sub-scale Corrected Item-total Correlation	Instrument Corrected Item-total Correlation
Factor 1: Progress Impeded		
5. I don't get frustrated when another driver will not heed my attempt to merge into traffic.	.61	.811
7. I don't get frustrated when a bicyclist is riding in the middle of the lane and slowing traffic down.	.59	.806
10. I don't get frustrated when a driver is holding up traffic by being slow to park.	.61	.809
11. I don't get frustrated when someone hastily pulls into oncoming traffic, causing the flow of traffic to unnecessarily slow.	.59	.806
16. I don't get frustrated when a slow vehicle on a winding road will not pull over to allow others to pass.	.66	.808
Sub-scale Alpha =	**.66**	
Factor 2: Irregular Traffic Flow		
39. I get frustrated when the driver in front of me makes a turn without signaling.	.64	.806
40. I get frustrated when someone runs a red light.	.67	.812
41. I get frustrated when the driver in front of me repeatedly drifts across the marked road lines.	.63	.808
29. I don't get frustrated when a portion of a vehicle which is pulled off to the side of the highway remains in my driving lane.	.65	.803
34. I get frustrated when the driver in front of me appears to be uncertain about his/her actions.	.67	.808
19. I don't get frustrated when I cannot pass another vehicle because a driver in the passing lane is driving too slowly.	.66	.803
Sub-scale Alpha =	**.69**	
Continued		

Table 5.4—'Driving Frustration' Sub-Scale and Instrument Reliability Estimates Continued

Item by Factor	Sub-scale Corrected Item-total Correlation	Instrument Corrected Item-total Correlation
Factor 3: Law Enforcement Presence		
51. I get frustrated when a law enforcement official pulls me over.	.58	.811
27. I get frustrated when I see a law enforcement official watching traffic from a hidden position.	.57	.808
28. I don't get frustrated when a law enforcement official appears to be following me.	.70	.809
Sub-scale Alpha =	**.71**	
Factor 4: Road Construction		
9. I get frustrated when I encounter road construction which halts my progress.	-	.809
12. I don't get frustrated when I encounter road construction with detours.	-	.806
Sub-scale Alpha =	**.70**	
Factor 5: Discourteous Driving Behavior		
36. I don't get frustrated when at night, the person immediately behind me is driving with their bright lights on.	.44	.811
25. I don't get frustrated when at night, a driver who is approaching does not dim their bright lights.	.60	.807
22. I get frustrated when someone backs out in front of me without looking.	.61	.808
Sub-scale Alpha =	**.65**	
Factor 6: Restricted Field of Vision		
17. I don't get frustrated when the condition of the roadway is so poor that it is difficult to see its markings.	.48	.804
18. I don't get frustrated when my defroster is unable to keep my windshield clear at all times.	.53	.806
54. I get frustrated when it is raining so heavily that it is difficult to see.	.50	.806
6. I don't get frustrated when a vehicle remains in my "blind spot" for an extended period.	.66	.815
Sub-scale Alpha =	**.61**	
Instrument Alpha =		**.81**

Spearman-Brown prophecy formula,[6] we can estimate the number of items required to obtain a desired reliability estimate of .90 for each sub-scale and the instrument. Thus, the sub-scales **progress impeded, irregular traffic flow, law enforcement presence, road construction, discourteous driving behavior**, and **restricted field of vision** would require a total of 10, 10, 7, 6, 8, and 10, respectively, for each to achieve a reliability of .90. Therefore, the 23-item form would need to be increased to 51 items following the prescriptions of the Spearman-Brown prophecy formula. Similarly, the instrument's reliability could be increased to .90 with only 3 additional items, **ceteris paribus**.

Model "Fit"

The ultimate worth of any scale is determined by its ability to reveal relationships among variables. The development of scales through factor analytic techniques employed here attempts to condense the variance shared among variables and define the number of factors needed to best describe the observed data. Thus, a primary goal of principal axis factor analysis is to maximize the proportion of variance explained by identifying groups of variables which correlate more highly with variables within than outside a given cluster. As a result, the most popular method for evaluating model "fit" is the assessment of the proportion of variance explained by the factor structure. For example, with regard to the driving frustration scale, 45 separate scales would exactly replicated the data and account for 100% of the variance. By employing factor analysis we attempt to minimize the number of scales while maximizing the amount of variance explained through identification of groups of variables.

As mentioned previously, oblique rotations provide clearer factor solutions but obfuscate interpretation due to "overlap" of variance accounted for among the correlated factors. Assessing the amount of variance accounted for through orthogonal rotations is easily accomplished through summation of the sums of squares loadings.

---

[6] $k = \dfrac{r_{kk}(1 - r_{11})}{r_{11}(1 - r_{kk})}$ where r_{kk} = desired reliability; r_{11} = reliability of existing

test; k = number of items test would have to be lengthened to obtain a reliability of r_{kk}.

Conversely, oblique rotations provide rather convoluted means for estimating for the proportion of variance explained. We may, however, attempt to estimate the proportion of variance accounted for by examining the proportion of variance accounted for by each factor—as that remains unchanged (Nunnally & Bernstein, 1994: 500)—and then assess the relative degree of correlation between the factor structures to provide an estimation.

The proportion of variance accounted for in the un-rotated solution indicates the following proportions of variance explained by the six factors: **progress impeded** = 19.47; **irregular traffic flow** = 6.21; **law enforcement presence** = 5.30; **road construction** = 4.15; **discourteous driving behavior** = 4.10; and **restricted field of vision** = 3.51 (see Appendix B). Cumulatively, these six factors account for 43.74% of the variance in the un-rotated solution. In the rotated solution, these variances overlap; thus, the proportion of variance explained will be less than their sum, or less than 43.74%. A review of the factor correlation matrix (see Appendices C and D) reveals moderate to negative correlations among the six factors; therefore, we can reasonably confident that the six-factor solution containing 23 items accounts for at least 40% of the total variance.

Conclusion

Two dominant general theories on crime and delinquency purport to explain traffic violations and at fault automobile accidents as their respective theoretical vantages account for why individuals engage in a host of behaviors that serve to increase their deviance from lawful and safe conduct. Self-Control Theory has received considerable empirical support and has become one of the most widely tested theories as noted in a recent review of the **Social Science Citation Index** by Unnever, Cullen, and Pratt (2003). Their analysis indicated that the theory has been cited over 300 times since its introduction in 1990. The empirical support and scholarly attention enjoyed by this theory can in part be traced to the conceptual clarity of the theory precipitating from the espousal of the parsimonious rational choice tradition and positivist tradition which recognizes individual differences in propensities to engage in crime and delinquent behaviors.

According to the architects of the self-control paradigm, the essence of crime and delinquency is the pursuit of simple and immediate pleasure through force or fraud, irrespective of context-specific political definitions. What must vary then, are individual levels of self-control and structural opportunities, because all individuals are equally motivated and tempted. The conceptual clarity enjoyed by this tradition has lead to construction of a 24-item self-control scale (Grasmick et al., 1993) which has accounted for significant proportions of variation in a wide-range of criminal and delinquent behaviors. The Grasmick et al. (1993) scale and factor structure has been replicated to varying degrees through subsequent confirmatory and **a priori** exploratory approaches (Delisi et al., 2003; Piquero et al., 2000) and it has demonstrated factorial invariance among different ages and over four nations (Vazsonyi et al., 2001).

General Strain Theory has, in contrast, suffered from conceptual obscurity and measurement difficulties. The core elements of the theory are regularly operationalized in various manners and applied to specific contexts without adequate conceptual modification. This chapter has attempted to document the existence of a construct rooted deep in the loam of General Strain Theory, and sought to assess the psychometric properties of a proposed measurement model. *Driving frustration*—which recognizes that frustration can lead to a host of driving delinquent behaviors for instrumental, escapist, or retaliatory reasons—appears to exist as a multi-dimensional latent construct with "effects" that manifest themselves through variations in individual reactions to the blockage, removal, or introduction of various positive and negative stimuli found in the driving experience.

These indicators suggest a measurement model consisting of the clustering of context-specific variables identified through the use of the most conservative psychometric techniques—form construction and factor rotation, extraction, and interpretation—available. This conservative approach was undertaken to create a Driving Frustration scale that would meet the psychometric standards of construct and predictive validation necessary to further investigate the role of this construct in forms of driving delinquency, and to assess its explanatory power in relation to its rival Self-Control Theory.

CHAPTER 6

A Test of Two General Theories of Crime/Delinquency in the Context of Driving

INTRODUCTION

The previous chapters have accomplished the following objectives: 1) identified a program theory upon which contemporary traffic safety education programs rest; 2) summarized the theoretically and empirically relevant variables contributing to the overrepresentation of young drivers in automobile accidents as identified and discussed in previous investigations; 3) examined the theoretical relation that two competing theories of crime and deviance may share with this phenomenon; and 4) described the development of a potential measurement model allowing for a test of General Strain Theory. As a result of these efforts, several testable propositions were advanced which may increase our understanding of those factors that contribute to this pressing social problem by either confirming or refuting previous findings, and offering a novel test of competing (or possibly complimentary) theoretical frameworks prominent in the Criminal Justice literature.

These competing (or possibly complimentary) theoretical frameworks claim to be 'general" theories, meaning that their explanatory power is not hemmed by political definitions or limited to particular forms of crime/deviance. Thus, extension of both these theories to driving delinquency—and more distally to accidents and citations—should be tenable. Fortunately, the theoretical cognates of low self-control and strain while operating a motor vehicle—driving delinquency—are quite similar making a simultaneous test possible provided the existence of a valid delinquency measurement model.

'Driving Delinquency': Development of a Measurement Model

The architects of Self-Control Theory argue that low self-control and accidents are the result of a host of driving behaviors that increase an individual's risk for at fault accidents—among them being speeding, drinking, tail-gating, inattentive driving, and high frequency of risk-taking (Gottfredson & Hirschi, 1990: 42). The implications of this proposition are important. The argument is that the role of self-control in accidents is **mediated** by driving delinquent behaviors: self-control → delinquent driving behaviors → accidents. Attempting to assess the influence of low self-control on accidents (self-control → accidents) without recognizing the mediating role of driving behaviors may provide biased and/or unstable estimates (R. Baron & Kenny, 1986: 1176). In this regard, General Strain theorists have been silent on the role that that their key variable may share with accidents.

Drawing from the core tenets of General Strain Theory along with definitions of stress drawn from the literature in psychology (see Chapter 5), the possible role that strain might play in the operation of a motor vehicle with respect to automobile accidents can be direct **and/or** indirect. Directly, the cognitive processes of an individual who experiences high levels of strain while operating a motor vehicle may become sufficiently disturbed to become disoriented, and in the process become vulnerable to involvement in an accident. Indirectly, individuals may become motivated to respond to the removal and/or blockage of positively valued goals, or the introduction of negative stimuli, and respond in a retaliatory, escapist, and/or instrumental manner (see Chapter 5). Thus, we would be interested in measuring an individual's level of strain experienced while operating a motor vehicle and the direct relation shared with their number of automobile accidents and citations (inadvertent violation of traffic laws) after controlling for other important variables (strain → accidents and citations). Indirectly, strain would lead to driving behaviors that are retaliatory, escapist, and/or instrumental in manner: speeding, tail-gating, risk-taking could be the results of strain, and these behaviors in turn increase the risk of accident (strain → delinquent driving behaviors → accidents and citations). Thus, the theoretical cognates of General Strain Theory are similar to those of Self-Control Theory, the only difference is the hypothesized source of the behaviors. One theoretical perspective views these behaviors flowing from "motivation' (retaliation or instrumental), and the other theoretical perspective views these behaviors as manifestations of an enduring predisposition (low self-control). Failure to measure these intervening variables (driving delinquent behaviors) would result in model misspecification to possibly confound results and disadvantage these theories during empirical testing.

Because the corpus of this investigation does **not** necessarily include the development of a novel **psychometrically sound** driving delinquency scale, relatively little discussion will be devoted to describing its development. This rationale is also rooted in the relative conceptual simplicity of identifying driving delinquent behaviors that likely correlate in nature, while being assisted and informed by existing potential measures (Joireman, 2004; Kidd & Huddleston, 1994). To reduce the likelihood of capitalizing on chance with sample specific results, the 18 driving behaviors appearing on the Washington Driver's Experience Survey (see Appendix G, items 53-70) were administered during the factor extraction phase of the 'Driving Frustration'' scale described in Chapter 5. The results were subsequently subjected to an exploratory factor analysis to serve as the hypothesized measurement model.

To summarize the sample characteristics described in considerable detail in Chapter 5, the subjects were 237 (140 males, 97 females) ranging in age from 18 to 24 years, with the mean, median, and mode ages = 20.53, 20, and 19, respectively.[7]   Similar to the development of the 'Driving Frustration' scale, sample size for the development of the 'Driving Delinquency' scale achieved the minimum five-to-one

---

[7] Courses at Washington State University that participated during this second phase of the 'Driving Frustration' scale development that ultimately served to assist in the simultaneous development of a 'Driving Delinquency' measurement model were: CRM J 105 (Realizing Justice in a Multi-Cultural Society) N = 22; CRM J 420 (Law of Evidence and Criminal Procedure) N = 30; CRM J 150 (Organizational Environment of Criminal Justice) N = 51; POL S 305 (Gender and Politics) N = 20; CRM J 330 (Crime Control Policies) N = 61; CRM J 101 (Introduction to the Administration of Criminal Justice) N = 53.

ratio recognized to sufficiently minimize the chance of "overfitting" the data, or deriving factors that are sample-specific (Hair et al., 1995: 373-74).

Principal Component Extraction

Using SPSS 11.5.1, responses to the 18 items were subjected to a principal component factor analysis. Although, the alternative method—principal axis factor analysis—is often preferred for its ability to provide more accurate point estimates, to produce smaller residual correlations, and to generate smaller root mean square errors (Nunnally & Bernstein, 1994; Snook & Gorsuch, 1989) by accounting for unique variance (u^2), this method could not provide an admissible solution (convergence of the estimated and observed matrices was not achieved). Consequently, principal component factor analysis was employed which substitutes a value of 1 into the communality estimates (h^2) of the variance/covariance matrix. Convergence was achieved in six iterations, and the solution was subjected to an oblique rotation [Promax with Kappa 4—or the power most commonly used (Loehlin, 1998; Nunnally & Bernstein, 1994)]. The solution yielded six factors with eigenvalues > 1 that cumulatively explained 72.3% of the variance prior to rotation (see Appendix H).

Factor Selection

The **latent root** criterion, the **scree test**, and the **salient variable** rule were all employed to determine the appropriate number of factors to extract. According to the latent root criterion, only those factors with eigenvalues greater than one are considered significant (Guttman, 1954; Kaiser, 1970). According to this rationale, any individual factor should account for the variance of at least a single variable if it is to be retained for interpretation. In all, six factors were eligible for extraction (see Appendix H). Because the Kaiser-Guttman rule has been shown to be biased upwards to account for less variance than purported (Cliff, 1988), the scree test and salient variable rule were also employed.

The scree test is used to identify the optimum number of factors that can be extracted before the amount of unique variance begins to dominate the common variance structure. This is achieved by plotting the latent roots against the number of factors in their order of extraction—which are extracted in order of their proportion of common variance accounted for—and identifying the point at which too large a proportion of unique variance would be included. An inspection of the scree plot was not definitive, but did suggest that the optimum number of factors to be extracted is three. As a result, the Kaiser-Guttman rule, scree test, and salient variable[8] rule were all employed to determine the appropriate number of factors to select. The salient variable rule recognizes the practical, rather than statistical, significance of a variable's relation to a factor.

Because the factor loading of a variable represents the correlation of a variable to the factor, the squared loading is the amount of the variable's total variance accounted for by the factor. Thus, a loading of .30 translates to approximately 10 percent explanation, while .5 translates to approximately 25 percent explanation. Because principal component factor analysis assumes no unique variance, estimates are often biased upwards. Thus, observing the salient variable rule during factor extraction favors the latter level of practical significance (.5), although .3 is a standard of practical significance commonly recognized in the social sciences. A review of the pattern matrix (see Appendix I)—in conjunction with the extraction techniques previously discussed—indicates that a three-factor solution is most appropriate (note that the decision to retain variable 63 with a loading of .376 was made in order to make the measure stable). Similarly, variable 64 appeared to be cross-loading with factors 2 and 3, but was retained on factor 2 for the purpose of clarification that **may** result in re-specification during confirmation of the factorial validity of the measurement model. Although factor four had two salient variables, the third variable was not within the range of practical significance (.034). Thus, termination of factor extraction occurred after factor three. The principal component oblique rotation factor solution is summarized in Table 6.1 with the pattern (**B**) elements.

---

[8] A salient is a variable having a value on a factor of at least .3, with .5 being preferred (Nunnally & Bernstein, 1994).

Table 6.1—Driving Delinquency Scale Items

Item by Factor	Pattern Element
Factor 1: Law Violation	
Eigenvalue = 6.19	
59 (57). I drive over the speed limit in clear weather.	.951
72 (70). I drive over the speed limit.	.932
56 (54). I drive 5 to 10 mph over the speed limit.	.862
61 (59). I drive over the speed limit at night.	.821
58 (56). I do things against the law when it is safe.	.644
Factor 2: Aggressive Driving	
Eigenvalue = 2.12	
66 (64). I give other drivers a nonverbal gesture.	.881
65 (63). I let people know when I'm unhappy with their driving.	.877
68 (66). I use my horn a lot.	.751
64 (62). I get back at people with my car	.478
Factor 3: Risk Taking	
Eigenvalue = 1.34	
70 (68). I run red lights.	.867
71 (69). I race in my car.	.790
63 (61). I drive on people's bumpers.	.376

†Note that the item numbers appearing in ( ) are those that appeared on the final probability sample survey (Washington Driver's Experience).

Sample Characteristics

The Washington Driver's Experience Survey (see Appendix G) was mailed to 2,000 licensed drivers 16 to 24 years of age during the months of October to December, 2004. The sample was stratified by age, and the participants were randomly selected within age strata by the Washington State Department of Licensing. Mailings occurred in two waves that ultimately achieved a response rate of 18.3%.

The subjects are N = 366 (156 males, 209 females) ranging in age from 16 to 24 years, with the mean, median, and mode ages = 19, 19.3, and 16, respectively. The percentage of drivers by age within the sample are: 16 years = 19.7%; 17 years = 12.6%; 18 years = 14.8%; 19 years = 8.7%; 20 years = 10.7%; 21 years = 8.5%; 22 years = 6.8%; 23 years = 9.3%; and 24 years = 8.7%.

Control Variables

Previous investigations have identified a number of environmental, opportunity, and individual level variables that either empirically or theoretically contribute to accident and citation rates among young drivers (see Chapter 1). These variables were also included in the Washington Driver's Experience Survey, and they appear as items 74 through 83 (see Appendix G). The response frequencies for the categorical (Table 6.2) and the continuous variables (Table 6.3) are described below.

Table 6.2—Categorical Control Variable Frequency Distribution

Variable:	Yes	No	Percent
Own Vehicle	251	112	99.2%
Urban Driving	237	112	95.4
Economy Car	241	123	99.5
Graduated Driver Licensing Program (GDL)	154	211	99.7
Gender: Male	156	209	99.7
Ethnicity: Caucasian	291	62	96.4

Table 6.3—Continuous Control Variable Data Distribution

Variable	Mean	Median	Mode	Minimum	Maximum
Miles per Week	18	170	125	1	850
Months Driving Experience	39.49	33	6	2	105
Licensing Exam Score	82.31	80	80	80	100

Assumptions of Asymptotic Theory and Maximum Likelihood Estimation

A preferred estimation procedure employed during structural equation modeling is that of Maximum Likelihood estimation (ML). ML as an estimation procedure is often preferred (compared to unweighted least squares; generalized least squares; and asymptotically distribution free (weighted least squares) for its relative superiority in generating accurate and correct results for multivariate, normally distributed data (Chou & Bentler, 1995). Furthermore, ML estimation is preferred for its relative robustness to minor violations of multivariate normality, should they occur (Bollen, 1989; Chou & Bentler, 1995; Raykov & Marcoulides, 2000). It is because of this relative superiority in accuracy of estimation and robustness to violations of multivariate normally distributed data that ML will be the method of both measurement and structural model estimation.

Maximum Likelihood estimation is grounded in large-sample (i.e., asymptotic) theory, however. Large-sample theory relies on the assumption that data employed are both continuous and normally distributed (Bollen, 1989; Byrne, 2001; Chou & Bentler, 1995; Hu & Bentler, 1995; Satorra & Bentler, 1990; West, Finch, & Curran, 1995). The reality is, however, that many forms of data included in structural equation modeling fail to meet fully these **scaling** and **normality** assumptions (West et al., 1995). Thus, it is important to assess the extent of departures from these assumptions, and consider potential remedies and consequences for their violation. In the absence of well-understood and widely available multivariate normality statistics, univariate skewness and kurtosis descriptive statistics can be examined as an acceptable alternative. The presence of univariate normality does not guarantee multivariate normality, but it is a necessary condition. Table 6.4 summarizes the skewness and kurtosis descriptive statistics for the observed variables to be included within the full structural model. A review of these statistics indicate that two variables, reported miles driven per week and self-reported number of automobile collisions and citations, are suffering from **extreme** skewness and/or kurtosis (or $\geq |2|$). It is important to note that extreme skewness is not occurring within any coarsely categorized variables—or variables with 4 or fewer categories—as ML estimation can often absorb minor violations in one but not both (West et al., 1995). Lastly, extreme violations in normality appear in the continuous level variable number of self-reported accidents and citations.

Table 6.4—Observable Variable Skewness and Kurtosis Descriptive Statistics

Observable Variable Skewness and Kurtosis Descriptive Statistics

	N	Skewness	Kurtosis
	Statistic	Statistic	Statistic
Ethnicity: Caucasian (0 = No / 1= Yes)	353	-1.712	.937
Gender: Male (0 = No / 1 = Yes)	365	.295	-1.924
Economy Car (0 = No / 1 = Yes)	364	-.688	-1.535
Urban Driving (0 = No / 1 = Yes)	349	-.771	-1.414
Own Vehicle (0 = No / 1 =Yes)	363	-.832	-1.314
Self-Report GDL (0 = No / 1 = Yes)	365	.318	-1.910
Miles Per Week	348	1.796	**3.739**
Months Driving Experience	362	.595	-.721
Age	365	.354	-1.167
Self-Reported Accidents and Citations	365	**2.498**	**9.593**
TSE x Strain (MMR)	184	-.230	.945

In a similar vein, the continuous variables contained within the three "construct" measurement models need to be examined. To this end, each variable within the 'Driving Frustration,' 'Driving Delinquency,' and 'Self-Control' measurement models were inspected for noteworthy departures in normality. A review of the univariate skewness descriptive statistics with the 'Driving Frustration' model revealed a range of |.451| to |1.78|, while the kurtosis statistics revealed that only one variable (v14) suffered extreme kurtosis with a value of 3.22. Similarly, the 'Driving Delinquency' scale revealed that three variables (v62), (v68), and (v69) were extremely skewed with values of 2.27, 2.52, and 2.78, while reporting kurtosis values of 5.13, 10.45, and 8.31, respectively. Lastly, the 'Self-Control' measurement model contained no variables that suffered extreme skewness or kurtosis.

Remedies for Categorical Data and Departures in Normality

Clearly the data within the covariance structure do not meet the scaling and normality assumptions upon which ML estimation rests. With respect to scaling, there are six dichotomous control variables. It is important to note, however, that none of these six categorical variables suffers extreme skewness or kurtosis (see Table 6.4). With respect to the normality of the continuous variables, one control variable (self-reported accidents and citations) suffers extreme departures from normality, while three variables within the 'Driving Delinquency' measurement model suffer an extreme departure from normality. The extreme skewness witnessed within self-reported accidents and citations variable is likely related to the nature of the variable that tends to follow a Poisson distribution—a higher number of observed frequencies at the low end of the distribution—which is not atypical for some variables within the social sciences, e.g., amount of substance abuse (West et al., 1995).

Departures in normality witnessed in the construct measurement models present a dilemma. Such nonnormally distributed data can often be the result of mistakes made during data entry, or the result of **outliers** within the data. A review of the covariance structure indicated that two cases (180 and 235) were contributing to this extreme skewness within the 'Driving Delinquency' measurement model. These extreme responses in the covariance structure were an accurate representation of the responses contained within the survey, however, and as a consequence could not be excluded with any theoretical justification.

Remedies for this violation of normality include the use the Asymptotically Distribution Free (ADF) or the Scaled χ^2 Statistic and Robust Errors estimators. The ADF estimator is computationally demanding (often failing to achieve convergence with models containing more than 25 variables) and requires extremely large samples (N > 1,000) (West et al., 1995), however, while the Scaled χ^2 and Robust Errors estimator could not achieve convergence where intercepts and slopes had to be simultaneously estimated because of missing data in the control and outcome variables. Lastly, given that the structural equation modeling software to be employed for this estimation (Analysis of Moment Structures 4.0) does not include the option of analyzing data that are categorical in nature (CVM—continuous/categorical variable methodology) it is important to understand the potential implications for model estimation.

To recapitulate, Maximum Likelihood estimation procedures are relatively robust to modest violations in multivariate normality, which is the case here (For more on relatively extreme departures in multivariate normality see Byrne, 2001: 272). Moreover, use of ML to estimate models which treat all data as continuous in scale is less problematic when the covariance, rather than correlation matrix, is analyzed; analysis of the latter can yield incorrect standard error estimates (Byrne, 2001: 72). Second, using CVM to estimate models with variables having only two categories does not produce substantial benefits unless the data are poorly distributed—which is not the case here (all categorical variables are free of **extreme** skewness) (West et al., 1995: 63-4; 74-5). Thus, although some departures in normality are present in the data used here, these departures are relatively minor. Because the categorical data are not poorly distributed, no significant advantages would be realized with a CVM estimator.

Control Variable Zero-Order Correlations

Previous investigations of young driver accidents and various forms of traffic delinquency have identified several variables that share a significant relation with automobile collisions and citation frequencies. Among them is an individual's *exposure* (Bergdahl & Norris, 2002; Carroll et al., 1971). Exposure is often measured in both the *amount* and *type* of driving conditions experienced by young drivers. Those who drive more miles, and who drive in densely populated areas, are at a higher risk for collisions and citations then drivers who travel fewer miles and drive in uncongested traffic conditions. The high mileage and urban area means drivers are more likely to experience traffic events that carry a risk for an accident and are more likely to receive a formal citation for violation of traffic laws because of local law enforcement deployment priorities (Gaines & Kappeler, 2003) and policing styles (Wilson, 1968).

Graduated Driver Licensing (GDL) programs represent a recent attempt by state governments to limit exposure to high-risk driving conditions disproportionately experienced by young drivers. GDL programs restrict the range of driving behaviors in an attempt to limit a youthful driver's exposure to high-risk environments. Young drivers are more likely than others to drive during nighttime conditions, driving situations which both limit visibility and tend to be associated with the use of drugs/alcohol. They are also likely to have teenage passengers that often distract their attention (McCartt et al., 2003). GDL programs attempt to reduce exposure to such high risk environments by restricting the driver's behavior during their first few months of driving. Those who either have participated in or are currently participating in GDL programs would theoretically be expected to report fewer accidents and citations than those who did not drive under these restrictions.

Vehicle ownership and type of vehicle are also theoretically related to an individual's rate of involvement in accidents and citations. Those operating smaller, fuel efficient (or economy) cars are less likely to respond to traffic events in an instrumental manner (passing a slow moving vehicle on a mountain road), while increasing the perceived potential costs associated with retaliatory (tail-gating) driving behaviors, as larger more powerful cars create both the opportunity and greater sense of safety not enjoyed by those operating economy cars (Porter, 1999). In addition, those who rely on the barrowed transportation of others would include in their calculation potential social costs (guilt and embarrassment) associated with their behaviors not experienced by those who own their own vehicle. Lastly, gender and ethnicity likely share a relation with young driver accidents and citations as a result of socialization, values, beliefs, and physiology (see Chapters 1 and 4).

To test the relation between these theoretically and empirically previously identified control variables—for the purpose of confirming or refuting past findings—and to ensure proper model specification for accuracy in the main effects estimates of "strain" and "self-control," bi-variate zero-order correlations were employed to measure association for these variables with an index variable created from their self-reported number of accidents and citations. The results of this analysis are presented in the theoretic analytic model (not to be confused with SEM estimation) in Figure 6.0. All solid paths indicated are statistically significant at the $p < .01$ level and substantively significant (or revealing magnitudes $> .10$)(J. Cohen, 1988). Generally, hypothesis 1 (see Chapter 4) is confirmed with the relation of all control variables to self-reported accidents and citations in the theorized direction, with the exception of ethnicity (which is nonsignificant).

Measurement Model Factorial Validity

<u>Driving Delinquency</u>

Consistent with the goals and methods of logical positivism—to discover functional relations between variables that exist in nature for the purpose of control, explanation, and prediction—investigators must minimize the probability of capitalizing on sample-specific results. Structural Equation Modeling techniques in contrast to classical modeling techniques (which are inherently descriptive in nature) offer an advantage in this respect by not fitting the model to the data as occurs in classical linear modeling techniques, but instead assess the plausibility of the specified relations existing in the population based upon the observed data (variance/covariance matrix). Before the investigator can state with confidence that a functional relationship exists *between* the variables of interest, they must ensure that their measures are reliable.

Adhering to the confirmatory nature (hypothesis testing versus description) of Structural Equation Modeling techniques, the measurement models previously identified—namely, 'Low Self-Control' (Grasmick et al., 1993), 'Driving Frustration' (see Chapter 5) and 'Driving Delinquency'—can be represented by a series of hypotheses that can be confirmed or refuted using Confirmatory Factor Analysis, a statistical technique belonging to the family of Structural Equation Modeling. Based on the previous description of the development of a 'Driving Delinquency' measurement model, a confirmatory model based on the exploratory findings of the convenience sample can be tested for its goodness-of-fit with the hypothesized population level model estimated from the data provided

Figure 6.0—Control Variable Zero-Order Correlations

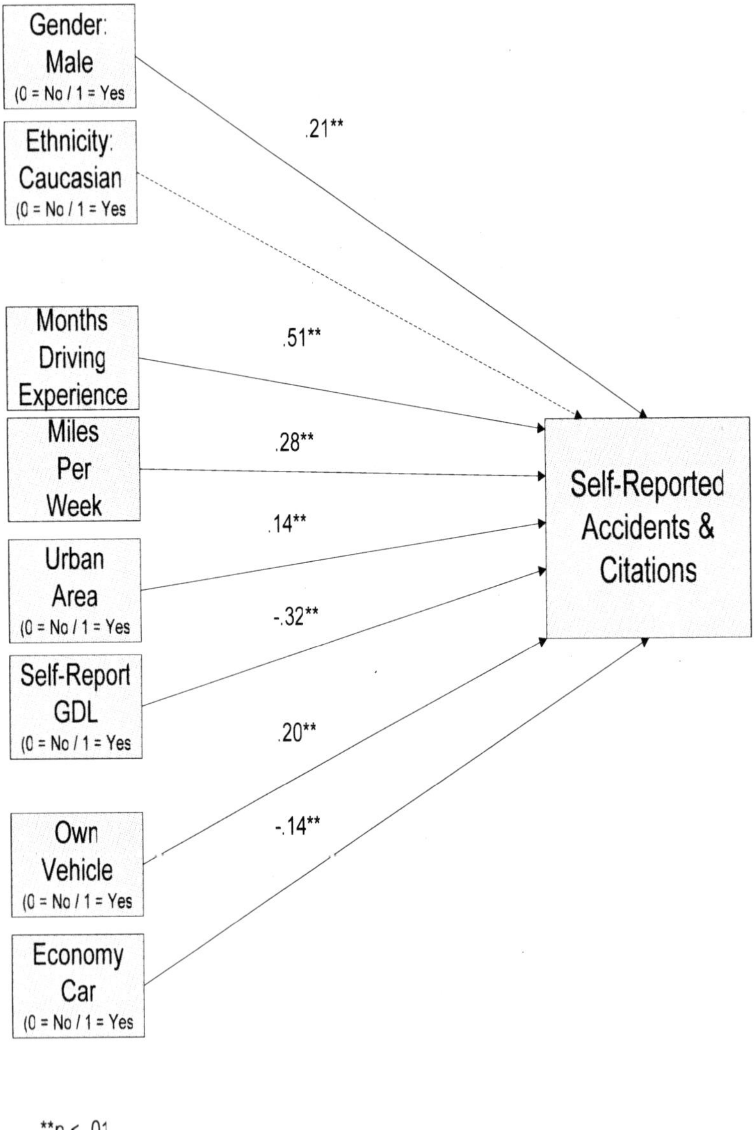

Gender: Male (0 = No / 1 = Yes)

Ethnicity: Caucasian (0 = No / 1 = Yes)

.21**

Months Driving Experience — .51**

Miles Per Week — .28**

.14**

Urban Area (0 = No / 1 = Yes)

-.32**

Self-Report GDL (0 = No / 1 = Yes)

.20**

Own Vehicle (0 = No / 1 = Yes) — -.14**

Economy Car (0 = No / 1 = Yes)

Self-Reported Accidents & Citations

**p < .01

by the probability sample. This step in the analysis represents an attempt to reduce the likelihood that the results reported on relationships among variables of interest are entirely sample specific. Based on the results of the exploratory analysis, we can hypothesize that 'Driving Delinquency" is best represented as a second-order construct consisting of three first-order factors—Law Violation, Aggressive Driving, and Risk-Taking. Each observable variable identified in Table 6.1 can also be hypothesized to share a statistically significant relationship with a non-zero loading on its respective construct. The series of statements just hypothesized can be graphically represented as illustrated in Figure 6.1.

Figure 6.1—Hypothesized 'Driving Delinquency' Measurement Model

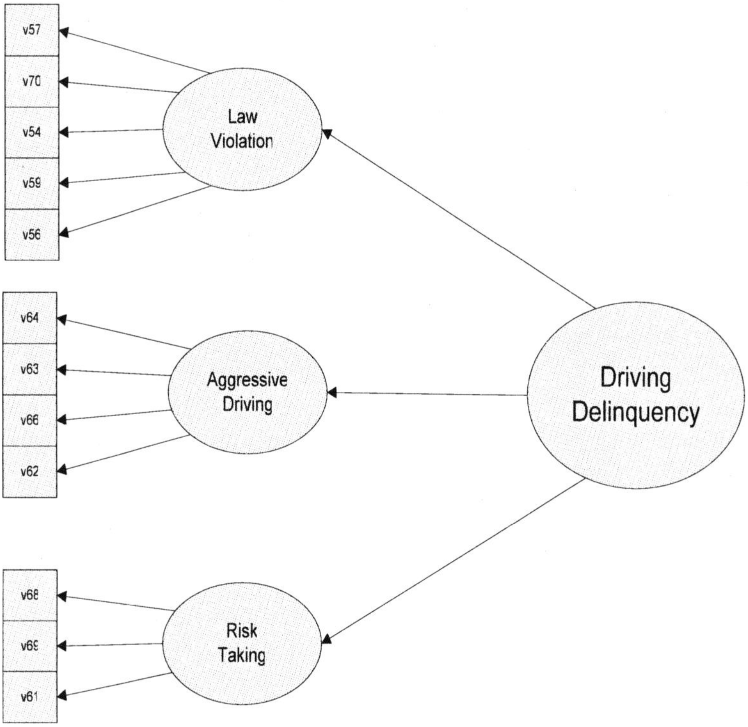

The results of the analysis are based on the sample previously described. Fortunately, there were no missing data for any of the observable variables; thus, no special estimation procedures (EM algorithm to be discussed later) had to be employed. The model was overidentified—meaning that there is more empirical information than parameters to be estimated for the purpose of providing a unique solution—with 51 *degrees of freedom* (df). Univariate skewness statistics reveal that three variables: v68, v69, v62 suffer extreme skewness with values of |2.5|, |2.7|, and |2.2|, respectively. The covariance matrix as a whole does not suffer extreme skewness, however, with the average univariate skewness statistic = |1.23| (For more on extreme covariance matrix skewness see Byrne, 2001: 272). Maximum Likelihood estimation was employed for its ability to absorb minor violations in normality, and for its relative precision in estimation. The results of the analysis support the hypotheses that each item designed to measure the first-order constructs shares a significant non-zero relationship with the construct it was designed to measure, and that each first-order construct shares a significant non-zero relationship with the second-order construct 'Driving Delinquency' (see Figure 6.2).

In reviewing the goodness-of-fit statistics also provided in Figure 6.2, we see that the inferential chi-square index—which tests the null hypothesis that the model fits the analyzed covariance matrix perfectly—is highly significant at the .000 level, leading us to reject the $H_o = \Sigma = \Sigma (\theta)$ and conclude that the postulated model does not hold in the population. Because the analysis of covariance structures is grounded in large sample theory—large samples are critical to obtaining precise parameter estimates, as well as to the tenability of asymptotic distributional approximations (MacCallum, Browne, & Sugawara, 1996)—and because χ^2 is a function of sample size (N − 1) that necessarily leads to rejection as the sample size grows, it is often unreliable (Byrne, 2001; Raykov & Marcoulides, 2000). Thus, we can examine alternative fit indices that do not suffer absolute (reject or retain) evaluations likely to lead to incorrect decisions as samples become large.

The Goodness-of-Fit (GFI) is a measure of the relative amount of variance and covariance in *S* (the observed covariance matrix) that is jointly explained by Σ (the population covariance matrix). The GFI and

AGFI (which differs from the GFI only in that it adjusts for the number of degrees of freedom in the specified model) are both absolute fit indices because they compare the hypothesized model with no model at all (Hu & Bentler, 1995: 82). As a result, these fit indices are analogous to R^2 in that they quantify the extent to which the variation and covariation in the data are accounted for by a model. These fit indices have maximum values of 1.00, with values $\geq .90$ being indicative of a good fit. The Comparative Fit index is an incremental or comparative fit index that differs from absolute fit indices (such as the GFI and AGFI) in that while absolute fit indices are based on a comparison of the hypothesized model against a standard based on no model, incremental fit indices use a standard which represents a baseline model (typically the independence or null model—in which all the observed variables are uncorrelated) (Bentler & Bonett, 1980; Byrne, 2001; Hu & Bentler, 1995). The CFI, like the GFI and AGFI, ranges from 0 to 1.00 with values $\geq .90$ being indicative of a well-fitting model.

In attempting to discern if the 'Driving Delinquency' measurement model—and 'Self-Control' and 'Driving Frustration' to be discussed later—can/should be represented as first- or second-order constructs, tightly reasoned theory, parsimonious sets of concepts, and model fit should all guide the investigator. According to the logic of first-order measurement models, all items from the various scales are measuring the same thing. In this instance, law-violation, aggressive driving, and risk-taking all are measuring 'Driving Delinquency,' and thusly all items of each scale are highly correlated with each other (inter-item reliability) and the various scales—law-violation, aggressive driving, and risk-taking—are highly correlated with each other because they are assessing the same construct 'Driving Delinquency' (Hull, Tedlie, & Lehn, 1995).

In contrast to a first-order one-factor model, in a *higher-order factor model* the individual scales are associated with discriminable dimensions of a higher-order construct. According to the logic of higher-order factor measurement models, the reason that items from a *particular* scale are highly correlated with each other is that they all measure the same somewhat **specific** construct. The reason that these specific constructs—law violation, aggressive driving, risk-taking— correlate with each other is that they are all related to a single, **general**

Figure 6.2—Driving Delinquency CFA

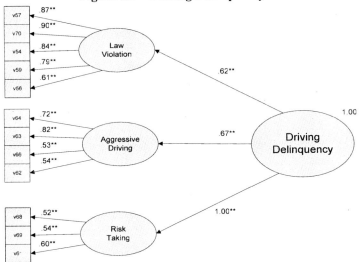

Final Model
$\chi^2(51, 126.865) = 0.000$, CFI = .96, GFI = .95, RMSEA = .06

**p < .01
†All Loadings are Standardized

construct. Despite sharing a significant amount of variation with this general construct, each specific construct retains a significant amount of variance that is unique, or unshared with the general construct (Hull et al., 1995: 219).

Theoretically, risk-taking, aggressive driving, and a general tendency to violate the law may explain a significant amount of unique variance that is not shared with 'Driving Delinquency.' Empirically, this proposition can be tested by examining the fit statistics for each model (first- and second-order). Based on the fit indices, rules of parsimony, and theory, the most appropriate measurement model can be advanced. An examination of the first- and second-order fit indices and model complexity expressed in degrees of freedom (df) (which serves as a measure of parsimony)(J. C. Anderson & Gerbing, 1988) in Table 6.5 indicate that the measurement model can be represented as either a first- or second-order factor structure without consequence. Indeed, the model complexity remains unchanged as do the absolute and incremental fit indices, while indicating a **minor** decrement in model fit expressed in the inferential χ^2 statistic. The choice to represent the 'Driving Delinquency' as a second-order construct in the full structural regression model is, therefore, based on the desire to achieve parsimony. To disaggregate the 'Driving Delinquency' scale would unnecessarily complicate the model in predicting the outcome variable of interest (self-reported accidents and citations).

Self-Control

Despite the admonition of the architects of Self-Control Theory (Gottfredson & Hirschi, 1990) not to view self-control as a personality trait, the first empirical test of the theory cast self-control as a personality trait predisposing individuals toward criminal acts by developing a 24-item psychometric scale consisting of the six components derived from Gottfredson and Hirschi's definition: Impulsivity, risk-taking, self-centeredness, preference for simple tasks, and frequent display of temper. Subsequent attempts to confirm the factorial validity of the scale using exploratory factor analysis (fitting the data to the model) have argued for presenting the construct as uni-dimensional (Nagin & Paternoster, 1993; Piquero & Tibbetts, 1996). Second-order Confirmatory Factor analysis models tested by Piquero et al. (2000) and Vazsonyi et al. (2001) found that Self-Control modeled as a multi-dimensional (second-order) construct yielded superior absolute and incremental fit indices. Moreover, the logic of self-control as a second-order construct is more consistent with Gottfredson and Hirschi's contention that self control should not be considered a personality trait requiring crime, but possibly only one of its by-products (Hirschi & Gottfredson, 1993).

 As a result of the theory of self-control and previous modeling efforts, a second-order measurement model was put forth for assessment. The model hypothesized that self-control was best represented as a second-order construct consisting of six first-order constructs: Impulsivity, simple tasks, risk-seeking, self-centered, and temper. Each of the first-order factors was hypothesized to share a significant non-zero loading with the higher-order general factor Self-Control, and that each observable item measuring the six first-order constructs would share a significant non-zero relationship with the trait that it was meant to measure. The hypothesized model is graphically represented in Figure 6.3. Results of the test indicated a relatively poor fitting model, with a GFI = .89, CFI = .86, and RMSEA = .06. Modification indices led to the correlation of two error terms, two residuals, and one error and residual term. The final fit indices suggest that the final model is well fitting with a GFI, CFI, and RMSEA of .91, .90, and .05, respectively (see Figure 6.4). What's more, all hypothesized paths were statistically significant.

To assess if the model would be more appropriately designated as a first-order factor, a second model was tested wherein the second-order self-control construct and first-order residuals were removed from the specified model. A comparison of the fit-indices and model complexity are set forth in Table 6.5. These results indicate a relatively superior CFI index level for the second-order model, while the complexity is statistically justified with a significant decrement in model fit as evidenced in $\Delta\chi2$ (4, 366) = 16.834.

Driving Frustration

The 'Driving Frustration' measurement model developed in Chapter 5 represents a social psychological context-specific measure attempting to assess the role of General Strain Theory in young driver accidents and driving delinquency. From a theoretical vantage, the conceptualization of the measure (context-specific) implies that there are specific conditions or events that frustrate or strain drivers, and that these contexts—although related to a higher-order general factor—possibly account for unique variance not part of the general higher-order 'Driving Frustration' construct. To test the factorial validity of the measurement model created to test General Strain Theory with respect to driving delinquency and traffic accidents and citations and examine the likelihood that the model was sample-specific, the

Figure 6.3—Hypothesized 'Self-Control' Measurement Model

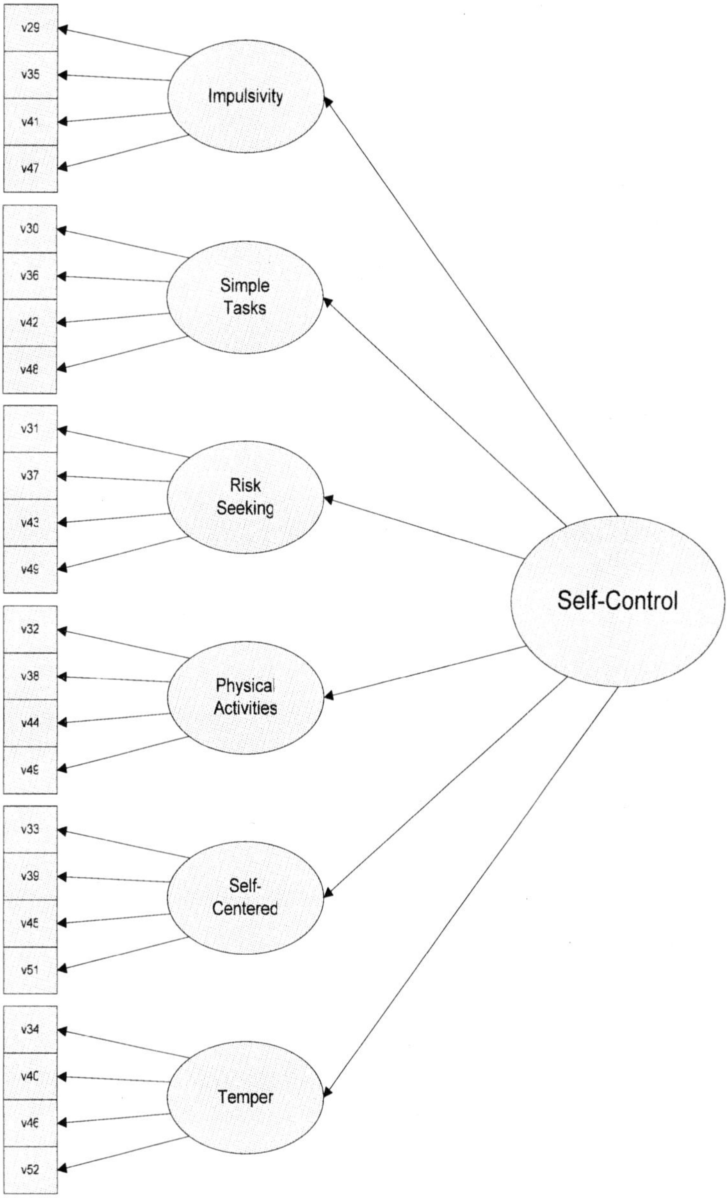

Figure 6.4—Self-Control CFA

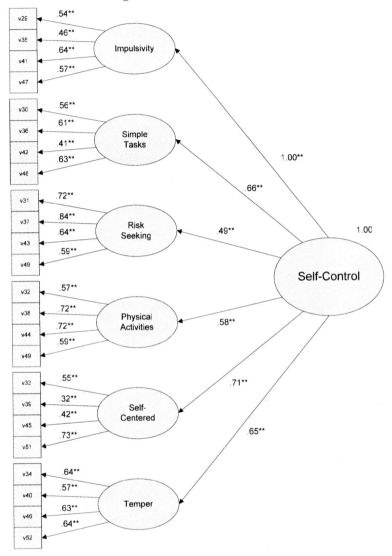

Final Model

$\chi^2(241, 445.842) = 0.000$, CFI = .91, GFI = .90, RMSEA = .05

**p < .01
†All Loadings are Standardized

hypothesized model derived from Chapter 5 was tested anew: Specifically, the 'Driving Frustration' measurement model was hypothesized to be best represented as a second-order construct consisting of the six first-order constructs identified in Chapter 5: Progress impeded, irregular traffic flow, law enforcement presence, road construction, discourteous driving behavior, and restricted field of vision. Each first-order factor was hypothesized to share a significant non-zero loading with the higher-order 'Driving Frustration' factor, and each variable attempting to measure the first-order factors would have a significant non-zero loading with the factor it was meant to measure.

The hypothesized model is graphically represented in the Figure 6.5. Results of the initial model indicate that it is relatively poor-fitting. Indeed, the GFI = .85, AGFI = .81, and RMSEA = .07. Each of the first-order factors shared a significant non-zero loading with the higher-order factor 'Driving Frustration,' and each indicator on the first-order factors had a significant non-zero loading on the factor it is was meant to measure. It is important to note that although the absolute fit indices reported for the hypothesized model indicate a relatively poor fit, this is likely a consequence of the specificity of the items within the scale. To be sure, theoretically the factorial structure of the measurement model was replicated per the hypothesized model developed from the exploratory work in Chapter 5. The source(s) of this poor fit cannot therefore be traced to theoretical misspecification, but instead to two potential sources of systematic error.

To be sure, the modification indices reported for the initial model indicate the poor fit is likely attributable to the context-specific nature of the measurement model or the omission of a small factor. Evidence in support of the first proposition is revealed by the modification indices which point to a large number of correlated error terms rather than any re-specification of the relation among observables and constructs (or regression weights)—or theoretical revision. Correlated error terms are a form of systematic error that often result from a high degree of overlap in item content (Byrne, 2001: 106-7) and/or the omission of a small factor (Aish & Joreskog, 1990). After correlating the error terms and residuals suggested by the modification indices, a well fitting model was achieved with a GFI = .93, AGFI = .90, and a RMSEA = .04 (see Figure 6.6).

Figure 6.5— Hypothesized 'Driving Frustration' Measurement Model

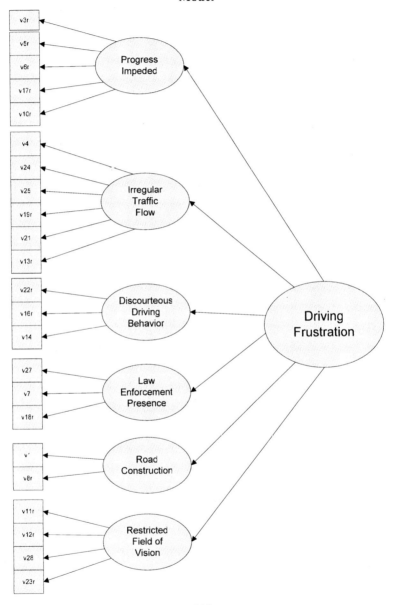

To assess the empirical considerations and implications for representing 'Driving Frustration' as a second-order construct (despite the theoretical justifications), the model complexity and fit indices were compared to a model representing the measure as a first-order construct after the deletion of the higher-order general construct and the related residuals. The results suggest that doing so produces a significant increment in the χ^2 as revealed in $\Delta\chi2$ (1, 366) = 115.704 (a significant decrement in model fit); while the absolute fit indices reveal the same (see Table 6.5).

Full Structural Regression Model

Up to this point, incomplete (or missing) data has not been a problem. Incomplete data is, however, almost an unavoidable occurrence in social science. In order to achieve generalizability of findings, it is necessary to have information for all respondents—obtained through probability sampling methods—for all data points. Individuals often do not provide information in survey research for a host of reasons. For example, individuals may not wish to disclose information on sensitive issues (i.e., drug use or income), they may not know the answer to the question being asked, may overlook a question, or poor survey design does not provide exhaustive categories (i.e., not applicable or the use of contingency questions) (J. Cohen et al., 2003; Neuman, 1997). The absence of complete data sets can seriously bias conclusions drawn from an empirical study, thus this problem must be addressed directly. When evaluating the data set for "missingness," two concerns direct inquiry: The extent (how much/many) and the pattern (random or systematic) of missing values.

The extent of missing data has implications for remedial action. Unfortunately, some disagreement exists regarding how much data need to be missing to constitute a large amount (Byrne, 2001). In fact, Kline (1998) suggested that missing data should not constitute more than 10% of the potential observation base, while others have suggested that missing data should not constitute more than 3% on any given variable, provided the sample is large (N > 200) (J. Cohen et al., 2003). Fortunately, more is known about the pattern of missing data, and the possible and appropriate remedies.

Figure 6.6—'Driving Frustration' CFA

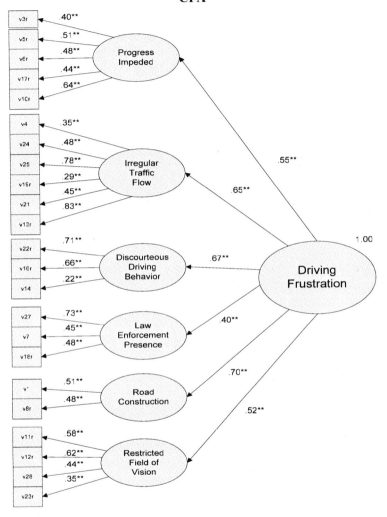

Final Model

$\chi^2(195, 336.18) = 0.000$, GFI = .93, AGFI = .90, RMSEA = .04

**p < .01
†All Loadings are Standardized

148

Table 6.5—First- and Second-Order Measurement Model Comparisons

Model:		df	χ2	GFI	AGFI	CFI	RMSEA	Δχ2
Driving	First-Order	51	126.507	.95	--	.96	.06	
Delinquency:	Second-Order	51	126.865	.95	--	.96	.06	(0) = .358
Self-	First-Order	237	462.676	.91	--	.89	.05	
Control:	Second-Order	241	445.842	.91	--	.90	.05	(4) = 16.834**
Driving	First-Order	194	451.883	.90	.86	--	.06	
Frustration:	Second-Order	195	336.179	.93	.90	--	.04	(1) = 115.704**

**p < .01

First, it is important to distinguish between situations wherein data are missing at random as opposed to absence as a result of a problem. Where the extent of missingness is less than 20%, and the data are missing at random, the researcher may substitute the arithmetic mean values and/or delete the cases using pairwise (deleting the case from a *particular* analyses involving variables for which there are unobserved scores) or listwise (deleting the case from the *entire* set of analyses where data are missing) deletion. Unfortunately, pairwise and listwise deletion can have the effect of reducing sample size—and consequently statistical power—and produce biased standard errors that can affect significance testing. Secondly, substitution of the arithmetic mean can substantially influence the distribution of frequencies to result in leptokurtic distributions as more cases are placed around the mean. These have been and continue to be the dominant remedies for random missing data within classical linear modeling techniques—each with attendant unfavorable consequences.

Where data are missing for systematic reasons (e.g., respondents are intentionally omitting information because of their value on the variable or some other outcome variable—for example, level of substance abuse and criminal convictions), the investigator is more restricted in their options. When respondents differ significantly in their response frequencies according to their level on a predictor variable, the data can be said to be missing for systematic reasons. Pairwise and listwise deletion, or substitution of the arithmetic mean, would in this instance significantly threaten the generalizability of the results.

In examining the extent of missing data, the only data missing on the construct measures was v2 of the 'Driving Frustration' scale. Fortunately, this variable was included as a "distracter" variable and was excluded from subsequent analyses. With respect to the control variables, three variables had values in excess of 3%: Miles per Week (4.9%); Urban Driving (4.6%); and Ethnicity: Caucasian (3.6%) (see Appendix K). To determine if the data are missing for systematic or random reasons, separate variance t-Tests were performed for these variables on all endogenous variables (Self-Control; Driving Frustration; Driving Delinquency; and Self-Reported Accidents and Citations) (see Appendix L). The results of the analysis indicate that Miles per Week and Ethnicity: Caucasian are missing for systemic reasons along several of the endogenous variables.

According to classical linear modeling techniques and the rationale of scientific generalization, imputation and pairwise/listwise deletion would threaten the generalizability of findings. Additionally, these remedies present unique problems for Structural Equation Modeling techniques—even if they were missing at random. To be sure, listwise and pairwise deletion decrease the statistical power of SEM, while increasing the risk of nonconvergent solutions and biasing standard errors (Arbuckle, 1996; Byrne, 2001; Marsh, Balla, & McDonald, 1988). To insert arithmetic mean would also present unique problems for SEM. In fact, doing so would increase the likelihood of invoking a leptokurtic distribution to possibly bias standard errors and produce misleading results. Thus, "means imputation" is not a recommended approach (Byrne, 2001).

In light of the systematic nature of the missing data, and the unique challenges that remedying incomplete covariance structures presents for SEM—for data missing at random—the author of AMOS 4.0 (Arbuckle, 1999) has provided Maximum Likelihood (ML) estimation procedures for incomplete covariance structures that employs the model-estimation (EM) algorithm. This method produces estimate statistics for the full sample that maximizes the differences between the final estimates and the complete data set (J. Cohen et al., 2003). This method of estimation does assume, however, that the missing data do not convey any new information—or that they are missing at random. When this assumption is true, the EM algorithm provides the best possible estimates of the population values. Even when this assumption isn't met, however, the ML estimation procedures exhibit the least bias (Byrne, 2001; J. Cohen et al., 2003; Little & Rubin, 1989). Thus, ML estimation will be used to substitute values for missing data—both random and systematic—that maximizes their likelihood within the population using the EM algorithm.

Subsequent to assessing the extent to which the assumptions necessary for accurate covariance structure modeling having been met, and assessing the theoretical validity and empirical status of the measurement models tapping the core constructs, the full structural regression model can be tested. Traffic safety education (TSE) programs have long been rooted in a theory which views the disproportionate representation of young drivers in the number of automobile collisions and traffic fatalities as resulting from the lack of knowledge, skills, sense of personal responsibility, and an understanding of the causes and consequences of accidents found in older, more experienced drivers. To this end, they have developed programs aimed at remedying these deficiencies and adopting state licensing exams to assess the level of the newly acquired knowledge and skills prior to issuing a state driver's license.

The effectiveness of the programs remains dubious, however, and investigators have identified a host of other variables residing at the individual, opportunity, and environmental levels that should be included during model specification to achieve accurate and stable estimates. *Vis-à-vis* the controversy surrounding the effectiveness of traffic safety education programs, two theories of crime and delinquency have been consulted that purport to operate at the individual level that may thwart or facilitate program outcomes and may be useful in explaining these discrepant findings. Moreover, each of these theories has implications for the programming of TSE activities, while claiming to be superior or related frameworks for investigating crime and delinquency. To investigate the role that each of the criminological theories play in traffic delinquency and accidents and citations—after partialling the important control variables previously identified in pursuit of accurate and stable point estimates—a full structural model can be proposed and tested.

Hypothesized Full Structural Regression Model

The hypothesized full structural model is represented in Figure 6.7. Omitted from the graphic representation for the purpose of interpretability, however, are those previously discussed statistically and substantively significant paths between the control variables and an individual's level of self-reported accidents and citations. According to the architects of Self-Control Theory, low self-control is related positively to automobile accidents—and presumably citations—by being correlated with a host of driving delinquent behaviors (or is mediated by driving delinquency). This hypothesis is represented with the causal arrow emanating from 'Self-Control' to 'Driving Delinquency'.

According to General Strain Theory and psychological definitions of stress, strain experienced while operating a motor vehicle shares a direct and indirect relationship with accidents and citations as individuals can respond in an instrumental or in a retaliatory manner to the blockage/removal of positively valued stimuli, or to escape negative stimuli through driving delinquent behaviors. This hypothesis is represented by the causal arrow emanating from 'Driving Frustration' to 'Driving Delinquency.' According to psychological definitions of stress, individuals who experience high levels of strain while driving may feel overwhelmed by situations and contexts to sufficiently disturb cognitive process so that their vulnerability to accidents and citations is increased (Barrett & Campos, 1991; Deffenbacher et al., 1994). This direct hypothesis is represented with the causal arrow emanating from 'Driving Frustration' to self-reported accidents and citations.

Self-Control theorists argue for the superiority of their variable, and assert that self-control predates other competing theories of crime/delinquency—social learning, control, life-course, and strain. They argue for the "master status" of their variable (Gottfredson & Hirschi, 1990). Accordingly, after accounting for individual levels of self-control any previous relationship between competing theories and crime/delinquency should disappear; they are "spurious." In contrast, General Strain theorists argue for potential integration of the two

Figure 6.7—Hypothesized Full Structural Regression Model

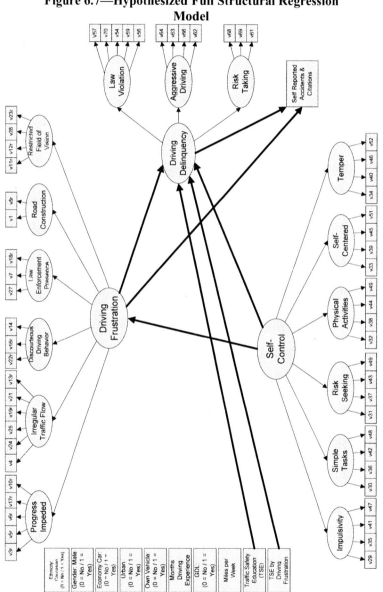

153

theories, inasmuch as previous studies measuring the psychological super-traits of "negative emotionality" and "constraint" have revealed a positive relationship. This type of finding suggests that several of the traits—impulsivity, risk-seeking, temper, egotism—measured by self-control may be tapping dispositional dimensions that "interplay" with situational traits (such as the emotions that result from strain experienced while operating a motor vehicle) to make those high in the latter more likely to engage in crime and delinquency (Agnew et al., 2002; Mazerolle & Piquero, 1998; Nunnally & Bernstein, 1994). This "interplay" hypothesis is represented with the causal arrow emanating from 'Self-Control' to 'Driving Frustration.'

Finally, traffic safety education programs are designed to infuse in 'novice drivers' sufficient knowledge and skills to decrease their risk of accidents and citations. These programs emphasize not only the rules that govern the operation of automobiles, but seek to promote an understanding of the causes of automobile accidents and enhance knowledge of state-sanctioned penalties for delinquent driving behaviors that increase risk for drivers and the public. These programs also attempt to instill in young drivers a sense of personal responsibility in the operation of a motor vehicle to modify driving behaviors in the direction of due caution and care while behind the wheel. Sufficient knowledge and skill are assessed with state proctored driving exams (Quenault & Sten, 1975), which in theory should predict an individual's likelihood for engaging in driving delinquency—especially if individual level variables (strain and self-control) do not assert such an overriding influence to render the effect of individual levels of knowledge and skill ineffective in determining driving behaviors.

A central hypothesis of this investigation is that the program theory of traffic safety education is perhaps valid, and that the conflicting, modest, and null results witnessed in the evaluation of traffic safety education programs (Harrington, 1971; Lovrich et al., 2003; McGuire, 1969; Schlesinger, 1972; Vernick et al., 1999) can in part be explained by failing to account for such individual level variables. To assess this assertion, individual Driver Licensing Exam Scores (denoted as TSE) were used as a measure of an individual's level of knowledge. If the program theory of traffic safety education is valid—that it is the absence of sufficient knowledge and skill that contributes to the overrepresentation of young drivers in automobile collisions—the direct path emanating from the TSE variable to 'Driving Delinquency' should be statistically and substantively significant. If, however, the impact of TSE is moderated by individual levels variables (which this investigation asserts is a function of individual levels of strain experienced while operating a motor vehicle) the path between the moderated multiple regression variable (denoted as TSE by Driving Frustration) and 'Driving Delinquency should be statistically and substantively significant.

Results and Discussion

The results of the simultaneous structural regression model estimation are represented in Figure 6.9. The measurement models (Self-Control, Driving Frustration, and Driving Delinquency) graphically represented were entered in their original hypothesized form—with no correlated errors terms or correlated residuals. All first-order constructs continued to share a significant non-zero loading with their respective higher-order factors, and each variable hypothesized to measure each first-order factor shared a significant non-zero loading with factor it was intended to measure (loading and significance denotations were omitted to enhance interpretability). All control variables were hypothesized to share a significant relationship with: Self-Reported Accidents and Citations, 'Driving Delinquency,' 'Driving Frustration,' and 'Self-Control.' Only the paths depicted remained statistically and substantively significant after accounting for individual levels of strain while operating a motor vehicle and self-control.

Model Fit

The model was *overidentified* with 2332 *degrees of freedom*, allowing for a unique solution. The inferential χ^2 statistic was significant at the .000 level (2332, 5390.18) leading us to reject the null: $H_0 = \Sigma = \Sigma (\theta)$, or that the postulated model holds in the population (The full AMOS 4.0 Output is available in Appendix M). Because χ^2 is a function of sample size (N-1), large samples necessarily increase the probability of incorrectly rejecting the null hypothesis. Because the model-estimation (EM) algorithm was used to estimate missing values for the observed

Figure 6.9—Full Structural Regression Model

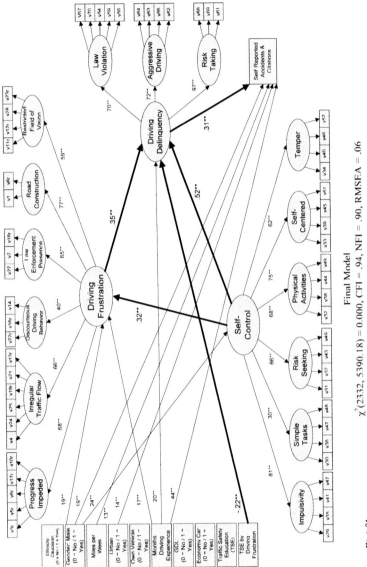

Final Model

$\chi^2 (2332, 5390.18) = 0.000$, CFI = .94, NFI = .90, RMSEA = .06

**p < .01
†All Loadings are Standardized

156

control and outcome variables, no absolute fit indices were reported with AMOS. Therefore, the NFI and CFI incremental fit indices were examined. The Normed Fit Index (NFI) was developed by Bentler and Bonnet (1980) and was the practical criterion of choice for the better part of a decade. The NFI ranges in value of 0 to 1.00, with a value > .90 being indicative of a well-fitting model. In recent years, some empirical evidence has emerged to suggest that the NFI tends to underestimate fit in small samples (Bentler, 1990). To address this concern, Bentler (1990) revised the NFI to take sample size into account with the development of the Comparative Fit Index (CFI). Similar to the NFI, the CFI ranges in value from 0 to 1.00, and it is derived from the comparison of a hypothesized model with the independence model. As such, it provides a measure of complete covariation in the data. Although a value of > .90 was originally considered to representative of a well-fitting model (Bentler, 1992), a revised cutoff value of close to .95 has recently been proposed (Byrne, 2001; Hu & Bentler, 1999). The NFI and CFI reported for the final model (after removing non-significant paths: those emanating from the control variables to all endogenous variables and the path from 'Driving Frustration → Self-Reported Accidents) are consistent in suggesting that the hypothesized model represents an adequate fit to the data. Similarly, the RMSEA, with a point and interval estimate of .06 and .058 - .062, respectively, indicate a relatively precise and efficient model.

Control Variables

In reviewing the influence of the control variables on formal outcomes (self-reported accidents and citations) after accounting for individual levels of strain experienced while operating a motor vehicle and self-control, several important findings come to light. First, several of the previously identified control variables that evidenced initial support in their hypothesized relationship with Self-Reported Accidents and Citations (see Figure 6.0—Control Variable Zero-Order Correlations) do not remain significant after accounting for these important individual level variables, while practical significance among several is reduced. To be sure, a review of Table 6.6 indicates several of the once statistically significant zero-order correlation coefficients become non-significant once accounting for individual level variables; these variables are Self-Report GDL, Own Vehicle, and Economy Car. Additionally, the practical significance of Gender, Months Driving Experience, and Miles per Week are reduced. The reduction to statistical non-significance and the diminishment of practical significance witnessed here suggests that the relationship between some of these previously identified control variables and accidents and citations is "spurious," and that when attempting to assess their true relationship models should consider including measures of strain and self-control.

Table 6.6—Control Variable Zero-Order and Structural Regression Model Correlation Comparison

Control Variable	Zero-Order Correlation	Structural Regression Model Correlation†
Gender: Male	.21**	.18**
Ethnicity: Caucasian	-.03	-.04
Months Driving Experience	.51**	.42**
Miles per Week	.28**	.13**
Urban Area	.14**	.14**
Self-Report GDL	-.32**	-.01
Own Vehicle	.20**	.08
Economy Car	-.14**	-.06

**p < .01
† Standardized Regression Weights

Driving Frustration, Driving Delinquency, and Accidents and Citations

According to the architect of General Strain Theory (Agnew, 1992), individuals vary in their "motivation" to engage in crime/delinquency based on their social psychological response to the removal/blockage of positively valued goals, or the introduction of negative stimuli. To retrieve, prevent loss, or escape, individuals may respond through criminal/delinquent acts based on the social situation and individual psychological responses. With respect to the operation of a motor vehicle, drivers may respond to the blockage/removal of positively valued goals, or the introduction of negative stimuli, in either an instrumental or retaliatory manner. The theoretical cognates of delinquent coping behaviors are similar to those associated with low self-control—namely, speeding, risk-taking, tailgating, etc. Thus, strain theorists argue for the direct relationship between individual levels of strain and driving delinquency. The results of this analysis support that proposition with a statistically and substantively significant path: Driving Frustration → Driving Delinquency.

Theoretically, high levels of strain can also share a direct relationship with accidents and citations as the cognitive process of the driver may become sufficiently disturbed as a result of feeling "stressed" or overwhelmed and incapable of overcoming the situation (Barrett & Campos, 1991; Deffenbacher et al., 1994). This direct relationship is not supported here. This could be a result, however, of the conceptualization of the construct 'driving frustration' and/or the method of measurement. Driving frustration as conceived here is more consistent with the construct of "stress," while anxiety is an affective response more consistent with disturbing sufficiently cognitive processes to lead to an accident or citation. Given this, observation and physiological measurement would seem a more appropriate method of investigation than the gathering of survey responses (Campbell & Fiske, 1959; Nunnally & Bernstein, 1994).

<u>Self-Control and Driving Delinquency</u>

The architects of Self-Control Theory Gottfredson and Hirschi (1990) argue that at the heart of politically defined forms of crime and delinquency lies an enduring predisposition to prefer simple and immediate self-serving pleasures at the cost of more distal and collective needs; some individuals are lower in self-control than others, are more likely to engage in criminal or delinquent behaviors. This personal trait is considered to be relatively stable after the age of eight and to be the result of several dimensions that tend to coalesce: Impulsivity, egocentrism, a preference for simple tasks and physical activities, and to seek risks and possess a temper. Low self-control leads to accidents—and presumably citations—as individuals low in self-control engage in a host of driving delinquent behaviors (Self-Control → Driving Delinquency). This proposition receives empirical support in this analysis, with a relative magnitude greater than the role of strain.

These architects of Self-Control Theory also argue for the "master status" of their core variable. According to them, positivistic criminology has led to endless (and needless) classifications that unnecessarily complicate theory testing and hinder theory development. They unite the classical and positivist traditions by recognizing that individual behavior is governed by both internal (individual desire to maximize utility) and external influences (position in and understanding of relevant sanctioning systems). What differs across people, since we are all rational utility maximizers, is our ability to exercise self-control in the face of temptation. It is this individual level propensity which predates other variables identified by positivist scholars as contributing to crime/delinquency; among those important variables are peer influences, strength of social bonds, social disadvantage, and even general strain. The advocates of Self-Control Theory argue that once we account for their master variable previously significant relationships should disappear; or those previously identified relationships are actually "spurious." The results of the analysis presented here indicate that even after accounting for individual levels of self-control, individual motivation continues to explain a significant amount of variation in driving delinquency; motivational factors continue to exert a significant independent influence even in the presence of self-control and control variables.

In contrast to self-control theorists, those working within the General Strain tradition have argued that not only does their variable continue to exert a significant influence after accounting for individual levels of self-control, but that there may exist an "interplay" between the two dimensions. To be sure, previous studies employing secondary data analysis on the role of "negative emotionality" and "constraint" identified by psychologists working on strain have revealed statistically significant levels of association. These two theories are also likely related as self-control can be viewed as a "dispositional" trait that may interplay with the "transitory" trait of general strain experienced while operating a motor vehicle. That is, individuals may possess certain "dispositional" characteristics (e.g., volatile temper) that may increase their likelihood for crime/delinquency when faced with "transitory" states (e.g., frustration while operating a motor vehicle) (Agnew, 1992;

Agnew et al., 2002; Mazerolle & Piquero, 1998; Nunnally & Bernstein, 1994). This proposition receives empirical support with the statistically and substantively significant path: Self-Control → Driving Frustration.

TSE and Driving Delinquency

Traffic safety education programs have been fashioned on a program theory that views the overrepresentation of young drivers in the annual number of automobile accidents and citations as resulting primarily from a level of knowledge, skill, and acceptance of personal responsibility that does not approximate that found in older, more experienced drivers. To this end, traffic safety education program activities have been designed to instill in young drivers the knowledge and skill necessary to safely operate a motor vehicle, and an understanding of state sanctions with the intent of eliminating some risky driving behaviors that threaten individual or public welfare. Prior to license issuance, driver license applicants must demonstrate an acceptable level of knowledge, skill, and understanding of the causes and consequences of accidents by passing a state exam proctored by the Department of Licensing. This exam consists of both a written and behind-the-wheel driving assessment. Unfortunately, data tapping the second dimension were not available. The role of individual knowledge of laws and the causes and consequences of accidents as assessed through the state exam were investigated, however, for their role in determining driving behaviors and accident and citation levels (predictive validity). The results reported here indicate that the individual's level of knowledge as measured by test score was not a significant predictor of driving behaviors or formal outcomes.

A central thesis of this investigation is that despite the best efforts of policymakers and program implementers to instill sufficient knowledge, skill, sense of personal responsibility, and understanding of the causes and consequences of automobile accidents through uniform pedagogy and curriculum, individual novice drivers may possess certain characteristics that may either thwart or facilitate program goals. That is, these individual level characteristics may present such an overriding influence that they nullify intervention efforts. To test this hypothesis with respect strain while operating a motor vehicle, an interaction effect was created using a Moderated Multiple Regression term (for more information on Interaction Effects in Structural Equation Modeling, see Stoolmiller, Duncan, & Patterson, 1995). To this end a multiplicative term was created using an individual's 'Driving Frustration" factor and written driving exam scores. The results observed indicate that the impact of traffic safety education on driving behaviors is in fact ***moderated*** by an individual's level of strain experienced while operating a motor vehicle.

Validation of the Driving Delinquency Measurement Model

In conclusion, this analysis has sought to examine the role of previously identified control and intervention variables in influencing young driver accidents and citations after including a variety of individual level measures. Because these individual measures exist in theory as constructs, and because the theoretical cognates of these constructs are also a construct (driving delinquency), from a policy perspective aimed at solving social problem—the overrepresentation of young drivers in the number of automobile collisions and fatalities—we should examine the practicality of the measures and models investigated here. From a practical perspective, these theoretical measures are of little utility if they do not predict an outcome of interest—namely, the overrepresentation of young drivers in automobile collisions and fatalities. Thus, although several theoretical relationships have been supported with this model, if these relationships fail to predict accidents and/or traffic citations (which are given as a form of "teaching" intended to reduce and individual's likelihood of having an accident) then the model is of little utility.

For example, if individuals who experience high levels of strain while operating a motor vehicle engage in driving delinquent behaviors, but these behaviors heighten an individual's sense of awareness and vehicle control—thereby reducing their likelihood for causing an accident (a discernable social harm with calculable costs), then the results reported here would have diminished relevance. It is important to note that the relationship that these constructs share with each other and driving behaviors does in fact predict an outcome of practical significance—an individual's number of automobile accidents and citations, despite the measurement bulwarks presented by the variable. That is, driving delinquent behaviors resulting from these individual level characteristics lead to many unreported and near accidents, while formal documentation of driving delinquent behaviors is a function of law enforcement levels and activities (e.g., behaviors may go undetected or be addressed through extralegal methods such as a verbal warning). Consequently, although this investigation has resided largely at the theoretical level, it has also documented a degree of practical relevance for those working in the area of accident prevention and analysis.

CHAPTER 7

Implications for Policy and Theory

INTRODUCTION

This investigation has explored the efficacy of our nation's concerted efforts to deal with a serious, troublesome problem associated with our widespread societal dependence upon the automobile for our personal and commercial transportation. The tragic toll taken of lives lost on the nation's roads and highways annually is indeed a serious continuing problem, with costs incurred in the form of devastated families, destroyed property, and substantial medical service charges. The fact that so many young people are involved in fatal and serious injury crashes makes the national problem more serious than it otherwise would be. Year in and year out, annual traffic safety statistics reveal that young drivers continually disproportionately experience the social and economic burdens associated with the use of automobiles, as measured in both human and economic costs. Traffic safety education programs are the most common countermeasure adopted by states in response to this profoundly costly perennial social problem. The theory informing traffic safety education program activities is one which views the problem as resulting from a lack of knowledge, poor driving skills, and inadequate acceptance of personal responsibility for safe vehicle operation found in older more experienced drivers. Consequently, state-sponsored intervention efforts have emphasized rather uniform pedagogy and curriculum aimed at overcoming this set of deficiencies.

Despite the concerted efforts of policymakers and program implementers alike, however, the efficacy of this form of public policy intervention remains somewhat dubious (Harrington, 1971; Lovrich et al., 2003; McGuire, 1969; Schlesinger, 1972); some evidence even exists which suggests that traffic safety education can be contributory to problematic traffic safety outcomes in some settings (Vernick et al., 1999). One reason that these traffic safety education programs may fail to demonstrate greater efficacy is that they are premised on the assumption that the target audience of novice drivers is a uniform one – that is, that this audience of learners does not vary considerably from learner to learner along psychological dimensions that may either thwart or facilitate educational program outcomes.

To deepen our collective understanding of potential individual-level characteristics that may significantly influence driving behaviors that contribute to this social problem, two prominent theories on crime and delinquency ("deviance" in the criminological literature) were consulted and tested. Not only do these major theories present in the Criminal Justice and Criminology literature offer promise in increasing our understanding of this social problem, but their application to this relatively unexplored area offers the promise of theoretical development and refinement on the limits, relationship, and/or relative superiority of these theories on deviance. To more fully understand and better appreciate the potential implications of the findings reported here for public policy development and for the further refinement of deviance theory, a brief review of the central theoretical frameworks and guiding questions is in order at this point.

Young Driver Accidents and Traffic Safety Education

Recognition of the increasing social and economic costs attendant to heavy reliance on the automobile for personal and commercial transportation initially led to numerous mechanical, technological, and structural (roadway design) interventions by both automobile manufactures and governmental authorities (Porter, 1999). Despite these important safety-promoting efforts, automobile use continued to extract costly economic and social tolls, especially among young drivers (16 to 24 years of age). In response, state governments began offering, and later requiring, traffic safety education programs in an attempt to decrease these costs. These programs (primarily based in public schools) were informed by an underlying theory of skill mastery which viewed the traffic safety problem as arising from a lack of knowledge, skill, acceptance of personal responsibility, and an understanding of the causes and consequences of young driver accidents ("Revised Code of Washington 28A.220", 1977) (see Figures 1.1, 1.2, 1.3, and 1.4 in Chapter 1). The adoption of standardized pedagogy and curriculum and the implementation of traffic safety education programs in local communities was thus seen as the most appropriate countermeasure by which state governments could address this pressing, ongoing social problem.

Systematic evaluations of the efficacy of traffic safety education program efforts have provided either mixed, conflicting, or null results, however (Harrington, 1971; Lovrich et al., 2003; McGuire, 1969; Schlesinger, 1972; Vernick et al., 1999). Looking beyond the role that vehicle operator knowledge and skill may play in young driver accidents, accident prevention researchers have identified a host of factors existing at the environmental, opportunity, and demographic levels that are important to take into consideration when specifying models which seek to isolate putative contributors to traffic accidents. The investigation reported here reveals that many of the previously identified conditioning variables—e.g., vehicle ownership, participation in Graduated Driver Licensing programs, type of vehicle driven, etc.— may in fact share a "spurious" relationship with young driver accidents. Moreover, the practical role that gender, months of driving experience, and miles driven per week share in young driver accidents are similarly reduced, indicating that individual-level variables reflecting driver predisposition toward frustration are capturing a significant amount of variation in driving behaviors and young driver accident and citation frequencies. Lastly, the role of an individual's level of knowledge regarding traffic laws and state sanctions aimed at eliminating behaviors that threaten individual and societal welfare—as measured in state-proctored licensing examination scores—does not appear to share any demonstrable relationship with driving behaviors or accident and citation rates (an absence of predictive validity).

Driving Frustration and Young Driver Accidents and Driving Delinquency

Contemporary criminologists working within the once-regnant *strain tradition* (classical strain) have revived researchers' interest in the psychological variable "motivation" by reconceptualizing and enhancing our appreciation of the sources of and responses to strain (Agnew, 1992; Cullen, 1983; Merton, 1938). This enhanced and augmented theoretical framework offers substantial promise in achieving the status of a "general" theory of crime/delinquency if scientists are able to address adequately the social psychological dimension of the theory through appropriate measurement of key constructs and subsequent systematic theory testing. Despite this great promise for the gaining of insight, the role of *General Strain Theory* in driving delinquency and involvement in accidents and the receipt of citations has been largely ignored in favor of more conventional conceptions of crime and delinquency, i.e., shoplifting, substance use/abuse, assault and battery, etc. This narrowness in focus can in part be traced to the measurement obstacles introduced with tests of the theory.

Testing the role of *General Strain Theory* thusly required the development of a novel assessment instrument. Considerable effort was directed toward developing a psychometrically sound instrument that would predict driving behaviors and outcomes in a probability sample of novice drivers. The novel scale developed here achieved this significant goal, and this accomplishment permits a more nuanced understanding of the role that these previously identified control variables share with young driver accidents, traffic safety education, and motivation to engage in delinquent driving behaviors.

The results of the analysis reported in the previous chapter indicate that individuals do indeed vary considerably in their motivation to engage in delinquent driving behaviors, and that this motivation likely increases their likelihood for becoming involved in accidents and receiving traffic citations. As a measure, this scale is more predictive and informative than existing state driver licensure measures which tap individual levels of knowledge regarding traffic laws and state sanctions for criminal behaviors. Perhaps more importantly, this trait was found to interact with individual levels of traffic safety knowledge to suggest that failure to attend to individual-level characteristics during formal traffic safety education programming may have the effect of nullifying otherwise efficacious intervention efforts.

Self-Control and Young Driver Accidents and Driving Delinquency

As a general theory of crime and delinquency, *Self-Control Theory* has become one of the most popular theories used to explain a wide range of adult criminal and juvenile delinquent behaviors (Pratt & Cullen, 2000; Tittle, Ward, & Grasmick, 2003a; Unnever et al., 2003; Vazsonyi et al., 2001). According to the architects of the theory, all individuals—because they are rational—are equally motivated to engage in crime and delinquency. What differs across persons, then, is each individual's ability to exercise control in the face of temptation (Gottfredson & Hirschi, 1990). This general theory of crime was crafted in response to the seemingly endless proliferation of quite narrow classifications of choice situations flowing from the prominence of the positivistic criminology. Separate analyses of street crime, white-collar crime, elder abuse, illegal drug use, domestic violence, etc. seemed to point to the need for separate and distinct theories for each type of crime. By conceiving of all types of criminal and delinquent acts as a result of an individual's unwillingness to subordinate immediate and tangible benefits to distal and uncertain consequences for the individual **and** the collective weal, low self-control was identified as the "master variable" that was the essence of criminal and delinquent acts, regardless of political context and precise definitions of criminal acts.

In asserting that self-control is the "master variable," the proponents of *Self-Control Theory* argue that the ability to exercise self-control predates many of the popular variables previously identified by positivist criminologists—social learning, social control, life-course, and General Strain Theory—and that once accounted for, previously identified conditioning variables should become nonsignificant (that is, their relationship with crime is "spurious"). This theoretical proposition is intended to serve as a counterpoise to the centrifugal tendencies of positivist criminology by identifying the putative "master variable" overlooked by competing traditions. As a result, criminologists could approach the study of crime and delinquency with a single framework that would facilitate the accumulation of scientific knowledge and permit more efficacious crime prevention actions.

The potential consequence of this form of reasoning about crime for rival theories is considerable—potential relegation to the 'theory dustbin' to languish without provincial claim to knowledge. General Strain theorists are suspicious of such bold claims of universality, and they tend to argue that self-control possibly pre-dates strain, but strain phenomena continue to enjoy the position of rival theoretic explanation by accounting for significant amounts of variation after considering self-control. Approached from this vantage point, these two major theories are at once competitors and possibly cousins in a synthesized reconceptualization of deviance.

The results of the analysis presented here do **not** offer unqualified support for the "spuriousness" thesis. Motivation to engage in driving delinquent behaviors continues to explain a significant amount of variation in driver behaviors after accounting for individual levels of self-control, and therefore *General Strain Theory* should not be relegated to the theory dustbin of Criminology and Criminal Justice. That said, what has been observed is that self-control is a more powerful predictor of driving delinquency than is strain when the two are considered simultaneously in an analysis of the driving records of young, novice drivers. The reasons for this observation could possibly be traced to the tautological orientation of the theory previously noted by scholars (Akers, 1991; Reed & Yeager, 1996), however. Support is found for the hypothesized "dispositional" and "transitory" relationship between the two theories (Agnew et al., 2002), a relationship that offers the promise of theoretical integration (Liska et al., 1989). The analysis presented here suggests that there is considerable overlap between self-control and driving frustration. Low-self control operates indirectly through strain, whereby the "disposition" interplays with "situation" to significantly increase an individual's likelihood to respond to driving context-specific strain through delinquent behaviors.

Driving Delinquency and Accidents and Citations

From a practical perspective, the social constructs of 'self-control,' 'driving frustration,' and 'driving delinquency' are of diminished utility if their predictive validity cannot be documented against an outcome of societal interest. Traffic safety education was fashioned in response to an undesirable social state—namely, the over-representation of young drivers in the official annual statistics on automobile accidents and fatalities. From a theoretical perspective, the relationship between delinquent driving behaviors and traffic accidents and fatalities appears axiomatic—they increase the likelihood of being involved in an automobile collision through deleterious driving behaviors. Such an assertion is somewhat presumptuous, however, in that driving delinquent behaviors may actually temporarily heighten concentration and motor skills to reduce the actual financial and social costs associated with accidents, or perhaps result in behaviors that may be undesirable but not illegal (such using one's horn frequently in response to undesirable conditions). The question thus becomes, to what extent does the measure which is related to the constructs under investigation—i.e., self-control and driving frustration—share with the real world outcome that traffic safety education was meant to address?

This central question can be answered by evaluating the ability of measures of self-control and strain to predict values on a 'driving delinquency' scale in a probability sample of young drivers, and that scale in turn showing a strong connection to accidents experienced and citations received. Individuals may experience high levels of strain while operating a motor vehicle which in turn predicts driving delinquent behaviors, but does this result in accidents and other theoretical cognates—traffic safety citations—that may eventually lead to the undesirable outcome? Despite the substantial measurement obstacles associated with using this observable variable as a proxy for these undesirable consequences and behaviors that contribute to the social problem (i.e., many accidents and near accidents go unreported, while law violations often go undetected or resolved through extra-legal methods), the 'driving delinquency' scale demonstrates predictive validity with a sizeable magnitude. In this regard, there is considerable relevance of the findings reported here for policymakers, for program implementers, for traffic safety educators, and for investigators working within the areas of accident prevention and analysis.

Theoretical and Applied Implications

Future Research on the Role of GST and Self-Control in
Crime/Delinquency

The positivistic tradition which began to dominate criminological inquiry in the early part of the 20th century has precipitated numerous categorizations and groupings of independent variables and politically defined dependent variables that have painted a deterministic portrait of the offender while producing competing conceptions of crime to divide disciplines (see Chapter 2). The application of these two general theories to conventional crimes, and through methods not favoring simultaneous estimation procedures, has overlooked and ignored the bounds of applicability and potential relation among these possibly complimentary theories of crime and delinquency. The results of this analysis—which considers these two issues—present some implications for the future study of conventional crime/delinquency through an integrated General Strain (GST) and Self-Control Theory.

First, tests of GST must recognize and capture the context-specific nature of strain and the important mediating role of both delinquent/criminal and/or nondelinquent/noncriminal coping strategies. Where tests of GST employ context-specific measures—as did here—the theory continues to enjoy empirical support. Despite the theory's explanatory promise where issues in measurement are addressed, the theory should not be considered in isolation. In fact, the predictive validity of the theory and our understanding of the causal mechanisms by which strain and low self-control are translated into crime/delinquency can be enhanced when considered simultaneously.

In fact, considering the total effects of low self-control on crime/delinquency is potentially enhanced by recognizing the direct and indirect effects of self-control as it translates directly into crime/delinquency and indirectly as individuals low in self-control are significantly more likely to experience higher levels of strain. This phenomenon should not be limited theoretically to traffic experiences, but should instead apply to other areas of crime and delinquency. To be sure, individuals low in self-control may engage in various forms of crime/delinquency, i.e., drug/alcohol abuse, vandalism, fighting, and theft, to cope with felt levels of strain (indirect causal mechanism), or because some individuals have predisposing personality traits that are impulsive and egocentric (direct mechanism). Investigating conventional forms of crime/delinquency from truancy to white-collar crime would appear to be aided from an integrated theoretical framework which recognizes that some individuals may tend to engage in crime/delinquency not only for the immediate and tangible benefits perceived to flow from these acts, but because they may at the same time be predisposed to experience higher levels of strain that at once favor the delinquent/criminal coping behaviors also favored by their impulsive and egocentric predisposition. The fragmentation witnessed within the field of criminology with the rise of the positivistic tradition has enhanced our understanding of the sources and causes of crime and delinquency, but it has been simultaneously implicated in hampering progress toward the development of a general theory within the field. Future research should continue toward integration wherever practicable, however, so that knowledge may accumulate with greater speed and possess greater relevance for practitioners and consumers of criminological research. The experience of this research project suggests that such attempts may bear fruit for both theorists and practitioners alike.

Implications for the Progressive Standardization of Traffic Safety Education

Traffic safety education as a public policy response to a high rate of young driver accidents has experienced a rather long-lived trend toward progressive standardization since its inception. This progressive standardization occurred as a result of our collective deepening of understanding of the effectiveness of various pedagogical approaches (e.g., simulator instruction, behind-the-wheel coaching, etc.) and the importation of topics covered in curricula which are grounded in theoretical or empirical anchors. The progressive professionalization of traffic safety education has similarly enhanced the standardization of curriculum and instructional practices. Standardization in pedagogy and curricula is desirable to the extent that implementer discretion is sufficiently protected to ensure democratic accountability (school board buy-in). In pursuit of instructional standardization, some questionable assumptions have been made regarding learners within the target instructional population, however. Program formulators by-and-large have assumed that individual learners do not vary significantly along predispositional dimensions that may either nullify or facilitate program instructional goals. The results of the analysis reported here suggest that this assumption may be incorrect, and that more effective outcomes could be attained through the appropriate individualization of instruction.

The implications for contemporary traffic safety education practice to be deduced from these findings are rather broad-based. To be sure, the psychometrically sound instrument developed in Chapter 5, and validated in Chapter 6, offers promise as a diagnostic tool that could achieve acceptable standards of reliability for practical application with minimal effort now that the factor structure has been documented and is more fully understood. Such an instrument could be administered by traffic safety education instructors during service delivery and by parents supervising their children during the completion of state-mandated Graduated Driver Licensing programs. Results of these assessments could then be shared with novice drivers and their parents/guardians for appropriate remedial action.

Fortunately, the effects of strain while operating a motor vehicle on driving delinquent behaviors is theorized to be mediated by situational variables that lie within the reach of governmental and parental manipulation (Agnew, 1992). How individuals cope with strain is in part a function of available coping skills, coping resources, self-efficacy, level of social control, and association with delinquent peers. Our knowledge of these factors gained from the study of juvenile delinquency would seem to have important implications for programming and parental/guardian roles and responsibilities in preventing young driver accidents. The administration of the 'driving frustration' scale is the first step in identifying those at risk for adopting delinquent coping behaviors in response to undesirable stimuli encountered while driving a motor vehicle. Once identified in-class and behind-the-wheel instructors can tailor program activities to reduce the likelihood that those suffering high levels of strain will respond in a delinquent manner. Similarly, parents and guardians who have a responsibility for novice driver training in states where Graduated Driver License Programs are in force can benefit from knowing how their learners are characterized with respect to the 'driving frustration' scale assessment.

Drivers often cope with strain experienced behind-the-wheel through instrumental or retaliatory behaviors that increase their risk for involvement in traffic accidents. Instructors in the classroom setting, in the field driving experience, and in the observation of simulator performance can acknowledge the existence of stressful driving conditions and emphasize to those high in the inventory alternative nondelinquent coping skills. For example, individuals may respond delinquently to a driver immediately behind them who is driving with bright lights at night in an instrumental (speeding to increase distance) or retaliatory (slamming on their breaks) manner that increases their risk for an accident. Alternatively, they may simply pull over and allow the offensive driver to pass. It is possible to identify a number of such strain-rich situations and to tailor program activities aimed at increasing coping skills for those students most likely to require such reinforcement. This knowledge offers promise as a remedial action that would facilitate program goals of preparing novice drivers for their driving challenges.

Parents and guardians informed of the presence of the disposition toward driving frustration would shoulder an increased burden in teaching safe driving habits and/or limiting and supervising driving opportunities and conditions that may increase risk. For example, parents might impose driving restrictions beyond those promulgated by the state during the Graduated Driver License period regarding number of vehicle occupants or amount and type (area and environmental conditions) of driving permitted. Similarly, the type and condition of the motor vehicle provided to the novice driver—those that are less powerful and in good condition—would theoretically reduce the likelihood of coping delinquently and decreasing perceived stress in less than optimum driving conditions.

Lastly, the efficacy of traffic safety education programs should be evaluated for their effectiveness **after** controlling for these important individual-level variables. Recent trends to privatize programs resulting from unsupportive program evaluations may serve to both subvert what may in fact be a valid program theory by diluting the intervention activities in pursuit of economic survival (Mikesell, 1995; Provan & Milward, 2001) and attenuating control through third-party principal-agent delivery mechanisms (Kettl, 2000; Moe, 1984). Furthermore, private provision may seriously bias service delivery demographically insofar as for-profit organizations target economies of scale in metropolitan areas while imposing regressive fees in more problematic markets. The potential consequence is the exacerbation of the public problem as many individuals are potentially "trained to state exams," or move beyond the reach of government influence by waiting until 18 years of age before applying for a state driver's license.

Study Design and Methodology Caveats

This investigation of the role of strain, self-control, and institutions and processes in young driver accidents and driving delinquency has deepened our understanding of both theory and practice. We must temper our enthusiasm with a balanced discussion of the limitations in design and method that characterize this study, however. As with most research agendas, finite resources—in the form of limited time and a shortfall of research money—means that investigators must make numerous design and methodology decisions which may limit the utility and applicability of findings. This is not say that the findings presented here should be viewed with undue suspicion, only that their limits should be recognized so that future researchers and practitioners can facilitate the further acquisition and application of knowledge.

Limits on time and money necessarily required that artificial boundaries be drawn with respect to the population of interest. Young driver accidents are not endemic to the state of Washington, but to the nation and in other modern industrialized societies. Ideally, the population from which the sample was drawn would have included the nation and/or other modern industrialized nations where the problem of young driver accidents is in evidence. Limits on time and money necessarily required that the research effort be narrowed. Researchers wishing to make generalizations beyond the sample do so at their own peril and must rely on logic when doing so. Logically, we would not expect young drivers in the state of Washington to differ from other young drivers found in states across the country or in other modern industrialized nations, yet to make such a statement is purely speculative and generalizations made beyond this sample may not hold in different populations.

The results contained herein are based on a response rate of 18.3% of 2,000 sampled subjects. When response rates are not adequate, the results can differ significantly from what they would be if everyone responded. Unfortunately, researchers disagree on what is *adequate*. Adequacy in response rates is, therefore, a judgment call that depends on the population, practical limitations, and the topic. The population of interest (young drivers 16 to 24 years of age), limits on time and money, and the social psychological nature and length of the survey all presented hurdles to achieving a high response rate. Attempts to overcome these hurdles were met with a financial incentive encouraging participation and early completion, and a follow-up survey to non-respondents. Despite the fact that many feel that response rates less than 50% are poor, response rates for mail surveys of 10% to 50% are not, however, uncommon (Neuman, 1997).

Methodological heterogeneity also hems our understanding and application of the knowledge derived from this investigation. Documentation of "latent" constructs follows a conservative and incremental approach, to avoid the endless proliferation of novel assessments (Campbell & Fiske, 1959) and narrow definitions of constructs whose properties are confounded with the choice of method (Houts, Cook, & Shadish, 1986). Before we can validate the existence of a novel construct—in this instance 'Driving Frustration'— psychological research encourages that *convergent* and *divergent* validity be documented through a multitrait-multimethod approach (Campbell & Fiske, 1959). That is, we must document the divergent validity of this instrument with other existing measures, i.e., general frustration scales—as evidenced in low correlations between the two measures—and convergent validity by employing different methods, i.e., observational measures—as evidenced in high correlations between the two—before we can justify the existence of this construct (for more on multitrait-multimethod construct validation see Nunnally & Bernstein, 1994: 92-4). This investigation has provided the basis from which methodological heterogeneity can now be pursued.

The novel 'Driving Frustration' psychometric scale presented in Chapter 5—and subsequently validated in Chapter 6—has met the minimum reliability requirement for basic research concerned with predictive or construct validation as evidenced in an $\alpha = .81$. If the instrument is to be used for making decisions regarding individuals—

identification and treatment activities—the reliability must be increased to a minimum of .90, with .95 being more desirable (Nunnally & Bernstein, 1994: 265). Because reliability is a function of test length, and now that the factor structure has been elucidated, increasing reliability to .90 could be achieved with only 3 additional items—assuming that the average correlation among the new items is no less than the average correlation of the existing items (see Chapter 5).

Lastly, the conceptualization of 'Driving Frustration' in relation to young drivers (16 to 24 years of age) suggests that these individuals differ significantly from older more experienced drivers either in terms of their experienced levels of strain and/or preferred coping mechanisms. That is, inexperienced youthful drivers may be more sensitive to frustrating stimuli encountered while operating vehicle than those who have been exposed to a wider range of frustrating stimuli more frequently, and/or who may prefer maladaptive coping behaviors which is in part a function of their low self-control—or inability or unwillingness to consider the distal and collective consequences of their behavior.

To document the influence of time (or age in this instance), repeated measures beginning at the issuance of a driver's license and occurring at regular intervals (say 1 year) until the age of twenty-four seems to be more congruent with the 'spirit" of the theory. Structural Regression Latent Change Analysis would aid in capturing the chronometric nature of these variables and would be far more informative in understating how individual levels of frustration change over time, as well as the influence of frustration on maladaptive (delinquent) coping behaviors with experience gained. The novel assessment instrument presented here offers promise to this end where sufficient time and research support are present.

Appendices

Instructions: For each of the statements below, please indicate whether or not the statement is characteristic of you. If the statement is extremely uncharacteristic of you (not at all like you) please write "1" in the space provided to the left of the statement; if the statement is extremely characteristic of you (very much like you) please write "7" in the space provided. And, of course, use the numbers in the middle if you fall between the two extremes.

1	2	3	4	5	6	7
Extremely Uncharacteristic	Moderately Uncharacteristic	Slightly Uncharacteristic	Uncertain	Slightly Characterisitc	Moderately Characterisitc	Extremely Characterisitic

_____ 1. I get frustrated when a driver in front of me does not immediately begin moving when the light turns green.

_____ 2. I don't get frustrated when a driver speeds up when I try to pass.

_____ 3. I get frustrated when "stuck" behind a large vehicle which I cannot see around.

_____ 4. I don't get frustrated when a driver is driving well above the posted speed limit.

_____ 5. I don't get frustrated when another driver will not heed my attempt to merge into traffic.

_____ 6. I don't get frustrated when a vehicle remains in my "blind spot" for an extended period.

_____ 7. I don't get frustrated when a bicyclist is riding in the middle of the lane and slowing down traffic.

1	2	3	4	5	6	7
Extremely Uncharacteristic	Moderately Uncharacteristic	Slightly Uncharacteristic	Uncertain	Slightly Characterisitc	Moderately Characterisitc	Extremely Characterisitic

8. I get frustrated when a law enforcement official is driving in close proximity to me for an extended period.

9. I get frustrated when I encounter road construction which halts my progress.

10. I don't get frustrated when a driver is holding up traffic by being slow to park.

11. I don't get frustrated when someone hastily pulls out into oncoming traffic, causing the flow of traffic to unnecessarily slow.

12. I don't get frustrated when I encounter road construction with detours.

13. I get frustrated when someone shouts at me about my driving.

14. I don't get frustrated when the driver in front of me frequently changes speeds.

15. I get frustrated when a driver passes me on the "right," or the non passing lane.

16. I don't get frustrated when a slow vehicle on a winding road will not pull over to allow others to pass.

17. I don't get frustrated when the condition of the roadway is so poor that it is difficult to see its markings.

18. I don't get frustrated when my defroster is unable to keep my windshield clear at all times.

1	2	3	4	5	6	7
Extremely Uncharacteristic	Moderately Uncharacteristic	Slightly Uncharacteristic	Uncertain	Slightly Characerisitc	Moderately Characerisitc	Extremely Characterisitic

19. I don't get frustrated when I cannot pass another vehicle because a driver in the passing lane is driving too slowly.

20. I don't get frustrated when the driver behind me is following too closely.

21. I get frustrated when a driver is driving more slowly than is reasonable for the traffic flow.

22. I get frustrated when someone backs out in front of me without looking.

23. I don't get frustrated when a driver appears to be engaged in activities not related to driving (e.g., talking on cell phone, putting on makeup, eating).

24. I don't get frustrated when a driver at a four-way stop goes before his/her turn.

25. I don't get frustrated when at night, a driver who is approaching does not dim their bright lights.

26. I don't get frustrated when a driver honks their horn at me.

27. I get frustrated when I see a law enforcement official watching traffic from a hidden position.

28. I don't get frustrated when a law enforcement official appears to be following me.

29. I don't get frustrated when a portion of a vehicle which is pulled off to the side of the highway remains in my driving lane.

1	2	3	4	5	6	7
Extremely	Moderately	Slightly	Uncertain	Slightly	Moderately	Extremely
Uncharacteristic	Uncharacteristic	Uncharacteristic		Characterisitc	Characterisitc	Characterisitic

_____ 30. I get frustrated when driving behind a truck which has material flapping around in the back.

_____ 31. I get frustrated when I'm at a stoplight which is malfunctioning.

_____ 32. I don't get frustrated when a driver in front of me changes directly into my lane without the use of their signal.

_____ 33. I get frustrated when a driver cuts in and takes the parking spot I have been waiting for.

_____ 34. I get frustrated when the driver in front of me appears to be uncertain about his/her actions.

_____ 35. I get frustrated when someone runs a stop sign.

_____ 36. I don't get frustrated when at night, the person immediately behind me is driving with their bright lights on.

_____ 37. I get frustrated when "stuck" behind a vehicle which is emitting noxious fumes.

_____ 38. I don't get frustrated when someone makes an obscene gesture towards me about my driving.

_____ 39. I get frustrated when the driver in front me makes a turn without signaling.

_____ 40. I get frustrated when someone runs a red light.

1	2	3	4	5	6	7
Extremely	Moderately	Slightly	Uncertain	Slightly	Moderately	Extremely
Uncharacteristic	Uncharacteristic	Uncharacteristic		Characterisitc	Characterisitc	Characterisitic

_____ 41. I get frustrated when the driver in front of me repeatedly drifts across the marked road lines.

_____ 42. I get frustrated when a pedestrian walks slowly across the middle of the street, slowing me down.

_____ 43. I get frustrated when the driver in front of me keeps applying their brakes for no apparent reason.

_____ 44. I don't get frustrated when the driver in front of me appears to be lost.

_____ 45. I get frustrated when water from the roadway is being sprayed onto my windshield from another vehicle, making it difficult to see.

_____ 46. I get frustrated when I hit a deep unmarked pothole.

_____ 47. I get frustrated when a responding Emergency Services Vehicle (e.g., police, fire, ambulance) disrupts traffic flow.

_____ 48. I get frustrated when my vehicle lacks the power to keep up with traffic flow.

_____ 49. I get frustrated when after waiting for an oncoming vehicle to pass through an intersection before making my left hand turn, the vehicle instead slows to make a right turn.

_____ 50. I get frustrated when my windshield wipers are unable to maintain my clear field of vision.

_____ 51. I get frustrated when a law enforcement official pulls me over.

1	2	3	4	5	6	7
Extremely	Moderately	Slightly	Uncertain	Slightly	Moderately	Extremely
Uncharacteristic	Uncharacteristic	Uncharacteristic		Characterisitc	Characterisitc	Characterisitic

52. I don't get frustrated when a driver is driving too fast for road conditions.

53. I don't get frustrated when the sun is shining in my eyes to such an extent that it is difficult to see.

54. I get frustrated when it is raining so heavily that it is difficult to see.

Appendix B
'Driving Frustration' Factor Extraction Eigenvalues and Variance Explained

Total Variance Explained

Factor	Initial Eigenvalues			Extraction Sums of Squared Loadings		
	Total	% of Variance	Cumulative %	Total	% of Variance	Cumulative %
1	8.760	19.467	19.467	8.220	18.267	18.267
2	2.794	6.209	25.676	2.285	5.077	23.344
3	2.387	5.304	30.980	1.865	4.143	27.487
4	1.869	4.153	35.133	1.364	3.031	30.518
5	1.844	4.098	39.231	1.295	2.878	33.396
6	1.578	3.506	42.738	1.050	2.333	35.729
7	1.504	3.341	46.079	.999	2.220	37.949
8	1.363	3.030	49.109	.843	1.873	39.823
9	1.251	2.779	51.888	.693	1.541	41.363
10	1.207	2.683	54.571	.650	1.445	42.809
11	1.173	2.606	57.177	.617	1.370	44.179
12	1.079	2.397	59.574	.509	1.131	45.309
13	1.000	2.222	61.796			
14	.990	2.199	63.996			
15	.945	2.100	66.096			
16	.902	2.004	68.100			
17	.849	1.887	69.987			
18	.831	1.846	71.833			
19	.794	1.765	73.597			
20	.758	1.683	75.281			
21	.743	1.651	76.932			
22	.694	1.543	78.474			
23	.673	1.497	79.971			
24	.617	1.372	81.343			
25	.604	1.342	82.685			
26	.592	1.315	84.000			
27	.572	1.270	85.271			
28	.542	1.205	86.476			
29	.504	1.119	87.595			
30	.489	1.087	88.682			
31	.472	1.049	89.730			
32	.453	1.006	90.737			
33	.439	.977	91.713			
34	.430	.955	92.668			
35	.410	.910	93.578			
36	.392	.871	94.449			
37	.368	.818	95.267			
38	.326	.725	95.993			
39	.318	.707	96.700			
40	.290	.644	97.344			
41	.268	.596	97.939			
42	.248	.552	98.492			
43	.245	.544	99.036			
44	.230	.511	99.547			
45	.204	.453	100.000			

Extraction Method: Principal Axis Factoring.

Appendix C
'Driving Frustration' Factor Pattern Matrix

Pattern Matrix [a]

	Factor						
	1	2	3	4	5	6	7
V5	**.731**	-.094	-.039	-.340	-.060	.240	-.019
V7	**.621**	-.075	.035	-.024	.078	.066	-.074
V10	**.509**	-.068	-.163	.208	-.032	.105	-.007
V11	**.471**	-.087	-.176	.088	.092	-.075	.138
V16	**.365**	.119	-.006	.074	-.066	.069	.050
V44	.236	.202	.096	.225	-.094	-.137	.207
V39	-.019	**.678**	-.035	-.100	-.072	.203	-.074
V40	-.253	**.656**	-.076	-.263	.068	-.096	.054
V41	-.140	**.578**	-.177	.013	.047	.004	.255
V29	.081	**.506**	.066	-.005	-.114	.180	-.065
V34	.233	**.470**	-.052	.144	.062	.013	-.046
V42	**.268**	**.341**	.175	.050	-.121	-.133	-.051
V19	.137	**.300**	.005	.101	-.088	.054	.141
V31	-.123	**.300**	.035	.251	.028	**.291**	.063
V51	-.003	-.269	**.814**	.003	-.064	-.095	.142
V27	-.021	.062	**.663**	-.071	-.128	.053	-.007
V28	-.172	.094	**.628**	.021	-.080	.139	-.084
V9	-.074	-.212	.001	**.842**	.129	-.038	.027
V12	-.003	.013	-.047	**.667**	-.122	.136	.047
V36	.020	-.108	-.180	-.005	**.727**	.051	.068
V25	-.165	-.023	-.032	.173	**.653**	-.042	-.029
V22	.207	.065	-.073	-.198	**.582**	-.167	.123
V46	.008	.103	.043	**.223**	**.337**	.204	-.129
V43	.090	.210	.214	.123	.296	-.049	-.108
V17	.220	-.065	.260	-.129	-.001	**.538**	.058
V18	.067	.073	.053	.042	.028	**.516**	.249
V54	.011	-.108	.029	.197	.032	**.462**	.113
V6	.133	.196	-.140	.076	-.119	**.454**	-.090
V50	-.197	.082	.080	-.049	.094	**.376**	**.292**
V37	-.053	.087	.022	-.058	.025	.085	.665
V48	.052	-.057	.018	.185	-.006	.080	.549
V33	.047	-.135	.051	.082	.087	-.017	.370
V21	.202	.026	.063	-.028	.232	-.127	.343
V26	.109	-.057	.037	.120	.164	.001	-.128
V38	.152	.114	-.050	-.071	-.174	-.091	.029
V20	-.056	.036	.007	-.106	.271	.158	.057
V45	-.001	.110	-.095	.333	-.098	.092	.041
V53	.113	.046	.111	-.046	.146	.081	-.180
V14	.134	.030	-.111	.140	.082	-.035	-.130
V2	.035	-.044	.176	-.037	-.021	-.057	.007
V3	.104	.067	.064	.170	-.049	-.013	.029
V1	.139	.047	.162	.202	.084	.038	-.072
V32	.208	.305	-.097	-.256	.156	.271	.027
V49	.004	.191	.243	-.011	.031	-.122	.193
V24	-.021	.216	.153	-.101	.253	-.119	-.120

Extraction Method: Principal Axis Factoring.
Rotation Method: Promax with Kaiser Normalization.
a. Rotation converged in 23 iterations.

Appendix D
'Driving Frustration' Factor Correlation Matrix

Factor Correlation Matrix

Factor	1	2	3	4	5	6
1	1.000	.552	.343	.418	.391	-.098
2		1.000	.397	.441	.550	.108
3			1.000	.471	.382	.226
4				1.000	.197	.033
5					1.000	.213
6						1.000

Extraction Method: Principal Axis Factoring.
Rotation Method: Promax with Kaiser Normalization.

Appendix E
Development of a 'Driving Frustration' Scale IRB Approval

WASHINGTON STATE UNIVERSITY

Office of Grant and Research Development

MEMORANDUM

TO: Steven Ellwanger
Political Science, WSU Pullman (4880)

FROM: Jamie Murphy (for) Cindy Corbett, Chair, WSU Institutional Review Board (3140)

DATE: 4 March 2004

SUBJECT: Approved Human Subjects Protocol - New Protocol

Your Human Subjects Review Summary Form and additional information provided for the proposal titled "Development of a Driving Frustration Scale." IRB File Number **6013-a** was reviewed for the protection of the subjects participating in the study. Based on the information received from you, the WSU-IRB **approved** your human subjects protocol on **4 March 2004**

IRB approval indicates that the study protocol as presented in the Human Subjects Form by the investigator, is designed to adequately protect the subjects participating in the study. This approval does not relieve the investigator from the responsibility of providing continuing attention to ethical considerations involved in the utilization of human subjects participating in the study.

This approval expires on 3 March 2005. If any significant changes are made to the study protocol you must notify the IRB before implementation. Request for modification forms are available online at http://www.ogrd.wsu.edu/Forms.asp

In accordance with federal regulations, this approval letter and a copy of the approved protocol must be kept with any copies of signed consent forms by the principal investigator for THREE years after completion of the project.

This institution has a Human Subjects Assurance Number FWA00002946 which is on file with the Office for Human Research Protections. WSU's Assurance of Compliance with the Department of Health and Human Services Regulations Regarding the Use of Human Subjects can by reviewed on OGRD's homepage (http://www.ogrd.wsu.edu/) under 'Electronic Forms.' OGRD Memorandum #6.

If you have questions, please contact the Institutional Review Board at OGRD (509) 335-9661. Any revised materials can be mailed to OGRD (Campus Zip 3140), faxed to (509) 335-1676, or in some cases by electronic mail, to ogrd@mail.wsu.edu

Review Type: NEW   OGRD No.: NF
Review Category: XMT   Agency: NA
Date Received: 26 February 2004

PO Box 641060, Pullman, WA 99164-3140
509-335-9661 • Fax: 509-335-1676 • ogrd@wsu.edu • www.ogrd.wsu.edu/

Appendix F
Modeling Young Driver Accidents: The Role of Strain, Self-Control, and Institutions and Process in Young Driver Accidents and Driving Delinquency IRB Approval

WASHINGTON STATE
UNIVERSITY

Office of Grant and Research Development

MEMORANDUM

TO: Steven J. Ellwanger
Political Science, WSU Pullman (4880)

FROM: Jamie Murphy (for) Cindy Corbett, Chair, WSU Institutional Review Board (3140)

DATE: 6 August 2004

SUBJECT: Approved Human Subjects Protocol - New Protocol

Your Human Subjects Review Summary Form and additional information provided for the proposal titled "Modeling Young Driver Accidents: The Role of Strain, Self-Control, and Institutions and Processes in Young Driver Accidents and Driving Delinquency." IRB File Number **8061**-a was reviewed for the protection of the subjects participating in the study. Based on the information received from you, the WSU-IRB **approved** your human subjects protocol on **6 August 2004**

IRB approval indicates that the study protocol as presented in the Human Subjects Form by the investigator, is designed to adequately protect the subjects participating in the study. This approval does not relieve the investigator from the responsibility of providing continuing attention to ethical considerations involved in the utilization of human subjects participating in the study.

This approval expires on 5 August 2005. If any significant changes are made to the study protocol you must notify the IRB before implementation. Request for modification forms are available online at http://www.ogrd.wsu.edu/Forms.asp

In accordance with federal regulations, this approval letter and a copy of the approved protocol must be kept with any copies of signed consent forms by the principal investigator for THREE years after completion of the project.

This institution has a Human Subjects Assurance Number FWA00002946 which is on file with the Office for Human Research Protections. WSU's Assurance of Compliance with the Department of Health and Human Services Regulations Regarding the Use of Human Subjects can by reviewed on OGRD's homepage (http://www.ogrd.wsu.edu/) under "Electronic Forms." OGRD Memorandum #8.

If you have questions, please contact the Institutional Review Board at OGRD (509) 335-9661. Any revised materials can be mailed to OGRD (Campus Zip 3140), faxed to (509) 335-1676, or in some cases by electronic mail, to ogrd@mail.wsu.edu.

Review Type: NEW   OGRD No. NF
Review Category: XMT   Agency: NA
Date Received: 29 July 2004

PO Box 641060, Pullman, WA 99164-3140
509-335-9661 • Fax: 509-335-1676 • ogrd@wsu.edu • www.ogrd.wsu.edu

Appendix G
Washington Driver's Experience Survey

WASHINGTON STATE
UNIVERSITY

WASHINGTON DRIVER'S
EXPERIENCE SURVEY

2004

You are being asked to take part in a statewide survey which is being sponsored by Washington State University of 2,000 drivers to assess your experiences and preferences while driving. We fully expect that different people will have different experiences and preferences, and are interested in knowing what you have experienced and what you prefer. This survey was designed by researchers at Washington State University. Your participation is very important and entirely **VOLUNTARY** and your answers are completely **CONFIDENTIAL**. Only researchers from Washington State University will see your answers and comments. The survey should take 15 to 20 minutes to complete. Please seal and mail the completed survey in the enclosed pre-addressed and postage-paid envelope. Your participation in this survey is greatly appreciated and will help us better understand driver attitudes, preferences, and experiences in our state. Responses received by October 29, 2004, will automatically be entered to win one of five $100.00 awards.

If you agree to participate in this survey project please indicate that you have read this statement by signing below. *If you are under 18 years of age, your parent or guardian must also sign this consent.* Please read the directions carefully and complete the questions in the order that they appear using the indicated scale. This study has been reviewed and approved for human participation by the WSU Institutional Review Board (IRB). If you have any questions regarding your rights as a participant, you man contact them at 509-335-9661. Note that if you have any questions regarding this project, you may contact the project investigators whose names and contact information are listed below the signature lines.

_____   _____
(respondent signature)   (parent or guardian signature)

_____   _____
Nicholas P. Lovrich, Jr.   Steven J. Ellwanger, A.B.D., M.P.A.
Director   Principal Investigator
Division of Governmental Studies and Services   Washington State University
Claudius and Mary Johnson Distinguished Prof.   Vancouver, WA 98686
Pullman, WA 99164   (360) 546-9495
(509) 335-3329

Note: *The processing number on this questionnaire is used only to coordinate mailings. When you return your survey your number is checked off our mailing list and you will not be bothered by follow-up mailings.*

Mail Processing Number _____

DIRECTIONS: For each of the statements below, please indicate whether or not the statement is characteristic of you. If the statement is extremely uncharacteristic of you (not at all like you) please write "1" in the space provided to the left of the statement; if the statement is extremely characteristic of you (very much like you) please write "7" in the space provided. And, of course, use the numbers in the middle if you fall between the two extremes.

1	2	3	4	5	6	7
Extremely Uncharacteristic	Moderately Uncharacteristic	Slightly Uncharacteristic	Uncertain	Slightly Characteristic	Moderately Characteristic	Extremely Characteristic

_____ 1. I get frustrated when I encounter road construction which halts my progress.

_____ 2. I don't get frustrated when a driver is driving well above the posted speed limit.

_____ 3. I don't get frustrated when another driver will not heed my attempt to merge into traffic.

_____ 4. I get frustrated when the driver in front of me makes a turn without signaling.

_____ 5. I don't get frustrated when a bicyclist is riding in the middle of the lane and slowing down traffic.

_____ 6. I don't get frustrated when a driver is holding up traffic by being slow to park.

_____ 7. I get frustrated when I see a law enforcement official watching traffic from a hidden position.

_____ 8. I don't get frustrated when I encounter road construction with detours.

_____ 9. I get frustrated when a driver passes me on the "right," or the non-passing lane.

_____ 10. I don't get frustrated when a slow vehicle on a winding road will not pull over to allow others to pass.

_____ 11. I don't get frustrated when the condition of the roadway is so poor that it is difficult to see its markings.

_____ 12. I don't get frustrated when my defroster is unable to keep my windshield clear at all times.

_____ 13. I don't get frustrated when I cannot pass another vehicle because a driver in the passing lane is driving too slowly.

_____ 14. I get frustrated when someone backs out in front of me without looking.

_____ 15. I don't get frustrated when a driver appears to be engaged in activities not related to driving (e.g., talking on cell phone, putting on makeup, eating).

1	2	3	4	5	6	7
Extremely Uncharacteristic	Moderately Uncharacteristic	Slightly Uncharacteristic	Uncertain	Slightly Characteristic	Moderately Characteristic	Extremely Characteristic

_____ 16. I don't get frustrated when at night, a driver who is approaching does not dim their bright lights.

_____ 17. I don't get frustrated when someone hastily pulls out into oncoming traffic, causing the flow of traffic to unnecessarily slow.

_____ 18. I don't get frustrated when a law enforcement official appears to be following me.

_____ 19. I don't get frustrated when a portion of a vehicle which is pulled off to the side of the highway remains in my driving lane.

_____ 20. I get frustrated when driving behind a truck which has material flapping around in the back.

_____ 21. I get frustrated when the driver in front of me appears to be uncertain about his/her actions.

_____ 22. I don't get frustrated when at night, the person immediately behind me is driving with their bright lights on.

_____ 23. I don't get frustrated when a vehicle remains in my "blind spot" for an extended period.

_____ 24. I get frustrated when someone runs a red light.

_____ 25. I get frustrated when the driver in front of me repeatedly drifts across the marked road lines.

_____ 26. I get frustrated when a responding Emergency Services Vehicle (e.g., police, fire, ambulance) disrupts traffic flow.

_____ 27. I get frustrated when a law enforcement official pulls me over.

_____ 28. I get frustrated when it is raining so heavily that it is difficult to see.

DIRECTIONS: For each of the statements below, please indicate your level of agreement. If you strongly agree with the statement (is very much like you) please write "5" in the space provided to the left of the statement; if you strongly disagree with the statement (is not at all like you) please write "1" in the space provided. And, of course, use the numbers in the middle if you fall between the two extremes.

1	2	3	4	5
Strongly Disagree	Somewhat Disagree	Uncertain	Somewhat Agree	Strongly Agree

29. I often act on the spur of the moment without stopping to think.

30. I frequently try to avoid projects that I know will be difficult.

31. I like to test myself every now and then by doing something a little risky.

32. If I had a choice, I would almost always rather do something physical than something mental.

33. I try to look out for myself first, even if it means making things difficult for other people.

34. I lose my temper pretty easily.

35. I don't devote much thought and effort to preparing for the future.

36. When things get complicated, I tend to quit or withdraw.

37. Sometimes I will take a risk just for the fun of it.

38. I almost always feel better when I am on the move than when I am sitting and thinking.

39. I'm not very sympathetic to other people when they are having problems.

40. Often, when I'm angry at people I feel more like hurting them than talking to them about why I am angry.

41. I often do whatever brings me pleasure here and now, even at the cost of some distant goal.

42. The things in life that are easiest to do bring me the most pleasure.

43. I sometimes find it exciting to do things for which I might get in trouble.

44. I like to get out and do things more than I like to read or contemplate ideas.

45. If things I do upset people, it's their problem not mine.

1	2	3	4	5
Strongly Disagree	Somewhat Disagree	Uncertain	Somewhat Agree	Strongly Agree

_____ 46. When I'm really angry, other people better stay away from me.

_____ 47. I'm more concerned with what happens to me in the short run than in the long run.

_____ 48. I dislike really hard tasks that stretch my abilities to the limit.

_____ 49. Excitement and adventure are more important to me than security.

_____ 50. I seem to have more energy and a greater need for activity than most other people my age.

_____ 51. I will try to get things I want even when I know it's causing problems for other people.

_____ 52. When I have a serious disagreement with someone, it's usually hard for me to talk calmly about it without getting upset.

DIRECTIONS: Using the scale shown below, please indicate the extent to which you engage in each driving behavior. Please place your response in the space provided to the left of the item.

1	2	3	4	5
Never	Rarely	Sometimes	Often	Always

_____ 53. I speed up to turn on a yellow light.

_____ 54. I drive 5 to 10 mph over the speed limit.

_____ 55. I take risks when driving.

_____ 56. I do things against the law when it is safe.

_____ 57. I drive over the speed limit in clear weather.

_____ 58. I play the radio very loud.

_____ 59. I drive over the speed limit at night.

_____ 60. I eat or drink beverages while driving.

_____ 61. I drive on people's bumpers.

1	2	3	4	5
Never	Rarely	Sometimes	Often	Always

_____ 62. I get back at people with my car.

_____ 63. I let people know when I am unhappy with their driving.

_____ 64. I give other drivers a nonverbal gesture.

_____ 65. I slow down when someone is trying to pass.

_____ 66. I use my horn a lot.

_____ 67. I speed up to get through a yellow light.

_____ 68. I run red lights.

_____ 69. I race in my car.

_____ 70. I drive over the speed limit.

Please write the appropriate response in the space provided:

71. How many speeding tickets have you received? _____

72. Not counting speeding tickets, how many other moving violations (e.g., running a red light) have you received? _____

73. In how many automobile accidents have you been involved as the driver? _____

74. Approximately how many miles do you drive during a typical week? _____

75. What percentage of your weekly miles is related to recreation or leisure activities?
    _____ (0% - 100%)

76. Approximately how long have you been in possession of a driver's license?
    _____ Years and _____ Months

77. What is your age? _____ Years

Please check the appropriate response:

78. Do you own your own vehicle?   _____ Yes   _____ No

79. How would you characterize the area in which the majority of your driving occurs?

_____ Urban   _____ Rural
(City)   (Country)

80. Would you characterize the type of vehicle which you drive as an economy car (small fuel efficient car)?

_____ Yes   _____ No

81. Are you/have you ever participated in a Graduated Licensing Program (a program which restricted your driving activities, e.g., a driving curfew, between 16 and 18 years of age)?

_____ Yes   _____ No

82. Gender: _____ Male   _____ Female

83. Ethnicity: _____ African American

_____ Asian American

_____ Caucasian (White)

_____ Hispanic

_____ Native American

_____ Other

7

Appendix H
'Driving Delinquency' Factor Extraction Eigenvalues and Cumulative Variance Explained

Total Variance Explained

Component	Initial Eigenvalues		Extraction Sums of Squared Loadings		Rotation Sums of Squared Loadings[a]	
	Total	Cumulative %	Total	Cumulative %	Total	Cumulative %
1	6.186	34.367	6.186	34.367	5.305	
2	2.123	46.162	2.123	46.162	3.152	
3	1.342	53.619	1.342	53.619	3.551	
4	1.217	60.380	1.217	60.380	3.428	
5	1.125	66.628	1.125	66.628	2.756	
6	1.015	72.265	1.015	72.265	1.528	
7	.759	76.483				
8	.682	80.273				
9	.590	83.549				
10	.565	86.688				
11	.501	89.474				
12	.389	91.637				
13	.351	93.589				
14	.313	95.329				
15	.276	96.864				
16	.218	98.075				
17	.182	99.084				
18	.165	100.000				

Extraction Method: Principal Component Analysis.

a. When components are correlated, sums of squared loadings cannot be added to obtain a total variance.

Appendix I
'Driving Delinquency' Factor Pattern Matrix

Pattern Matrix [a]

	Component			
	1	2	3	4
V59	**.951**	.059	-.144	-.018
V72	**.932**	.015	-.090	.019
V56	**.862**	.013	-.136	.105
V61	**.821**	.014	.019	-.152
V58	**.644**	-.044	.338	.050
V57	**.515**	-.091	.332	.160
V66	.021	**.881**	-.065	-.005
V65	.060	**.877**	-.095	-.007
V68	-.037	**.751**	.015	.095
V64	-.029	**.478**	**.464**	-.081
V70	-.209	-.113	**.867**	.061
V71	.200	.012	**.790**	-.174
V63	-.074	.097	**.376**	.191
V55	-.004	.045	.005	**.910**
V69	.074	.010	-.073	**.909**
V60	-.054	.100	-.087	-.034
V62	.115	-.189	.009	.032
V67	.028	-.076	-.079	-.012

Extraction Method: Principal Component Analysis.
Rotation Method: Promax with Kaiser Normalization.

a. Rotation converged in 6 iterations.

Appendix J
'Driving Delinquency' Factor Correlation Matrix

Component Correlation Matrix

Component	1	2	3
1	1.000	.251	.449
2		1.000	.323
3			1.000
4			
5			
6			

Extraction Method: Principal Component Analysis.
Rotation Method: Promax with Kaiser Normalization.

Appendix K
Univariate Missing Data Frequencies

Univariate Statistics

	N	Mean	Std. Deviation	Missing Count	Missing Percent
MPERWEEK	348	169.95	153.783	18	4.9
MONTHDRV	362	39.49	29.439	4	1.1
SLFREPDE	365	1.6767	2.24334	1	.3
STRAIN	366	111.5546	17.13719	0	.0
SELFCONT	366	58.1803	13.44192	0	.0
DRVDELIN	366	26.1667	6.62267	0	.0
OWNVEHC	363			3	.8
URBAN	349			17	4.6
ECONOMY	364			2	.5
SELFGDL	365			1	.3
GENDRMAL	365			1	.3
ETHCAUS	353			13	3.6

Appendix L
Missing Data Separate Variance t-Tests

Separate Variance t Tests [a]

		MPERWEEK	MONTHDRV	SLFREPDE	STRAIN	SELFCONT	DRVDELIN
MPERWEEK	t	.	6.7	5.0	1.9	-.3	2.9
	df	.	25.9	31.2	18.7	18.9	20.1
	P(2-tail)	.	.000	.000	.066	.804	.008
	# Present	348	345	348	348	348	348
	# Missing	0	17	17	18	18	18
	Mean(Present)	169.95	40.57	1.7299	111.9598	58.1408	26.3477
	Mean(Missing)	.	17.59	.5882	103.7222	58.9444	22.6667
MONTHDRV	t	.3	.	-.6	1.5	-.8	-1.2
	df	2.0	.	2.0	3.1	3.0	3.0
	P(2-tail)	.762	.	.587	.234	.481	.333
	# Present	345	362	362	362	362	362
	# Missing	3	0	3	4	4	4
	Mean(Present)	170.20	39.49	1.6657	111.6492	58.0994	26.1022
	Mean(Missing)	141.67	.	3.0000	103.0000	65.5000	32.0000
URBAN	t	-1.3	-.5	-.2	-.8	-1.6	-.7
	df	13.6	15.8	17.0	17.9	21.1	17.9
	P(2-tail)	.224	.634	.878	.411	.136	.523
	# Present	334	346	349	349	349	349
	# Missing	14	16	16	17	17	17
	Mean(Present)	167.12	39.28	1.6734	111.4011	58.0344	26.1203
	Mean(Missing)	237.57	44.06	1.7500	114.7059	61.1765	27.1176
ETHCAUS	t	.1	1.0	2.5	.4	.2	.6
	df	11.7	13.8	14.8	12.5	12.9	12.8
	P(2-tail)	.910	.318	.026	.731	.812	.580
	# Present	336	349	352	353	353	353
	# Missing	12	13	13	13	13	13
	Mean(Present)	170.15	39.72	1.7102	111.6374	58.2125	26.2068
	Mean(Missing)	164.58	33.31	.7692	109.3077	57.3077	25.0769

For each quantitative variable, pairs of groups are formed by indicator variables (present, missing).

a. Indicator variables with less than 1% missing are not displayed.

Appendix M
Full Structural Regression Model AMOS 4.0 Output

Full Structural Model N = 366

Friday, December 17, 2004 03:08:39

Amos

by James L. Arbuckle

Version 4.01

****

Title

Full structural model n = 366: Friday, December 17, 2004   03:08 PM

Your model contains the following variables

v10r	observed	endogenous
v17r	observed	endogenous
v6r	observed	endogenous
v5r	observed	endogenous
v3r	observed	endogenous
v13r	observed	endogenous
v21	observed	endogenous
v19r	observed	endogenous
v25	observed	endogenous
v24	observed	endogenous
v4	observed	endogenous
v14	observed	endogenous
v16r	observed	endogenous
v22r	observed	endogenous
v18r	observed	endogenous
v7	observed	endogenous
v27	observed	endogenous
v8r	observed	endogenous
v1	observed	endogenous
v23r	observed	endogenous
v28	observed	endogenous
v12r	observed	endogenous
v11r	observed	endogenous
v57	observed	endogenous
v70	observed	endogenous
v54	observed	endogenous
v59	observed	endogenous
v56	observed	endogenous
v64	observed	endogenous
v63	observed	endogenous
v66	observed	endogenous
v62	observed	endogenous
v68	observed	endogenous
v69	observed	endogenous
v61	observed	endogenous
slfrepde	observed	endogenous
v47	observed	endogenous
v41	observed	endogenous
v35	observed	endogenous
v29	observed	endogenous
v48	observed	endogenous

v42	observed	endogenous
v36	observed	endogenous
v30	observed	endogenous
v49	observed	endogenous
v43	observed	endogenous
v37	observed	endogenous
v31	observed	endogenous
v50	observed	endogenous
v44	observed	endogenous
v38	observed	endogenous
v32	observed	endogenous
v51	observed	endogenous
v45	observed	endogenous
v39	observed	endogenous
v33	observed	endogenous
v34	observed	endogenous
v40	observed	endogenous
v46	observed	endogenous
v52	observed	endogenous
strtsemm	observed	exogenous
gendrmal	observed	exogenous
Monthdrv	observed	exogenous
urban	observed	exogenous
mperweek	observed	exogenous
writexam	observed	exogenous
ethcaus	observed	exogenous
ownvehc	observed	exogenous
selfgdl	observed	exogenous
Economy	observed	exogenous
Progress Impeded	unobserved	endogenous
Irregular Traffic Flow	unobserved	endogenous
Discourteous Driving Behavior	unobserved	endogenous
Law Enforcement Presence	unobserved	endogenous
Road Construction	unobserved	endogenous
Restricted Field of Vision	unobserved	endogenous
Driving Frustration	unobserved	endogenous
Law Violation	unobserved	endogenous
Aggressive Driving	unobserved	endogenous
Risk Taking	unobserved	endogenous
Driving_Delinquency	unobserved	endogenous
Self Control	unobserved	endogenous
Impulsivity	unobserved	endogenous
Simple Tasks	unobserved	endogenous
Risk Seeking	unobserved	endogenous
Physical Activities	unobserved	endogenous
Self-Centered	unobserved	endogenous
Temper	unobserved	endogenous
err10r	unobserved	exogenous
err17r	unobserved	exogenous
err6r	unobserved	exogenous

err7r	unobserved	exogenous
err3r	unobserved	exogenous
err13r	unobserved	exogenous
err21	unobserved	exogenous
err19r	unobserved	exogenous
err25	unobserved	exogenous
err4	unobserved	exogenous
err14	unobserved	exogenous
err16r	unobserved	exogenous
err22r	unobserved	exogenous
err18r	unobserved	exogenous
err7	unobserved	exogenous
err27	unobserved	exogenous
err8r	unobserved	exogenous
err1	unobserved	exogenous
err23r	unobserved	exogenous
err28	unobserved	exogenous
err12r	unobserved	exogenous
err11r	unobserved	exogenous
res RF	unobserved	exogenous
res RC	unobserved	exogenous
res LE	unobserved	exogenous
res DDB	unobserved	exogenous
res IT	unobserved	exogenous
res PI	unobserved	exogenous
err6	unobserved	exogenous
err57	unobserved	exogenous
err70	unobserved	exogenous
err54	unobserved	exogenous
err59	unobserved	exogenous
err56	unobserved	exogenous
err64	unobserved	exogenous
err63	unobserved	exogenous
err66	unobserved	exogenous
err62	unobserved	exogenous
err68	unobserved	exogenous
err69	unobserved	exogenous
crr61	unobserved	exogenous
res LV	unobserved	exogenous
res AD	unobserved	exogenous
res RT	unobserved	exogenous
res DD	unobserved	exogenous
res Self Report Delinquency	unobserved	exogenous
res Driving Frustration	unobserved	exogenous
res Self Control	unobserved	exogenous
err 47	unobserved	exogenous
err 41	unobserved	exogenous
err 35	unobserved	exogenous
err 29	unobserved	exogenous
err 48	unobserved	exogenous

err 42	unobserved	exogenous
err 36	unobserved	exogenous
err 30	unobserved	exogenous
err 49	unobserved	exogenous
err 43	unobserved	exogenous
err 37	unobserved	exogenous
err 31	unobserved	exogenous
err 50	unobserved	exogenous
err 44	unobserved	exogenous
err 38	unobserved	exogenous
err 32	unobserved	exogenous
err 51	unobserved	exogenous
err 45	unobserved	exogenous
err 39	unobserved	exogenous
err 33	unobserved	exogenous
err 34	unobserved	exogenous
err 40	unobserved	exogenous
err 52	unobserved	exogenous
res Impulsivity	unobserved	exogenous
res ST	unobserved	exogenous
res RS	unobserved	exogenous
res PA	unobserved	exogenous
res SC	unobserved	exogenous
res T	unobserved	exogenous

Number of variables in your model:	166
Number of observed variables:	70
Number of unobserved variables:	96
Number of exogenous variables:	88
Number of endogenous variables:	78

Summary of Parameters

	Weights	Covariances	Variances	Means	Intercepts	Total
Fixed:	93	0	7	0	0	100
Labeled:	0	0	0	0	0	0
Unlabeled:	72	0	81	10	60	223
Total:	165	0	88	10	60	323

NOTE:
  The model is recursive.

Sample size: 366

Model: Default model

Computation of degrees of freedom

Number of distinct sample moments: 2555
Number of distinct parameters to be estimated: 223

Degrees of freedom: 2332

Minimum was achieved

Chi-square = 5390.182
Degrees of freedom = 2332
Probability level = 0.000

Maximum Likelihood Estimates

Regression Weights:	Estimate	S.E.	C.R.
Self Control <------------- gendrmal	0.493	0.125	3.960
Driving Frustration <-- Self Control	0.337	0.083	4.038
Driving Frustration <------ gendrmal	-0.408	0.144	-2.840
Driving Frustration <------ Monthdrv	0.006	0.002	2.736
Driving_Delinquency <-- Self Control	0.797	0.129	6.158
Driving_Delinque <- Driving Frustrat	0.506	0.117	4.344
Driving_Delinquency <------ strtsemm	-0.000	0.000	-2.936
Driving_Delinquency <------ Monthdrv	0.011	0.003	3.738
Progress Impeded <- Driving Frustrat	0.849	0.106	8.041
Irregular Traffi <- Driving Frustrat	0.824	0.102	8.068
Discourteous Dri <- Driving Frustrat	0.404	0.079	5.129
Law Enforcement <- Driving Frustrat	0.779	0.105	7.416
Road Constructio <- Driving Frustrat	0.683	0.102	6.712
Restricted Field <- Driving Frustrat	0.426	0.084	5.097
Law Violation <- Driving_Delinquency	0.388	0.045	8.684
Aggressive Drivi <- Driving_Delinque	0.311	0.038	8.143
Risk Taking <--- Driving_Delinquency	0.161	0.022	7.363
Temper <--------------- Self Control	0.494	0.063	7.838
Self-Centered <-------- Self Control	0.524	0.054	9.756
Physical Activities <-- Self Control	0.332	0.052	6.349
Risk Seeking <--------- Self Control	0.410	0.048	8.480
Simple Tasks <--------- Self Control	0.308	0.066	4.634
Impulsivity <---------- Self Control	0.520	0.054	9.607

v10r <------------- Progress Impeded	1.000		
v17r <------------- Progress Impeded	0.573	0.071	8.051
v6r <-------------- Progress Impeded	0.591	0.084	7.005
v5r <------------- Progress Impeded	0.649	0.089	7.312
v3r <-------------- Progress Impeded	0.465	0.081	5.774
v13r <------- Irregular Traffic Flow	1.000		
v21 <-------- Irregular Traffic Flow	0.518	0.079	6.590
v19r <------- Irregular Traffic Flow	0.530	0.081	6.570
v25 <-------- Irregular Traffic Flow	0.411	0.076	5.387
v24 <-------- Irregular Traffic Flow	0.373	0.088	4.255
v4 <--------- Irregular Traffic Flow	0.513	0.081	6.291
v14 <- Discourteous Driving Behavior	1.000		
v16r <- Discourteous Driving Behavio	1.066	0.091	11.698
v22r <- Discourteous Driving Behavio	1.087	0.095	11.437
v18r <----- Law Enforcement Presence	1.000		
v7 <------- Law Enforcement Presence	0.935	0.131	7.138
v27 <------ Law Enforcement Presence	0.856	0.117	7.296
v8r <------------- Road Construction	1.000		
v1 <-------------- Road Construction	0.877	0.177	4.960
v23r <--- Restricted Field of Vision	1.000		
v28 <---- Restricted Field of Vision	1.207	0.244	4.950
v12r <--- Restricted Field of Vision	1.381	0.260	5.316
v11r <--- Restricted Field of Vision	1.297	0.247	5.255
v57 <----------------- Law Violation	1.000		
v70 <----------------- Law Violation	0.943	0.040	23.534
v54 <----------------- Law Violation	0.878	0.041	21.267
v59 <----------------- Law Violation	0.893	0.047	18.973
v56 <----------------- Law Violation	0.708	0.053	13.332
v64 <------------ Aggressive Driving	1.000		
v63 <------------ Aggressive Driving	1.248	0.098	12.714
v66 <------------ Aggressive Driving	0.621	0.069	9.060
v62 <------------ Aggressive Driving	0.489	0.052	9.403
v68 <-------------------- Risk Taking	1.000		
v69 <-------------------- Risk Taking	1.725	0.230	7.491
v61 <-------------------- Risk Taking	1.788	0.234	7.634
slfrepde <------ Driving_Delinquency	0.411	0.075	5.448
v47 <-------------------- Impulsivity	1.000		
v41 <-------------------- Impulsivity	1.162	0.130	8.960
v35 <-------------------- Impulsivity	0.935	0.118	7.952
v29 <-------------------- Impulsivity	0.989	0.128	7.754
v48 <------------------- Simple Tasks	1.000		
v42 <------------------- Simple Tasks	0.447	0.060	7.460
v36 <------------------- Simple Tasks	0.538	0.057	9.367
v30 <------------------- Simple Tasks	0.623	0.068	9.206
v49 <------------------- Risk Seeking	1.000		
v43 <------------------- Risk Seeking	1.364	0.139	9.777
v37 <------------------- Risk Seeking	1.755	0.162	10.857
v31 <------------------- Risk Seeking	1.410	0.138	10.178
v50 <----------- Physical Activities	1.000		
v44 <----------- Physical Activities	1.813	0.268	6.766

v38 <----------- Physical Activities	1.774	0.263	6.754
v32 <----------- Physical Activities	1.555	0.242	6.438
v51 <----------------- Self-Centered	1.000		
v45 <----------------- Self-Centered	0.724	0.107	6.748
v39 <----------------- Self-Centered	0.462	0.093	4.953
v33 <----------------- Self-Centered	0.818	0.109	7.530
v34 <------------------------ Temper	1.000		
v40 <------------------------ Temper	0.888	0.108	8.219
v46 <------------------------ Temper	0.973	0.114	8.560
v52 <------------------------ Temper	1.045	0.123	8.512
slfrepde <----------------- gendrmal	0.849	0.185	4.589
slfrepde <----------------- Monthdrv	0.032	0.003	9.718
slfrepde <-------------------- urban	0.642	0.199	3.232
slfrepde <----------------- mperweek	0.002	0.001	3.069

Standardized Regression Weights:	Estimate
Self Control <------------- gendrmal	0.237
Driving Frustration <-- Self Control	0.322
Driving Frustration <------ gendrmal	-0.187
Driving Frustration <------ Monthdrv	0.173
Driving_Delinquency <-- Self Control	0.518
Driving_Delinque <- Driving Frustrat	0.345
Driving_Delinquency <------ strtsemm	-0.216
Driving_Delinquency <------ Monthdrv	0.205
Progress Impeded <- Driving Frustrat	0.675
Irregular Traffi <- Driving Frustrat	0.664
Discourteous Dri <- Driving Frustrat	0.399
Law Enforcement <- Driving Frustrat	0.649
Road Constructio <- Driving Frustrat	0.766
Restricted Field <- Driving Frustrat	0.593
Law Violation <- Driving_Delinquency	0.665
Aggressive Drivi <- Driving_Delinque	0.724
Risk Taking <--- Driving_Delinquency	0.968
Temper <--------------- Self Control	0.619
Self-Centered <-------- Self Control	0.747
Physical Activities <-- Self Control	0.684
Risk Seeking <--------- Self Control	0.656
Simple Tasks <--------- Self Control	0.302
Impulsivity <---------- Self Control	0.815
v10r <------------- Progress Impeded	0.693
v17r <------------- Progress Impeded	0.517
v6r <-------------- Progress Impeded	0.444
v5r <-------------- Progress Impeded	0.464
v3r <-------------- Progress Impeded	0.363
v13r <------- Irregular Traffic Flow	0.718
v21 <-------- Irregular Traffic Flow	0.420

v19r <------- Irregular Traffic Flow	0.418
v25 <-------- Irregular Traffic Flow	0.341
v24 <-------- Irregular Traffic Flow	0.268
v4 <--------- Irregular Traffic Flow	0.400
v14 <- Discourteous Driving Behavior	0.627
v16r <- Discourteous Driving Behavio	0.708
v22r <- Discourteous Driving Behavio	0.682
v18r <----- Law Enforcement Presence	0.663
v7 <------- Law Enforcement Presence	0.560
v27 <------ Law Enforcement Presence	0.591
v8r <------------- Road Construction	0.545
v1 <-------------- Road Construction	0.480
v23r <--- Restricted Field of Vision	0.414
v28 <---- Restricted Field of Vision	0.471
v12r <--- Restricted Field of Vision	0.583
v11r <--- Restricted Field of Vision	0.556
v57 <----------------- Law Violation	0.869
v70 <----------------- Law Violation	0.900
v54 <----------------- Law Violation	0.850
v59 <----------------- Law Violation	0.796
v56 <----------------- Law Violation	0.626
v64 <------------ Aggressive Driving	0.724
v63 <------------ Aggressive Driving	0.828
v66 <------------ Aggressive Driving	0.531
v62 <------------ Aggressive Driving	0.552
v68 <-------------------- Risk Taking	0.523
v69 <-------------------- Risk Taking	0.577
v61 <-------------------- Risk Taking	0.597
slfrepde <------ Driving_Delinquency	0.294
v47 <-------------------- Impulsivity	0.626
v41 <-------------------- Impulsivity	0.655
v35 <-------------------- Impulsivity	0.547
v29 <-------------------- Impulsivity	0.528
v48 <----------------- Simple Tasks	0.878
v42 <----------------- Simple Tasks	0.424
v36 <----------------- Simple Tasks	0.531
v30 <----------------- Simple Tasks	0.522
v49 <----------------- Risk Seeking	0.602
v43 <----------------- Risk Seeking	0.670
v37 <----------------- Risk Seeking	0.819
v31 <----------------- Risk Seeking	0.714
v50 <----------- Physical Activities	0.419
v44 <----------- Physical Activities	0.711
v38 <----------- Physical Activities	0.705
v32 <----------- Physical Activities	0.606
v51 <----------------- Self-Centered	0.711
v45 <----------------- Self-Centered	0.461
v39 <----------------- Self-Centered	0.321
v33 <----------------- Self-Centered	0.535
v34 <----------------------- Temper	0.630

```
v40 <---------------------- Temper      0.589
v46 <---------------------- Temper      0.629
v52 <---------------------- Temper      0.623
slfrepde <--------------- gendrmal      0.190
slfrepde <---------------- Monthdrv     0.423
slfrepde <------------------ urban      0.135
slfrepde <---------------- mperweek     0.129
```

Means:	Estimate	S.E.	C.R.
gendrmal	0.427	0.026	16.463
Monthdrv	39.575	1.548	25.568
strtsemm	9341.427	107.092	87.228
urban	0.679	0.025	27.163
mperweek	170.046	8.234	20.653
writexam	82.310	0.379	217.187
ethcaus	0.824	0.020	40.648
ownvehc	0.691	0.024	28.483
selfgdl	0.422	0.026	16.299
Economy	0.662	0.025	26.669

Intercepts:	Estimate	S.E.	C.R.
v10r	5.020	0.138	36.474
v17r	5.294	0.095	55.813
v6r	4.071	0.109	37.227
v5r	4.927	0.116	42.512
v3r	5.084	0.101	50.385
v13r	5.015	0.132	37.957
v21	4.871	0.098	49.580
v19r	4.550	0.101	45.204
v25	5.054	0.092	54.703
v24	4.985	0.103	48.257
v4	5.052	0.101	50.024
v14	5.842	0.101	57.616
v16r	5.437	0.098	55.353
v22r	5.689	0.103	55.195
v18r	4.399	0.133	33.190
v7	3.731	0.138	27.026
v27	4.689	0.122	38.452
v8r	4.044	0.119	34.097

v1	4.026	0.113	35.630
v23r	4.290	0.109	39.417
v28	4.326	0.118	36.567
v12r	4.648	0.116	40.224
v11r	4.689	0.112	41.714
v57	4.046	0.276	14.641
v70	3.851	0.260	14.811
v54	4.141	0.243	17.054
v59	3.183	0.248	12.825
v56	2.706	0.201	13.486
v64	2.170	0.223	9.730
v63	2.630	0.276	9.538
v66	1.931	0.143	13.506
v62	1.512	0.112	13.506
v68	1.493	0.117	12.803
v69	1.764	0.199	8.854
v61	1.962	0.206	9.534
slfrepde	-0.080	0.398	-0.202
v47	1.918	0.062	31.058
v41	2.078	0.069	30.054
v35	1.715	0.065	26.499
v29	2.381	0.070	33.802
v48	1.949	0.066	29.608
v42	2.285	0.059	38.908
v36	1.829	0.057	32.210
v30	2.468	0.067	36.870
v49	2.332	0.060	38.673
v43	2.396	0.075	31.983
v37	2.846	0.082	34.805
v31	3.105	0.073	42.255
v50	2.662	0.065	40.690
v44	3.349	0.074	45.041
v38	3.283	0.073	44.859
v32	2.820	0.073	38.638
v51	1.835	0.060	30.499
v45	1.967	0.063	31.045
v39	1.741	0.057	30.779
v33	1.956	0.063	31.264
v34	2.175	0.074	29.526
v40	1.938	0.069	27.919
v46	2.325	0.072	32.417
v52	2.569	0.078	33.052

Variances:	Estimate	S.E.	C.R.
gendrmal	0.245	0.018	13.491
res Self Control	1.000		
Monthdrv	867.117	64.518	13.440
res Driving Frustration	1.000		
strtsemm	2.16e+006	2.25e+005	9.585
res DD	1.000		
res DDB	1.000		
res IT	1.000		
res PI	1.000		
res ST	1.000		
res RF	0.390	0.130	3.009
res RC	0.382	0.194	1.971
res LE	0.968	0.227	4.262
res LV	0.476	0.057	8.376
res AD	0.220	0.038	5.720
res RT	0.004	0.007	0.655
res Impulsivity	0.145	0.040	3.620
res RS	0.235	0.045	5.236
res PA	0.133	0.039	3.423
res SC	0.230	0.059	3.918
res T	0.416	0.083	5.012
urban	0.218	0.017	13.192
mperweek	23556.100	1788.199	13.173
writexam	26.355	2.751	9.579
ethcaus	0.145	0.011	13.267
ownvehc	0.213	0.016	13.454
selfgdl	0.244	0.018	13.491
Economy	0.224	0.017	13.472
err10r	1.991	0.217	9.190
err17r	1.659	0.146	11.368
err6r	2.624	0.217	12.084
err7r	2.813	0.236	11.906
err3r	2.626	0.208	12.635
err13r	1.681	0.199	8.452
err21	2.246	0.184	12.209
err19r	2.364	0.193	12.219
err25	2.302	0.181	12.721
err4	2.471	0.200	12.357
err14	1.838	0.171	10.746
err16r	1.347	0.170	7.939
err22r	1.616	0.188	8.617
err18r	2.132	0.257	8.307
err7	3.200	0.305	10.493
err27	2.284	0.230	9.936
err8r	2.191	0.257	8.518
err1	2.376	0.234	10.171

err23r	2.912	0.245	11.892
err28	3.066	0.272	11.255
err12r	2.220	0.237	9.386
err11r	2.265	0.228	9.938
err6	3.210	0.246	13.048
err57	0.277	0.027	10.107
err70	0.177	0.020	8.806
err54	0.252	0.024	10.653
err59	0.395	0.034	11.645
err56	0.661	0.052	12.823
err64	0.419	0.042	10.033
err63	0.329	0.047	6.965
err66	0.454	0.037	12.358
err62	0.251	0.021	12.219
err68	0.185	0.016	11.831
err69	0.415	0.037	11.190
err61	0.402	0.037	10.888
res Self Report Delinquency	2.892	0.225	12.878
err 47	0.671	0.063	10.635
err 41	0.777	0.077	10.140
err 35	0.887	0.076	11.628
err 29	1.090	0.092	11.802
err 48	0.325	0.078	4.160
err 42	1.004	0.079	12.751
err 36	0.811	0.067	12.013
err 30	1.143	0.095	12.098
err 49	0.726	0.061	11.895
err 43	0.941	0.084	11.152
err 37	0.627	0.082	7.685
err 31	0.792	0.076	10.468
err 50	1.170	0.093	12.635
err 44	0.805	0.088	9.164
err 38	0.794	0.085	9.293
err 32	1.041	0.094	11.077
err 51	0.509	0.067	7.661
err 45	1.012	0.084	12.015
err 39	0.966	0.075	12.884
err 33	0.866	0.077	11.246
err 34	1.024	0.099	10.336
err 40	1.001	0.091	10.960
err 46	0.973	0.094	10.343
err 52	1.160	0.111	10.446

Summary of models

Model	NPAR	CMIN	DF	P	CMIN/DF
Default model	223	5390.182	2332	0.000	2.311
Saturated model	2555	0.000	0		
Independence model	70	55625.880	24850.000	22.385	

Model	DELTA1 NFI	RHO1 RFI	DELTA2 IFI	RHO2 TLI	CFI
Default model	0.903	0.897	0.943	0.939	0.942
Saturated model	1.000	1.000	1.000		
Independence model	0.000	0.000	0.000	0.000	0.000

Model	PRATIO	PNFI	PCFI
Default model	0.938	0.847	0.884
Saturated model	0.000	0.000	0.000
Independence model	1.000	0.000	0.000

Model	NCP	LO 90	HI 90
Default model	3058.182	2848.012	3275.610
Saturated model	0.000	0.000	0.000
Independence model	53140.880	52376.904	53911.232

Model	FMIN	F0	LO 90	HI 90
Default model	14.768	8.379	7.803	8.974
Saturated model	0.000	0.000	0.000	0.000
Independence model	152.400	145.591	143.498	147.702

Model	RMSEA	LO 90	HI 90	PCLOSE
Default model	0.060	0.058	0.062	0.000
Independence model	0.242	0.240	0.244	0.000

Model	AIC	BCC	BIC	CAIC
Default model	5836.182	5943.890		
Saturated model	5110.000	6344.048		
Independence model	55765.880	55799.689		

Model	ECVI	LO 90	HI 90	MECVI
Default model	15.990	15.414	16.585	16.285
Saturated model	14.000	14.000	14.000	17.381
Independence model	152.783	150.690	154.894	152.876

Model	HOELTER .05	HOELTER .01
Default model	166	169
Independence model	18	18

Execution time summary:

Minimization: 4.125
Miscellaneous: 0.234
Bootstrap: 0.000
Total: 4.359

References

Agnew, R. (1992). Foundation for a general strain theory of crime and delinquency. *Criminology, 30*, 47-87.

Agnew, R. (2001). Building on the foundation of general strain theory: Specifying the types of strain most likely to lead to crime and delinquency. *Journal of Research in Crime and Delinquency, 38*, 319-361.

Agnew, R., & Brezina, T. (1997). Relational problems with peers, gender and delinquency. *Youth and Society, 29*, 84-111.

Agnew, R., Brezina, T., Wright, J. P., & Cullen, F. T. (2002). Strain, personality traits, and delinquency: Extending general strain theory. *Criminology, 40*, 43-71.

Agnew, R., & White, H. R. (1992). An empirical test of general strain theory. *Criminology, 30*, 475-499.

Aish, A. M., & Joreskog, K. G. (1990). A panel model for political efficacy and responsiveness: An application of LISERAL 7 with weighted least squares. *Quality and Quantity, 19*, 716-723.

Akers, R. L. (1991). Self-control as a general theory of crime. *Journal of Quantitative Criminology, 7*, 201-211.

Allen, H. E., & Simonsen, C. E. (1989). *Corrections in America: An introduction.* New York, NY: Macmillan.

Almond, G. (1990). *A discipline divided: Schools and sects in political science.* Thousand Oaks, CA: Sage Publications.

Anderson, E. (1999). *Code of the street.* Philadelphia, PA: W. W. Norton.

Anderson, J. C., & Gerbing, D. W. (1988). Structural equation modeling in practice: A review and recommended two-step approach. *Psychological Bulletin, 103*, 411-423.

Annis, H. M. (1998). Effective treatment for drug and alcohol problems: What do we know? In T. J. Flanagan, J. W. Marquart & K. G. Adams (Eds.), *Incarcerating criminals: Prisons and jails in social and organizational context* (pp. 174-183). New York, NY: Oxford University Press.

Arbuckle, J. L. (1996). Full information estimation in the presence of incomplete data. In G. A. Marcoulides & R. E. Schumacker (Eds.), *Advanced structural equation modeling: Issues and techniques* (pp. 243-277). Mahwah, NJ: Lawrence Erlbaum Associates.

Arbuckle, J. L. (1999). *Amos 4.0 [Computer software].* Chicago, IL: Smallwaters.

Arneklev, B. J., Cochran, J. K., & Gainey, R. R. (1998). Testing Gottfredson and Hirschi's "low self-control" stability hypothesis: An exploratory study. *American Journal of Criminal Justice, 23*, 225-247.

Aseltine, R. H., Gore, S., & Gordon, J. (2000). Life stress, anger and anxiety, and delinquency: An empirical test of general strain theory. *Journal of Health and Social Behavior, 41*, 256-275.

Averill, J., R. (1982). *Anger and aggression.* New York, NY: Springer-Verlag.

Baerwald, J. E. (1965). *Traffic engineering handbook.* Washington, D.C.: Institute of Traffic Engineers.

Bandura, A. (1989). Human agency and social cognitive theory. *American Psychologist, 44*, 1175-1184.

Baron, R., & Kenny, D. A. (1986). The moderator-mediator variable distinction in social psychological research: Conceptual, strategic, and statistical considerations. *Journal of Personality and Social Psychology, 51*, 1173-1182.

Baron, S. (2003). Self-control, social consequences, and criminal behavior: Street youth and the general theory of crime. *Journal of Research in Crime and Delinquency, 40*, 403-425.

Barrett, K. C., & Campos, J. J. (1991). A diacritical function approach to emotions and coping. In M. E. Cummings, A. L. Greene & K. H. Karraker (Eds.), *Life-span developmental psychology: Perspectives on stress and coping.* Hillsdale, New Jersey: Lawrence Erlbaum Associates, Publishers.

Beccaria, C. (1819 [1764]). *An essay on crimes and punishment.* Philadelphia, PA: P. H. Nicklin.

Becker, H. S. (1963). *Outsiders.* New York, NY: Macmillan.

Bentler, P. M. (1988). Causal modeling via structural equation systems. In J. R. Nesselroade & R. B. Cattell (Eds.), *Handbook of multivariate experimental psychology* (2 ed., pp. 317-335). New York, NY: Plenum.

Bentler, P. M. (1990). Comparative fit indexes in structural models. *Psychological Bulletin, 107*, 238-246.

Bentler, P. M. (1992). On the fit of models to covariances and methodology to the Bulletin. *Psychological Bulletin, 112*, 400-404.

Bentler, P. M., & Bonett, D. G. (1980). Significance tests and goodness-of-fit in the analysis of covariance structures. *Psychological Bulletin, 88*, 588-606.

Bergdahl, J., & Norris, M. R. (2002). Sex differences in single vehicle fatal crashes: A research note. *The Social Science Journal, 39*, 287-293.

Block, J. (1995). A contrarian view of the five-factor approach to personality description. *Psychological Bulletin, 117*, 187-215.

Blumstein, A., Farrington, D. P., & Moitra, S. (1985). Delinquency careers. In M. Tonry & N. Morris (Eds.), *Crime and justice: A review of research.* Chicago, IL: University of Chicago Press.

Bohrnstedt, G. W., & Knoke, D. (1994). *Statistics for social data analysis* (3 ed.). Itasca, IL: F. E. Peacock Publishers, Inc.

Bollen, K. A. (1989). *Structural equations with latent variables.* New York, NY: Wiley.

Bonta, J. (1996). Risk-needs assessment and treatment. In A. T. Harland (Ed.), *Choosing correctional options that work: Defining the demand and evaluating the supply* (pp. 19-32). Thousand Oaks, California: Sage Publications.

Braithwaite, J. (1985). White collar crime. *Annual Review of Sociology, 11*, 1-25.

Braithwaite, J. (2002). *Restorative justice and responsive regulation.* New York, NY: Oxford University Press.

Broidy, L. M. (2001). A test of general strain theory. *Criminology, 39*, 9-35.

Bureau of the Census. (1995). *Statistical Abstract of the United States.* Washington, D.C.: U.S. Department of Commerce.

Burgess, E. W. (1928). The growth of the city. In R. E. Park & R. D. Mckenzie (Eds.), *The city.* Chicago, IL: University of Chicago Press.

Burton, V. S., Evans, T. D., Cullen, F. T., Olivares, K., & Dunaway, R. G. (1999). Age, self-control, and adults' offending behaviors: A research note assessing a general theory of crime. *Journal of Criminal Justice, 27*, 45-54.

Burton, V. S., Jr., & Cullen, F. T. (1992). The empirical status of strain theory. *Journal of Crime and Justice, 15*, 1-23.

Byrne, B. M. (2001). *Structural equation modeling with AMOS.* Mahwah, NJ: Lawrence Erlbaum Associates, Publishers.

Campbell, D. T., & Fiske, D. W. (1959). Convergent and discriminant validation by the multi-trait-multimethod matrix. *Psychological Bulletin, 56*, 81-105.

Capowich, G. E., Mazerolle, P., & Piquero, A. R. (2001). General strain theory, situational anger, and social networks: An assessment of conditioning influences. *Journal of Crime and Justice, 29*, 445-461.

Carlson, W. L., & Klein, D. (1970). Familial vs. institutional socialization of the young traffic offender. *Journal of Safety Research, 2*, 13-25.

Carroll, P. S., Carlson, W. L., McDole, T. L., & W., S. D. (1971). *Conditions of information on exposure and on non-fatal crashes.* Ann Arbor, MI: U.S. Department of Transportation.

Cauffman, E., Steinberg, L., & Piquero, A. R. (2005). Psychological, neuropsychological and physiological correlates of serious antisocial behavior in adolescence: The role of Self-Control. *Criminology, 43,* 133-175.

Chambliss, W. (1969). *Crime and legal process.* New York, NY: McGraw-Hill.

Chou, C.-P., & Bentler, P. M. (1995). Estimates and tests in structural equation modeling. In R. H. Hoyle (Ed.), *Structural equation modeling: Concepts, issues, and applications.* Thousand Oaks, CA: Sage Publications, Inc.

Cliff, N. R. (1988). The eigenvalues-greater-than-one rule and the reliability of components. *Psychological Bulletin, 103,* 276-279.

Cloward, R. A., & Ohlin, L. E. (1960). *Delinquency and opportunity: A theory of delinquent gangs.* New York: The Free Press.

Cohen, A. K. (1955). *Delinquent boys: The culture of the gang.* New York: The Free Press.

Cohen, J. (1988). *Statistical power analysis for the behavioral sciences* (2 ed.). Hillsdale, NJ: Erlbaum.

Cohen, J., Cohen, P., West, S. G., & Aiken, L. S. (2003). *Applied multiple regression/correlation analysis for the behavioral sciences* (3 ed.). Mahwah, NJ: Lawrence Erlbaum Associates, Publishers.

Cohen, L. E., & Felson, M. (1979). Social change and crime rate trends: A routine activity approach. *American Sociological Review, 44,* 588-608.

Cole, S. (1975). The growth of scientific knowledge: Theories of deviance as a case study. In L. A. Coser (Ed.), *The idea of social structure: Papers in honor of Robert K. Merton.* New York, NY: Harcourt Brace Jovanovich.

Compas, B. E. (1987). Coping with stress during childhood and adolescence. *Psychological Bulletin, 101,* 393-403.

Cronbach, L. J. (1951). Coefficient alpha and the internal structure of tests. *Psychometrika, 6,* 297-334.

Cronbach, L. J. (1990). *Essentials of psychological testing.* New York: Harper.

Cullen, F. T. (1983). *Rethinking crime and deviance theory: The emergence of a structuring tradition.* Totowa, NJ: Rowman and Allanheld.

Darwin, C. (1859). *The origins of species.* New York, NY: D. Appleton and Company.

Deffenbacher, J. L., Oetting, E. R., & Lynch, R. S. (1994). Development of a driving anger scale. *Psychological Reports, 74*, 83-91.

Delisi, M., Hochstetler, A., & Murphy, D. S. (2003). Self-control behind bars: A validation study of the Grasmick et al. scale. *Justice Quarterly, 20*, 241-263.

Doane, D. (2004). *Young drivers as a proportion of all licensed drivers in Washington State.* Olympia, WA: Washington State Traffic Safety Commission. October 15.

Durkheim, E. (1986). *The division of labor in society* (G. Simpson, Trans.). New York: The Free Press.

Elliot, D., Huizinga, D., & Ageton, S. (1985). *Explaining delinquency and drug use.* Beverly Hills, CA: Sage.

Elliot, D. S. (1962). Delinquency and perceived opportunity. *Sociological Inquiry, 32*, 216-227.

Ellwanger, S. J. (2002). Cruel and unusual punishment. In D. Levinson (Ed.), *Encyclopedia of crime and punishment* (Vol. 1, pp. 441-445). Thousand Oaks, California: Sage Publications.

Ellwanger, S. J. (2004a). *Washington State traffic safety education legislative and administrative authority.* Pullman, WA: Division of Governmental Studies and Services. [Working Paper].

Ellwanger, S. J. (2004b). *Washington State traffic safety education logic model.* Pullman, WA: Division of Governmental Studies and Services. [Working Paper].

Ellwanger, S. J. (2004c). *Washington State traffic safety education program impact theory.* Pullman, WA: Division of Governmental Studies and Services. [Working Paper].

Ellwanger, S. J. (2004d). *Washington State traffic safety education service utilization flow chart.* Pullman, WA: Division of Governmental Studies and Services. [Working Paper].

Etzioni, A. (1996). *The new golden rule.* Basic Books.

Evans, D. T., Cullen, F. T., Burton, V. S., Dunaway, R. G., & Benson, M. L. (1997). The social consequences of self-control: Testing the general theory of crime. *Criminology, 35*, 475-504.

Farnworth, M., & Leiber, M. L. (1989). Strain theory revisited: Economic goals, educational means, and delinquency. *American Sociological Review, 54*, 263-274.

Ferro, G. L. (1972 [1911]). *Criminal man according to the classification of Cesare Lombroso.* Putnam, NY: Patterson Smith,.

Fredricks, M., & Molnar, M. (1969). Relative occupational aspirations and aspirations of delinquents and non-delinquents. *Journal of Research in Crime and Delinquency, 6*, 1-7.

Friedson, E. (1970). *Professional dominance.* New York: Atherton Press.

Friedson, E. (1975). *Doctoring together.* New York: Elsevier.

Gaines, L. K., & Kappeler, V. E. (2003). *Policing in America* (4 ed.). Cincinnati, OH: Anderson Publishing Co.

Gendreau, P., Cullen, F. T., & Bonta, J. (1994). Intensive rehabilitation supervision: The next generation in community corrections? *Federal Probation, 58*, 72-78.

Gibbs, J. J., Giever, D., & Martin, J. S. (1998). Parental management and self-control: An empirical test of Gottfredson and Hirschi's general theory. *Journal of Research in Crime and Delinquency, 35*, 40-70.

Gluek, S., & Gluek, E. (1950). *Unraveling juvenile delinquency.* Cambridge, MA: Harvard University Press.

Goddard, H. H. (1972 [1914]). *Feeblemindedness: Its causes and consequences.* New York: Arno.

Gottfredson, M. R., & Hirschi, T. (1989). A propensity-event theory of crime. In W. Laufer & F. Adler (Eds.), *Advances in criminological theory* (Vol. 1). New Brunswick, NJ: Transaction Press.

Gottfredson, M. R., & Hirschi, T. (1990). *A general theory of crime.* Stanford, CA: Stanford University Press.

Grasmick, H. G., & Bursik, R. J. (1990). Conscience, significant others, and rational choice: Extending the deterrence model. *Law & Society Review, 24*, 837-861.

Grasmick, H. G., Tittle, C. R., Bursik, R. J., & Arneklev, B. J. (1993). Testing the core empirical implications of Gottfredson and Hirschi's general theory of crime. *Journal of Research in Crime and Delinquency, 30*, 5-29.

Guess, G. M., & Farnham, P. G. (2000). Problem identification and structuring. In *Cases in public policy analysis* (2 ed., pp. 22-63). Washington, D.C.: Georgetown Press.

Gulick, L. (1937). Notes on the theory of organization. In J. M. Shafritz & A. C. Hyde (Eds.), *Classics of Public Administration* (4 ed., pp. 81-89). Fort Worth, TX: Harcourt Brace.

Guttman, L. (1954). Some necessary conditions for common factor analysis. *Psychometrika, 19*, 149-161.

Hair, J. F., Anderson, R. E., Tatham, R. L., & Black, W. (1995). *Multivariate data analysis* (4 ed.). Upper Saddle River, New Jersey: Prentice Hall.

Harland, A. T. (1996). Correctional options that work: Structuring inquiry. In
    A. T. Harland (Ed.), *Choosing correctional options that work: Defining
    the demand and evaluating the supply* (pp. 1-17). Thousand Oaks,
    California: Sage Publications.

Harrington, D. M. (1971). *The young driver follow-up study* (No. Highway
    Research Report No. 38). Sacramento, CA: California Department of
    Motor Vehicles.

Hay, C. (2001). Parenting, self-control, and delinquency: A test of self-control
    theory. *Criminology, 39*, 707-736.

Hay, C. (2003). Family strain, gender, and delinquency. *Sociological
    Perspectives, 46*, 107-135.

Hendrickson, A. E., & White, P. O. (1964). Promax: A quick method for
    rotation to oblique simple structure. *British Journal of Statistical
    Psychology, 17*, 71-82.

Hirschi, T. (1969). *Causes of delinquency.* Beverly Hills, CA: University of
    California Press.

Hirschi, T., & Gottfredson, M. R. (1993). Commentary: Testing the general
    theory of crime. *Journal of Research in Crime and Delinquency, 30*, 47-
    54.

Hirschi, T., & Hindlelang, M. J. (1977). Intelligence and delinquency: A
    revisionist review. *American Sociological Review, 42*, 572-587.

Houts, A. C., Cook, T. D., & Shadish, W. R. (1986). The person-situation
    debate: A critical multiplist perspective. *Journal of Personality, 54*, 52-
    105.

Hoyle, R. H. (1995). The structural equation modeling approach: Basic
    concepts and fundamental issues. In R. H. Hoyle (Ed.), *Structural
    equation modeling: Concepts, issues, and applications* (pp. 1-15).
    Thousand Oaks, CA: Sage Publications, Inc.

Hu, L.-t., & Bentler, P. M. (1995). Evaluating model fit. In R. H. Hoyle (Ed.),
    Structural equation modeling: Concepts issues and applications (pp. 76-
    99). Thousand Oaks, CA: Sage Publications.

Hu, L.-t., & Bentler, P. M. (1999). Cutoff criteria for fit indexes in covariance
    structure analysis: Conventional criteria versus new alternatives.
    Structural Equation Modeling: A Multidisciplinary Journal, 6, 1-55.

Huesmann, L., Rowell, L., Lefkowitz, M., & Walder, L. (1984). Stability of
    aggression over time and generations. *Developmental Psychology, 20*,
    1120-1134.

Hull, J. G., Tedlie, J. C., & Lehn, D. A. (1995). Modeling the relation of personality variables to symptom complaints: The unique role of negative affectivity. In R. H. Hoyle (Ed.), *Structural equation modeling: Concepts, issues, and applications* (pp. 217-235). Thousand Oaks, CA: Sage Publications.

Hummel, R. P. (1994). *The bureaucratic experience: A critique of life in the modern organization* (4 ed.). New York, NY: St. Martin's Press.

Hunter, J. E., & Schmidt, F. L. (1990). *Methods of meta-analysis: Correcting error and bias in research findings.* Newbury Park, CA: Sage Publications.

International Automotive Engineering Congress. (1973). *Results of a study to determine accident causes.* Detroit, Michigan: Institute for Research in Public Safety.

Jesilow, P. D., Pontell, H. N., & Geis, G. (1985). Medical criminals: Physicians and white-collar offenses. *Justice Quarterly, 2,* 149-164.

Joireman, J. (2004). *Driving behaviors (Personal Interview).* Pullman, WA: Washington State University. April 2004.

Junger, M., & Tremblay, R. E. (1999). Self-control, accidents and crime. *Criminal Justice and Behavior, 26,* 485-501.

Kaiser, H. F. (1970). The application of electronic computers to factor analysis. *Educational and Psychological Measurements, 20,* 141-151.

Kaplan, D. (1995). Statistical power in structural equation modeling. In R. H. Hoyle (Ed.), *Structural equation modeling: Concepts, issues, and applications* (pp. 100-117). Thousand Oaks, CA: Sage Publications, Inc.

Kaplan, H. B. (1980). *Deviant behavior in defense of self.* New York, NY: Academic Press.

Keane, C., Maxim, P. S., & Teevan, J. J. (1993). Drinking and driving, self-control, and gender: Testing a general theory of crime. *Journal of Research in Crime and Delinquency, 30,* 30-46.

Kettl, D. F. (2000). *The global management revolution: A report on the transformation of governance.* Washington, D.C.: The Brookings Institution.

Kidd, P., & Huddleston, S. (1994). Psychometric properties of the driving practices questionnaire: Assessment of risky driving. *Research in Nursing & Health, 17,* 51-58.

King, G., Keohane, R. O., & Verba, S. (1994). *Designing social inquiry: Scientific inference in qualitative research.* Princeton, NJ: Princeton University Press.

Klein, D. (1971). The influence of societal values on rates of death and injury. *Journal of Safety Research, 3,* 2-8.

Kline, R. B. (1998). *Principles and practice of structural equation modeling.* New York, NY: Guildford Press.

Kornhauser, R. (1978). *Social sources of delinquency.* Chicago, IL: University of Chicago Press.

Lajunen, T., & Parker, D. (2001). Are aggressive people aggressive drivers? A study of the relationship between self-reported general aggressiveness, driver anger and aggressive driving. *Accident Analysis & Prevention, 33,* 243-255.

Lajunen, T., Parker, D., & Stradling, S. (1998). Dimensions of driver anger, aggressive and highway code violations and their mediation by safety orientation in UK drivers. *Transportation Research, F 1,* 107-121.

Landis, J. R., & Scarpitti, F. R. (1965). Perceptions regarding value orientation and legitimate opportunity: Delinquents and non-delinquents. *Social Forces, 44,* 83-91.

Lazarus, R., & Folkman, S. (1984). *Stress, appraisal, and coping.* New York, New York: Springer.

Leeper-Piquero, N., & Sealock, M. D. (2000). Generalizing general strain theory: An examination of an offending population. *Justice Quarterly, 17,* 449-484.

Likert, R., Roslow, S., & Murphy, G. (1993). A simple and reliable method of scoring the Thurstone Attitude Scales. *Personnel psychology, 46,* 689-690.

Lipsitt, P. D., Buka, S. L., & Lipsitt, L. P. (1990). Early intelligence scores and subsequent delinquency. *American Journal of Family Therapy, 18,* 197-208.

Liska, A. E. (1971). Aspirations, expectations, and delinquency: Stress and additive models. *Sociological Quarterly, 12,* 99-107.

Liska, A. E., Krohn, M. D., & Messner, S. F. (1989). Strategies and requisites for theoretical integration in the study of crime and deviance. In S. F. Messner, M. D. Krohn & A. E. Liska (Eds.), *Theoretical Integration in the study of deviance and crime: Problems and prospects.* Albany, NY: State University of New York Press.

Little, R. J., & Rubin, D. B. (1989). The analysis of social science data with missing values. *Sociological Methods and Research, 18,* 292-326.

Loehlin, J. C. (1998). *Latent variable models: An introduction to factor, path, and structural analysis* (3 ed.). Mahwah, NJ: Lawrence Erlbaum Associates, Publishers.

Longshore, D., & Turner, S. (1998). Self-control and criminal opportunity: Cross-sectional test of the general theory of Crime. *Criminal Justice and Behavior, 25,* 81-98.

Lovrich, N. P., Stehr, S., Ellwanger, S. J., & Lin, Y. (2003). *The impacts of traffic safety education.* Paper presented at the Annual Conference of the American Driver and Traffic Safety Education Association, Charlotte, NC, July 19-26.

MacCallum, R. C., Browne, M. W., & Sugawara, H. M. (1996). Power analysis and determination of sample size for covariance structure modeling. *Psychological Methods, 1,* 130-149.

Marsh, H. W., Balla, J. R., & McDonald, R. P. (1988). Goodness-of-fit indices in confirmatory factor analysis: The effect of sample size and model complexity. *Quality and Quantity, 28,* 391-410.

Matsueda, R. L. (1982). Testing control theory and differential association: A causal modeling approach. *American Sociological Review, 47,* 489-504.

Mayhew, D. R., & Simpson, H. M. (1991). New to the Road, young drivers and novice drivers: Similar problems and solutions? *Accident Analysis & Prevention, 12,* 124-137.

Mazerolle, P., & Piquero, A. R. (1997). Violent responses to situations of strain: A structural examination. *Justice Quarterly, 15,* 65-91.

Mazerolle, P., & Piquero, A. R. (1998). Linking exposure to strain with anger: An investigation of deviant adaptations. *Journal of Crime and Justice, 26,* 195-211.

Mazerolle, P., Piquero, A. R., & Capowich, G. E. (2003). Examining the links between strain, situational and dispositional anger, and crime: Further specifying and testing general strain theory. *Youth & Society, 35,* 131-157.

McCartt, A. T., Shabanova, V. I., & Leaf, W. A. (2003). Driving experience, crashes and traffic citations of teenage beginning drivers. *Accident Analysis & Prevention, 35,* 311-320.

McGuire, F. L. (1969). The doubt about driver education. *Educate, 9,* 31-38.

Merton, R. K. (1938). Social structure and anomie. *American Sociological Review, 3,* 672-682.

Merton, R. K. (1968). *Social theory and social structure.* Glencoe, IL: The Free Press.

Messner, S. F., & Rosenfeld, R. (2001). *Crime and the American dream* (3 ed.). Belmont, CA: Wadsworth / Thomas Learning.

Messrs, A., Tallqvist, A., Mäki, J., & Prigogine, J. (1975). Personality and other person-centered characteristics. In A. Messrs, M. Fell, G. Herrmann,

J. Marek, J. Prigogine & S. W. Quenault (Eds.), *Road research: young driver accidents* (pp. 97-119). Paris, France: Organization for Economic Co-operation and Development.

Mikesell, J. L. (1995). *Fiscal administration: Analysis and applications for the public sector* (4 ed.). Belmont, California: Wadsworth.

Miller, J. L., & Anderson, A. B. (1986). Updating the deterrence doctrine. *The Journal of Criminal Law & Criminology, 77*, 418-438.

Mills, R. (1975). Exposure and experience. In M. Fell, G. Herrmann, J. Marek, J. Prigogine & S. W. Quenault (Eds.), *Road research: young driver accidents* (pp. 23-43). Paris, France: Organization for Economic Co-operation and Development.

Moe, T. (1984). The new economics of organization. *American Journal of Political Science, 28*, 739-777.

Morris, N., & Hawkins, G. (1970). *The honest politician's guide to crime control*. Chicago, IL: University of Chicago Press.

Munsch, G. (1966). Physical maturity and mature driving. In H. B. Wolf & E. Forsberg (Eds.), *Proceedings of the 2nd Congress of the International Association of Accident and Traffic Medicine*. Malmo, Sweden: Kirurgiska Universitskliniken.

Nagin, D. S., & Paternoster, R. (1993). Enduring individual differences and rational choice theories of crime. *Law & Society Review, 27*, 467-496.

National Commission on Marijuana and Drug Abuse. (1973). *Drug use in America: Problem in perspective* (No. 5266-00003). Washington, D.C.: U.S. G.P.O.

National Highway Traffic Safety Administration. (2002). *Traffic safety facts 2002: Young drivers*. Washington, D. C.: National Center for Statistics and Analysis.

National highway Traffic Safety Administration. (2004). *Traffic safety facts: 2004 data*. Washington, D.C.: Department of Transportation.

National Highway Traffic Safety Administration. (2005). *Motor vehicle traffic crashes as a leading cause of death in the U.S., 2002--A demographic perspective*. Washington, D.C.: National Center for Statistics and Analysis.

Neuman, W. L. (1997). *Social research methods* (3 ed.). Boston, MA: Allyn and Bacon.

Newman, G. (1985). *The punishment response*. Albany, NY: Harrow & Heston.

Nunnally, J. C., & Bernstein, I. H. (1994). *Psychometric theory* (3 ed.). New York, NY: McGraw-Hill, Inc.

Palmore, E., & Hammond, P. (1964). Interacting factors in juvenile delinquency. *American Sociological Review, 29*, 848-854.

Park, R. E. (1936). Human Ecology. *American Journal of Sociology, 42*, 152.

Parry, M. H. (1968). *Aggression on the road.* New York, NY: Tavistock.

Paternoster, R., & Mazerolle, P. (1994). General strain theory and delinquency: A replication and extension. *Journal of Research in Crime and Delinquency, 29*, 561-585.

Paternoster, R., & Simpson, S. (1996). Sanction threats and appeals to morality: Testing a rational choice model of corporate crime. *Law & Society Review, 30*, 549-583.

Piquero, A. R., MacIntosh, R., & Hickman, M. (2000). Does self-control affect survey response? Applying exploratory, confirmatory, and item response theory analysis to Grasmick et al.'s self-control scale. *Criminology, 38*, 897-929.

Piquero, A. R., & Tibbetts, S. (1996). Specifying the direct and indirect effects of low self-control and situational factors in offenders' decision making: Toward a more complete model of rational offending. *Justice Quarterly, 13*, 481-510.

Popper, K. (1962). *On the structure of scientific revolutions.* Chicago, IL: Chicago University Press.

Porter, R. C. (1999). *Economics at the wheel: The costs of cars and drivers.* San Diego, CA: Academic Press.

Pratt, T. C., & Cullen, F. T. (2000). The empirical status of Gottfredson and Hirschi's general theory of crime: a meta-analysis. *Criminology, 38*, 931-964.

Pratt, T. C., Turner, M. G., & Piquero, A. R. (2004). Parental socialization and community context: A longitudinal analysis of the structural sources of low self-control. *Journal of Research in Crime and Delinquency, 41*, 219-243.

Preusser, D. G., Williams, A. F., Zador, P. L., & Blomberg, R. D. (1984). The effect of curfew laws on motor vehicle crashes. *Law and Policy, 6*, 115-128.

Prior, M. (1992). Childhood temperament. *Journal of Child Psychology and Psychiatry and Allied Disciplines, 33*, 249-279.

Provan, K., & Milward, H. B. (2001). Do networks really work? A framework for evaluating public-sector organizational networks. *Public Administration Review, 61*, 414-423.

Quenault, S. W., & Sten, T. (1975). Driver training. In A. Messrs, M. Fell, G. Herrmann, J. Marek, J. Prigogine & S. W. Quenault (Eds.), *Young driver accidents*. Paris, France: Organization for Economic Co-operation and Development.

Ragin, C. C. (1994). *Constructing social research*. Thousand Oaks, CA: Pine Forge Press.

Raykov, T., & Marcoulides, G. A. (2000). *A first course in structural equation modeling*. Mahwah, NJ: Lawrence Erlbaum Associates, Publishers.

Reed, G. E., & Yeager, P. C. (1996). Organizational offending and neoclassical criminology: Challenging the reach of a general theory of crime. *Criminology, 34*, 357-382.

Revised Code of Washington 28A.220, Washington State Legislature, 28A.220 Cong. Rec.(1977).

Rivera, R., & Short, J. F. (1967). Significant adults, caretakers, and structures of opportunity: An exploratory study. *Journal of Research in Crime and Delinquency, 4*, 76-97.

Rosenau, P. M. (1992). *Post-modernism and the social sciences: Insights, inroads, and intrusions*. Princeton NJ: Princeton University Press.

Rosenberg, M. (1990). Reflexivity and emotions. *Social Psychology Quarterly, 53*, 3-12.

Samaha, J. (1990). *Criminal Law* (3 ed.). St. Paul, MN: West Publishing Company.

Sampson, R., & Groves, B. (1989). Community structure and crime: Testing social disorganization theory. *American Journal of Sociology, 94*, 774-802.

Sampson, R., & Laub, J. H. (1990). Crime and deviance over the life course: The salience of adult social bonds. *American Sociological Review, 55*, 609-627.

Satorra, A., & Bentler, P. M. (1990). Model conditions for asymptotic robustness in the analysis of linear relations. *Computational Statistics and Data Analysis, 10*, 235-249

Schlesinger, L. (1972). Human factors in driver training and education. In T. W. Forbes (Ed.), *Human Factors in Highway Traffic Safety Research*. New York, NY: Wiley-Interscience.

Schuman, S. H., Pelz, D. C., Ehrlich, N. J., & Selzer, M. I. (1967). Young male drivers. *Journal of the American Medical Association, 200*, 12.

Shaw, C., & McKay, H. D. (1942). *Juvenile delinquency and urban areas.* Chicago, IL: University of Chicago Press.

Shaw, L., & Sichel, H. S. (1971). *Accident proneness: Research in the occurrence, causation, and prevention of road accidents.* New York, NY: Pergamon Press.

Shiner, D. (1998). Aggressive driving: The contribution of the drivers and situation. *Transportation Research, 1*, 137-160.

Short, J. F., Rivera, R., & Tennyson, R. A. (1965). Perceived opportunities, gang membership, and delinquency. *American Sociological Review, 30*, 56-67.

Sigfusdottir, I.-D., Farkas, G., & Silver, E. (2004). The role of depressed mood and anger in the relationship between family conflict and delinquent behavior. *Journal of Youth and Adolescence, 33*, 509-523.

Snook, S. C., & Gorsuch, R. L. (1989). Component analysis versus common factor analysis: A Monte Carlo study. *Psychological Bulletin, 106*, 148-154.

Stone, D. (2002). *Policy paradox: The art of political decision making* (2 ed.). New York: W. W. Norton & Company, Inc.

Stoolmiller, M., Duncan, T. E., & Patterson, G. R. (1995). Predictors of change in antisocial behavior during elementary school for boys. In R. H. Hoyle (Ed.), *Structural equation modeling: Concepts, issues, and applications* (pp. 236-253). Thousand Oaks, CA: Sage Publications, Inc.

Sutherland, E. H. (1973). Development of the theory. In K. Schuesssler (Ed.), *Edwin H. Sutherland on analyzing crime.* Chicago: University of Chicago Press.

Sykes, G. M., & Matza, D. (1957). Techniques of neutralization: A theory of delinquency. *American Sociological Review, 22*, 664-670.

Taylor, F. W. (1912). Scientific management. In J. M. Shafritz & A. C. Hyde (Eds.), *Classics of public administration* (4 ed., pp. 30-32). Fort Worth, Texas: Harcourt Brace.

Tellegen, A. (1985). Structures of mood and personality and their relevance to assessing anxiety, with an emphasis on self-report. In H. Tuba & J. Maser (Eds.), *Anxiety and the anxiety disorders.* Hillsdale, NJ: Erlbaum.

Tittle, C. R., & Botchkovar, E. V. (2005). Self-control, criminal motivation and deterrence: An investigation using Russian respondents. *Criminology, 43*, 307-353.

Tittle, C. R., Ward, D. A., & Grasmick, H. G. (2003a). Gender, age, and crime/deviance: A challenge to self-control theory. *Journal of Research in Crime and Delinquency, 40,* 426-453.

Tittle, C. R., Ward, D. A., & Grasmick, H. G. (2003b). Self-control and crime/deviance: Cognitive vs. behavioral measures. *Journal of Quantitative Criminology, 19,* 333-365.

Tryon, R. C., & Bailey, D. E. (1966). The BC TRY computer system of cluster and factor analysis. *Multivariate Behavioral Research, 1,* 95-111.

Unnever, J. D., Cullen, F. T., & Pratt, T. C. (2003). Parental management, ADHD, and delinquent involvement: Reassessing Gottfredson and Hirschi's general theory. *Justice Quarterly, 20,* 471-500.

Vazsonyi, A. T., Pickering, L. E., Junger, M., & Hessing, D. (2001). An empirical test of a general theory of crime: A four-nation comparative study of self-control and the prediction of deviance. *Journal of Research in Crime and Delinquency, 32,* 91-131.

Vernick, J. S., Li, G., Ogaitis, S., MacKenzie, E. J., Baker, S. P., & Gielen, A. C. (1999). Effects of high school driver education on motor vehicle crashes, violations, and licensure. *American Journal of Preventative Medicine, 16,* 40-46.

Voas, R. B. (1975). Alcohol and drugs. In A. Messrs, M. Fell, G. Herrmann, J. Marek, J. Prigogine & S. W. Quenault (Eds.), *Road research: Young driver accidents* (pp. 63-80). Paris, France: Organization for Economic Co-operation and Development.

Vold, G. B., Bernard, T. J., & Snipes, J. B. (2002). *Theoretical criminology* (5 ed.). New York: Oxford University Press.

Wagenaar, A. C. (1983). *Teen-age drivers, and traffic accidents.* Lanham, Maryland: Lexington Books.

Warr, M. (1993). Parents, peers and delinquency. *Social Forces, 72,* 247-264.

Washington Administrative Code 392-153, 392-153 (2001).

Washington State Patrol. (1971). *Teen-age drivers: Summary of traffic accidents.* Washington.

Washington Traffic Safety Commission. (2001). *State of Washington 1998 fatal traffic collisions in Washington state.* Olympia, WA: Washington Traffic Safety Commission.

Watson, D., Clark, L. A., & Harkness, A. (1994). Structures of personality and their relevance to psychopathology. *Journal of Abnormal Psychology, 103,* 18-31.

Weber, M. (1968). *Economy and Society.* New York: Bedminister Press.

West, S. G., Finch, J. F., & Curran, P. J. (1995). Structural equation models with nonnormal variables: Problems and remedies. In R. H. Hoyle (Ed.), *Structural equation modeling: Concepts, issues, and applications.* Thousand Oaks, CA: Sage Publications, Inc.

Wilson, J. Q. (1968). *Varieties of police behavior: The management of law and order in eight communities.* Cambridge, MA: Harvard University Press.

Wilson, J. Q., & Herrnstein, R. (1985). *Crime and human nature.* New York, NY: Simon and Schuster.

Wolfgang, M., Figlio, R., & Sellin, T. (1972). *Delinquency in a birth cohort.* Chicago, IL: University of Chicago Press.

Wright, B. R. E., Caspi, A., Moffitt, T. E., & Paternoster, R. (2004). Does the perceived risk of punishment deter criminally prone individuals? Rational choice, self-control, and crime. *Journal of Research in Crime and Delinquency, 41,* 180-213.

Index

A

B

C